THE STORY OF
SHEFFIELD

THE STORY OF
SHEFFIELD

TIM COOPER

For Joe and Ben,
Sheffield born and bred.

Front cover: Jarvis Cocker mural by Bubba2000 at Kelham Island.

First published 2021
Reprinted 2022

The History Press
97 St George's Place, Cheltenham,
Gloucestershire, GL50 3QB
www.thehistorypress.co.uk

British Library Cataloguing in Publication Data.
A catalogue record for this book is available from the British Library.

ISBN 978 0 7509 6763 1

Typesetting and origination by Typo•glyphix, Burton-on-Trent, DE14 3HE
Printed by TJ Books Limited, Padstow, Cornwall

CONTENTS

INTRODUCTION AND ACKNOWLEDGEMENTS

The commission to write a history of Sheffield was a pleasant surprise, coming more than ten years since I had last worked in detail on the city's past as historical consultant to the University's commercial archaeological unit. For the first time, it gave me the opportunity to look at Sheffield's story as a whole, not just as a collection of isolated sites and surveys. It also presented me with the occasion, as someone born and brought up in that other great metalworking city, Birmingham, to pay homage to a place I had first come to know in my early twenties and which has now been my home for more than half my life.

I say 'homage', because Sheffield for me was a love at first sight, and one that has grown over the years I have lived here. Yet at the same time, I like to think that writing the history of a place in which you do not have your roots allows some sense of detachment. From the start, I wanted to produce a narrative that sought out what was unique, or at least distinctive, in the story of Sheffield. All of us new to the city can remember our initial reactions to it. Mine included my first walk along Broad Lane from the University in search of the city centre. Looking around on Fargate, it took me a little while to realise that this was it! To someone brought up in a city like Birmingham, Sheffield seemed somehow lacking in buildings, with more of the look of a middle-sized provincial town than a great metropolis. One of the writers who recorded a similar reaction was George Orwell, who commented somewhat disparagingly that a town with a 'population of half a million … contains fewer decent buildings than the average East Anglian village'.

My other early, and enduring, reaction to Sheffield was not to its urban centre but its relationship to the natural landscape. An industrial city in which an hour's walk from its western suburbs would lead you through sublime scenery of woods and waterfalls and take you to the edge of the Peak District National Park. A city of hills, with none of the long, straight, suburban boulevards that characterise Birmingham or Manchester. The comment by the town's celebrated local historian Joseph Hunter is almost as true of the 2020s as it was of the 1820s, when he wrote that 'there is no street in Sheffield from which the country may not be seen'. A city made up of distinct communities separated by hills, each with its own spectacular views of the whole, or the rural uplands that surround it. A city of numerous rocky and wooded valleys with romantic names like Loxley and Rivelin.

As a Midlander, it seemed to me that Sheffield was where the south ended and the north began. As a historian, I knew that there was good reason to believe that populations that lived on boundaries between different jurisdictions – in Sheffield's case it was one between kingdoms, provinces and counties – often developed an independence of outlook and even a rebelliousness of spirit. In addition to the fact that Sheffield had grown at some distance from major cross-country communication routes, was this, I wondered, why so much about the city seemed to be different? A city whose main public square was dedicated to peace but simultaneously celebrated a political radical accused of attempting to take over the town by force of arms. A city that contained only two statues of dignitaries (both monarchs, one of which was moved from the city centre to a suburban park) but numerous memorials to social reformers. A city that confounded the British establishment with its support for the French Revolution and, in the late twentieth century, still seemed to be at war with the government in Westminster. This was a common thread that I hoped to uncover in my story.

In writing this book, my greatest debt is to those who have written histories of Sheffield before me, no more so than to David Hey, whose numerous publications were a constant source of reference when I first worked on the city's past myself. His death in February 2016, just as I was starting on my own history of Sheffield, was a great sadness and an immeasurable loss to the historical scholarship of Hallamshire. My debt to other historians of Sheffield will be apparent from a glance at the bibliography, and in a book that I wanted to keep free of footnotes, this is where I would point readers looking for the factual sources of my own narrative.

On a personal level, my greatest debt is to my wife, Pauline. Not only did she put up with me working on this book for more than five years, but her early suggestion that Sheffield's predominant culture has its roots in its working-class communities set me on a fruitful train of thought as to how the city differed from the likes of Leeds and Bradford, let alone Birmingham and Manchester. A number of friends have similarly influenced my thoughts about Sheffield, in particular Simon Linskill with whom I shared a flask of tea before work on many occasions and discussed the roots of the independent streak of his fellow Sheffielders. I am grateful also to Jon Dewey, Matthew Hunt, Olivia Johnstone and Paul Newman, who read part or all of the book at a late stage and made very helpful comments. Since 2013 I have built up a big debt of gratitude to the numerous international students of the University of Sheffield who have accompanied me in all weathers on my Local History Walks around the city, and whose perceptive comments and thought-provoking questions have served as a constant reminder of what an amazing place Sheffield is.

Indeed, my two sons will have lost count of the number of times I told them how fortunate they are to have been born in Sheffield. I hope they believe it to be true; whether or not that is the case, this book is for them.

A Note About the Illustrations

My intention in taking the photographs for this book myself is to place the historical narrative within the context of a present time – which, for the record, was between the summer of 2020 and early spring 2021. As such, I hope to have provided something of a snapshot of Sheffield at a fixed point in its story.

Chapter One

CRUCIBLE: 18,000 BCE–1750 CE

People on the Move

The story of Sheffield begins on the boundary between highland and lowland Britain. During the course of its history this was to become a frontier between peoples, kingdoms, shires and even the provinces of a distant imperial power. Being on such a significant boundary was to shape much of what is distinctive about Sheffield's story, from legends of dragons and outlaws to a fiercely proud political assertiveness and independent streak that persists even to this day.

The most prominent feature of this boundary was the River Don, its name (meaning 'water' or 'river') having origins in the distant Celtic past. Over

The confluence of the rivers Sheaf and Don; the land on the right was where the lords of Sheffield built the mighty castle around which the town coalesced.

time, settlement coalesced on a number of ridges that reached down from the uplands to the river valley below. The underlying geology meant that the numerous rivers and streams descending from the upland were fast moving and marked by many small waterfalls. The largest of the ridges, ending at the confluence of the rivers Sheaf and Don, formed the core of an ancient region of human habitation called Hallam, and it was at the end of this ridge that the town of Sheffield was to evolve. But that is to get ahead of our story.

A World of Ice and Stone

During the last Ice Age, between 50,000 and 10,000 years ago, the region lay at the very edge of enormous glaciers that stretched south from the Arctic. This ice was several kilometres thick and covered much of the northern hemisphere. To the south of these great rivers of ice was a vast expanse of permanently frozen land, similar in character to the Siberian tundra of our times. At the height of the last Ice Age, some 18,000 years ago, small family groups of people travelled east–west across the tundra, making temporary shelter in caves and overhanging rocks along the way. As they hunted and foraged for their food, they shared the plains and rocky outcrops with animals such as woolly mammoth and rhinoceros, giant deer, bison, bears, lions and hyenas. In modern times, very occasionally, archaeologists have come across the discarded stone tools they used for cutting up the animals they killed and cooked using one of our species' greatest technological accomplishments – the ability to start and control fire.

The First People

Just 22km south-east of modern Sheffield, some of the most spectacular remains of early human presence in northern Europe have been found. During the last Ice Age, Creswell Crags was one of the most northerly inhabited places on earth, providing people with shelter from the chilling winds in the form of a narrow gorge of limestone cliffs riddled with deep caves. Since the 1870s, antiquarians and archaeologists have found the stone implements and butchered animal bones that are all that remain of their desperate fight against the elements.

These finds include stone arrowheads and knives, the bones of woolly mammoth, rhinoceros and giant deer, and – most spectacularly – a bone decorated with a carving of a horse. In one of the caves, rock carvings and other forms of cave art have been discovered. These finds are unique in Britain and, together with the bone carving, represent the most northerly remains of early human creativity found anywhere in the world.

As the glaciers retreated in the face of global warming some 10,000 years ago, a greater expanse of Arctic-like tundra was laid bare. Over the course of a few hundred years, the ground thawed and dense forest and scrub slowly took over the land from the south. By this time, the mammoth and rhinoceros of the Ice Age had given way to aurochs (a large, extinct wild ox), wolves, bears, wild boar, red and roe deer, and smaller animals such as foxes, badgers, wildcats, otters and beavers.

During the Middle Stone Age (otherwise known as the Mesolithic era) from around 10,000 to 6,500 years ago, the population of Britain grew to a few thousand people. These people appear to have lived in small family groups but left little mark on the landscape. They were nomads who, between spring and autumn each year, moved across the land, much of it dense forest, gathering plants and hunting animals to eat. In winter they sheltered in caves. The distances covered by these first people were immense. Over the course of a season, the sparse archaeological remains of their encampments suggest that many of them travelled between the uplands to the west of Sheffield and the North Sea coast to the east. Over the generations, their journeys gradually became reduced, until they were effectively limited to annual movement between the hills and the valleys below. The greatest impact these first more settled communities had on the landscape was to start clearing the forests, which eventually gave rise to the expanses of elevated moorland that are familiar to us today.

Most of the movement of people was between winter shelters and summer camps, though occasionally more permanent resting places developed. Both types of settlement are evidenced by the remains of the inhabitants' distinctive tools made from flakes of flint and chert (a kind of quartz) glued with birch pitch to wooden or bone shafts to make spears and arrows, or used on their own as knives and edge tools. Due to later intensive urban development, relatively few remains of these people have been found in the valleys. Up on the moors, occasional finds of their flint tools and weapons are the only traces left by our Mesolithic ancestors. Much of what they used would have been made of organic materials such as animal bone, skin and wood, and, along with the temporary structures of their settlements, have long since decayed.

Remains of a temporary habitation, carbon-dated to about 8,500 years ago, have been found on Broomhead Moor in what is now the parish of Bradfield. It takes the form of five deep holes in the ground that would have held the frame of a wooden structure built to withstand the west wind. Behind this 'windbreak', a paved area was discovered that incorporated stone hearths where the people tended fire for cooking food and providing warmth, along with a scatter of almost 2,000 pieces of worked stone.

Evidence of a similar settlement from this time, in the form of an oval arrangement of quartzite blocks and sandstone paving slabs, was discovered at Deepcar. This, again, probably formed the foundation of a 'windbreak' shelter some 4m by 3m, within which were three hearths. Scattered around the stone hearths were no fewer than 23,000 flint and chert tools of various shapes and sizes. It could perhaps be said that this was Sheffield's first ever edge tool-making site. This ancient 'tool factory' would probably only have been used during the summer months, but nearby the remains of a more permanent settlement have been found where a family could have lived over winter. Similar settlements have been discovered at sites across the Sheffield area, including Burbage Valley, Wyming Brook, Hackenthorpe, Wybourn, Birley Spa, Whirlow and Wincobank. The people of the region were starting to settle down.

The First Farmers

Settled farming reached Britain from the Middle East and continental Europe about 6,000 years ago during the period we call the New Stone Age, or Neolithic era. People still lived in fairly small groups with others to whom they were related. For some time, these extended family groups remained largely mobile, but instead of just following prey animals such as deer they were also moving domesticated animals between their winter shelters and summer pastures. They maintained the clearings in the woodland by periodic burning, and over time these hunting grounds were turned into areas of cultivation for crops. The period saw increasing forest clearance by people, and the first major monuments to be built in the landscape in the form of large mounds, or 'barrows'. These were massive chambered burial mounds made of large stones and covered with earth. They were usually constructed on the highest points in the landscape and are often later recognised by the place-name element –*low* (from the Old English word for burial mound) in names such as Whirlow and Ringinglow.

The sites chosen for the barrows were likely to have been upland pastures to which families moved from wooded valleys during the course of the year. In these chambered mounds, family groups buried chosen representatives from among their dead, probably as a way of claiming rights and access to valuable land. The burials were often accompanied by objects such as flint axes and pottery vessels that seem to have been particularly valued, and group cohesion was likely to have been reinforced each time extended families moved back to the lands that had been claimed for their ancestors. The region between the Don Valley and the Peak District was extensively settled towards the end of the Neolithic period, leaving evidence such as groups of barrows on Broomhead Moor, Ewden, and other areas to the west of the region. In addition, stone tools from this period have been discovered at sites including Neepsend, Wybourn, Fulwood, Crookes, Whirlow, Walkley, Stocksbridge and Shirecliffe.

If the barrows provide evidence of family groups consolidating their seasonal relationship to the land, then the massive circular enclosures we call 'henges' are likely to have brought people together from further afield. The creation of these impressive structures would have required co-operation on a significant scale and they were probably used for large ceremonial gatherings of people from a wide area. Two surviving examples in the Peak District – Arbor Low and the Bull Ring – are both 30km west of Sheffield and probably served to bring people together from across the region, perhaps on an annual basis. Within these massive earth and stone structures we can imagine people feasting, exchanging livestock, polished stone axes and other valuable commodities. They may also have arranged 'marriage' partnerships and negotiated access to land for grazing and building camps. In general, the gatherings would have served to strengthen communal bonds among people who were still largely on the move. Undoubtedly, these impressive ceremonial gathering places were an important step on the journey from a nomadic to a more settled way of life in the region.

Discovering Metal

The end of the Neolithic period witnessed a huge growth in the construction of monuments, mainly in the form of burial mounds. This was an increase in activity that took place around the same time that metalworking was introduced to the

British Isles. The first evidence of this are the gold and copper artefacts that are found in the archaeological record from about 4,700 years ago. Around 4,000 years ago people started to mix tin with copper to make the more durable material we call bronze, and with this discovery a revolution in living was under way.

A Settled Population

Alongside bronze-working, a new style of pottery appeared at this time, known as 'beaker ware', which is found among the grave goods in burial mounds across the whole of Europe. This used to be interpreted as evidence of a distinct ethnic population of colonisers but it is now considered more likely that it represents a technological leap in both metalworking and ceramics associated with increasing population, itself largely the result of more favourable climatic conditions.

Within a few hundred years of the appearance of beaker ware we also find another type of food vessel known as 'collared urns'. It is notable that from burial deposits we can see that different groups of people seemed to prefer the different types of pottery, something that is probably best explained by the emergence of tribal groupings among the wider population. So, for example, while beakers are more commonly found in graves in the limestone areas of the Peak District, it was collared urns that were particularly favoured by settlers on the gritstone areas closer to what was to become Sheffield.

An important distinction between both groups and their predecessors who had built their burial mounds in prominent places across the landscape was their preference for cremation over inhumation as a means of disposing of their dead. However, there is little evidence that the emerging tribal organisation of the Sheffield region was dominated by the type of powerful chieftains who were buried with numerous gold grave goods in areas like the south-west of England. The evidence from the barrows in the Sheffield area, such as those at Grimesthorpe, is that they were constructed by ordinary farming families.

Technological advances and the probable emergence of tribal organisation went hand in hand with the development of more permanent settlements of circular huts with stone foundations, often associated with monuments in the form of round barrows and massive piles of stones known as 'cairns'. On top of the stone foundations the houses were timber-framed. Perhaps most dramatically, in the low irregular field walls of earth and stone, we see the first indication of the parcelling of land for individual family units.

Before peat completely took over the uplands, the soil was sufficiently fertile for growing cereals as well as for grazing livestock, possibly using a rotation system. Pollen preserved in peat bogs shows that woodland was gradually cleared over the course of a 2,000-year period from the early Bronze Age. Stones were cleared from the cultivable lands and piled up to form cairns on the marginal areas. Pollen analysis from the upland moors in the vicinity of Sheffield suggests that this move towards more permanent settlement began about 3,700 years ago and reached its greatest extent some 200 years later. In the Sheffield region, significant settlement remains from this period have been identified at sites including Hall Wood in Ecclesfield, Chapeltown, Ecclesall Woods, Rivelin and – most extensively – at Winyard's Nick on the south-western boundary near Hathersage.

When Did the Uplands Become Moorland?

Pollen analysis, combined with carbon dating, reveals that at the end of the last Ice Age, around 10,000 years ago, the uplands on the edge of Sheffield looked very different from today. As the great rivers of ice retreated, the climate quickly turned warmer. Scrub vegetation started to colonise the land, followed over the next 2,000 years by the development of woods and forests. Both forest and

Big Moor on the south-western outskirts of Sheffield, once the grassy pastures of early settlers.

scrub began to decline from about 7,500 to 7,000 years ago and peat began to take over the higher ground.

The reason for this dramatic change in the landscape is uncertain. Some archaeologists think it was the result of climate change, with wetter and colder conditions being the main cause. Others stress people themselves as the main agents in this dramatic transformation. This latter theory gains support from finds of charcoal in peat deposits that may be the remains of fires deliberately set to create woodland clearings. It is suggested that these grassy clearings would attract grazing animals such as deer, and being able to predict the whereabouts of your prey made it much easier to hunt.

In the long term, however, whatever the main cause of the deforestation, the loss of habitats eventually reduced the store of food available on the uplands, and from this time onwards settlement became increasingly concentrated in the valleys below.

Earth and Sky

In contrast to the first settlers who built large burial mounds to establish their relationship to the land, as the population increased, and communities became more permanent, people started to construct monuments that seem to have been an expression of their relationship to the stars and sky. These stone circles were considerably smaller than the massive henges built by their ancestors and appear to have been associated with rituals performed by smaller family units rather than the larger-scale gatherings at sites such as Arbor Low.

Just under thirty of these smaller monuments still survive on the higher ground of the Sheffield region, either in the form of small circles of standing stones set in a low earthen bank, or continuous banks of earth or stone known as 'ring cairns'. They typically have one or two entrances and sometimes a single upright stone outside the main enclosure. In the immediate vicinity of Sheffield there is a surviving example at Ash Cabin Flat on the moors above Wyming Brook. The circles were aligned to the setting or rising sun at the summer and winter solstices and are therefore likely to have been associated either with astronomical observations (perhaps with a mystical element) or rituals commemorating important stages in the agricultural year – or both. Like the earlier burial mounds, they would also have been a way of cementing social and familial bonds and, indeed, some circles combined these functions by incorporating cremations, sometimes in collared urns.

More usually, at the time that the stone circles were being built, people started to bury their dead under round mounds of earth that were considerably smaller, and in less prominent locations, than the earlier long barrows and chambered tombs. Dozens of examples of these mounds, and of the stone cairns, are to be found on the Hallam Moors above Sheffield, especially following the burning back of heather. Like the stone circles, these smaller round barrows appear to have been associated with more concentrated groups of people, probably based on family units. Again, this seems to be evidence that since the time of the first farmers, people were increasingly settling down.

Stone circle on Froggatt Edge near Sheffield: local families are likely to have come here to celebrate the passing seasons.

Bronze Age Settlement Case Study – Swine Sty

Situated some 14km south-west of Sheffield on Big Moor, archaeological surveys have revealed a small group of roundhouses with paved floors that can be dated from pottery remains to a period between 4,000 and 3,000 years ago. Excavation of one of the hut circles revealed its stone foundations and the probability that the main structure would have been built of timber and roofed with thatch or turf. The houses were about 7m in diameter.

Surrounding the houses were small plots of land enclosed by stone walls that have been interpreted as gardens or yards. Close by was a large scatter of worked shale that was discarded during the craft production of ornamental jewellery, mainly in the form of polished rings and bracelets. It is likely that these would have been used to trade for other commodities to supplement the families' subsistence from their crops and livestock.

Pollen analysis of this and nearby sites has revealed a considerable increase in the amount of grassland during the Bronze Age, so it is probable that the farming in this area was mainly pastoral, with flocks of sheep and goats and herds of cattle being grazed on upland pasture in the summer months. Over the years, stones that had been gathered from woodland clearings to create the small irregular fields were heaped on the edge of the settlement to form a large cairn, which in turn might have served as an identifier of land ownership. Some of the fields may have produced cereals after the land had been tilled with a simple 'ard' or scratch-plough.

It is possible that the occupants of these houses only lived there during the grazing periods and for the rest of the year dwelt in the valleys below. Unfortunately, the intensive development of lowland sites in the modern period has meant there is very little evidence from which we can draw firm conclusions. Each extended family or kin group probably had use of a particular group of barrows and one of the small stone circles that have been identified in the area. The barrows usually contain multiple burials of people with quite simple grave goods. These were the ordinary farming families who were among the first to lay down roots in the Sheffield area.

At around the same time that people began building settlements of round houses among fields they were also constructing impressive enclosures on prominent hilltops, often surrounded by stone walls and wooden palisades. At first sight these have the appearance of fortifications, and so the common term that has been used for them is 'hill forts'. There were at least seventeen of them constructed in the immediate vicinity of Sheffield. Traditionally, these hilltop enclosures were seen as evidence of a violent late Bronze Age society of warrior chieftains in which people had to seek refuge in high places behind strong walls. However, at the same time that the 'hill forts' were being constructed, the round houses that were being built among fields give the impression of a more peaceful society. Were the 'forts' there for the people of the fields to take refuge in times of danger? In most of the enclosures a water supply is lacking, so the sites would have been hard to defend for any length of time. And at only a minority of the sites, such as at Mam Tor, some 20km west of Sheffield, is there evidence of large-scale construction of dwellings within the enclosure.

More recent archaeological opinion has questioned the idea of a primary defensive purpose for these enclosures. In this view, sites such as Carl Wark (see below) were more likely to have been either ceremonial gathering places for people in the area similar to the earlier henges, or places where long-distance cattle-herders could congregate and make exchanges. At the same time, they might have had a 'political' function as a place where communities and their representatives came together to make important decisions. In practice, just as with the stone circles, they are likely to have fulfilled a combination of these functions, including a defensive one.

Carl Wark: A Bronze Age 'Hill Fort' in Sheffield

This rocky outcrop in the Burbage Valley (which itself means 'stream by the fortified place' in Old English) is about 230m long and 60m wide, and was enclosed around 3,000 years ago. On its northern flank the site makes use of the natural cliffs, while on the southern side a 3m-high embankment was constructed. Most impressively, on the narrow east side the people who made use of the site defended it with a substantial wall of massive stone blocks.

The interior of the enclosure is strewn with boulders, which means it could not have been used as a continuous settlement like the site on top of Mam Tor, some 12km to the west. Similarly, the lack of running water within the enclosed area itself would seem to make it unsuitable as a long-term defensive refuge. However, on the sandy soils to the south-west of the outcrop there is evidence of field boundaries dating from a similar period to the 'hill fort', together with more than seventy stone cairns, burial barrows and a ceremonial enclosure known as a 'ring cairn'. Taken together, these suggest a significant Bronze Age settlement of which Carl Wark was a prominent feature.

Carl Wark.

An Age of Iron

The forging of iron, which was to play such an important part in the story of Sheffield, became widespread in the British Isles around 2,700 years ago. This period, which includes the Roman occupation of Britain from 2,000 years ago, was a time of dramatic social and economic change that saw the end of Bronze Age patterns of subsistence farming in favour of more settled systems of agriculture and life in general. It was also a period of significant climate change and soil depletion, which in the Sheffield region was characterised by the unstoppable advance of peat in the upland areas and the creation of the desolate moorland that we know today.

Gradually, the upland fields became agriculturally unsustainable and settlement was increasingly concentrated in the valleys below. For this reason, we know less about the Iron Age inhabitants of the region than we do of their ancestors, as the remains of both their lowland fields and settlements have been largely obliterated by subsequent development. However, there is enough evidence to suggest that the population increased, and while the uplands were now used exclusively for summer grazing, the south-facing slopes and valley sides were the site of increasingly sophisticated farming settlements.

Celts and Romans

Equally sophisticated were the social and political arrangements of Iron Age Britain, which included a long period of colonisation by the Romans who came to dominate much of Europe in this period. By the time of the Roman invasion of Britain in 43 CE, the northern part of the region that was to become Sheffield was under the control of the Celtic people known as the Brigantes, whose centre of influence was at Aldborough in North Yorkshire. To the south-east, and separated by the River Don and its tributaries, were the tribal groupings of the Corieltauvi, and right up to modern times Sheffield lay on one of the most significant boundaries in Britain, a fact that was to have an important influence on its history and development and, arguably, even the character of its people.

By the late Iron Age, the region was quite extensively settled and cultivated, as can be seen in the complex field systems in Ecclesall Woods, at Ecclesfield, and an important site at Whirlow (see below). At the same time, we can see the development of the first 'industry' in the production of beehive-shaped, hand-operated millstones or 'querns' for grinding corn, at the nationally important site at Wharncliffe (meaning 'quern cliff'). Also from this period comes the first evidence of the metalworking for which the area was to become famous, with sites of early forges being known from a broad area from Barnsley and Doncaster in the east to Penistone and Sheffield itself in the west.

A major monument from this period is the massive 'hill fort' at Wincobank, which, when built around 2,500 years ago, would have dominated the Lower Don Valley and approaches to the uplands to the west. As with the similar enclosures from the Bronze Age, there is no direct evidence as to whether this structure was used militarily or as a place of ceremonial gatherings. However, there are signs that part of the earthwork was once subjected to intense heat, which might point to it having come under attack at some time in the past.

Wincobank hill fort was probably built by the Brigantes along the border with the neighbouring Corieltauvi to the south-east, as part of a defensive system that also included the so-called 'Roman Rig', a series of earthworks that extended north-eastwards towards Mexborough. Whatever its exact use, the site at Wincobank has the distinction of being the only Iron Age hill fort to survive within the boundaries of a major European city.

Eastern ring ditch of Wincobank Hillfort with its commanding views over the Lower Don Valley.

The Dragon of Wantley – Folk Memory of an Iron Age Foundation Myth?

There is some evidence from place-names and local folk tradition that the tale of *The Dragon of Wantley*, popularised from the sixteenth century, was based on medieval and earlier legends of a beast dwelling in the high crags at Wharncliffe to the north of Sheffield. According to legend, at the time of the annual festival of *Samhain* (or Celtic New Year, 31 October to 1 November) the dragon would do battle with a water monster emerging from pools in the Don Valley below. The festival itself was associated with the spirits that dwelt on the boundary between the worlds of the living and the dead. By the sixteenth century the legend had become more standardised, with myths quite common in Europe of a dragon that had to be slain before a town could be founded, or a similar undertaking begun. It is in this context that Sheffield Town Hall has a decorative stone frieze of a knight killing a dragon on the main stairway and a rather cute representation of the same beast above the main entrance.

The Dragon of Wantley, as depicted on the Town Hall main entrance.

Like the later Robin Hood legends (see below), the marginal lands on an important political boundary (here between the Celtic tribes of the Brigantes and the Corieltauvi) are just the kind of place we would expect the survival of stories associated with primal battles between elemental forces. Away from the realm of myth, we also know that Wharncliffe, Stocksbridge and Deepcar have some of the most important early remains of human settlement in the whole of the Sheffield region. It is perhaps equally significant that folk traditions associated with Halloween (itself based on the earlier Celtic festival of *Samhain*), such as 'soul-caking', persisted in Stocksbridge and Deepcar, in the shadow of Wharncliffe Craggs, right into the twentieth century.

Within little more than ten years following their invasion of Britain, the Romans had established roads and military installations in the Sheffield region. To the new arrivals, the lead mines of the Peak District were one of the main prizes of their conquered territory. At the same time, they took the opportunity of announcing their arrival to the British tribes in the area by building one of their arterial roads right through the sacred landscape centred on the stone circle at Arbor Low. The importance of establishing a military presence in the area was also due to the fact that the region formed the southern border of the powerful tribal confederation of the Brigantes. Later, this same border was probably used as the division between the two Roman provinces of *Maxima* and *Flavia Caesariensis* that were created by the Emperor Diocletian in the late third century CE.

Soon after establishing their foothold in Britain, the Romans had moved to subdue the powerful Deceangli tribes of North Wales. However, this campaign was abandoned in 47 CE due to the uprising of a number of the tribes of southern and midland Britain. Among these were the Catuvellauni, whose king, Caratacus, led a major rebellion against the invaders. Following his eventual defeat in 51 CE, Caratacus fled north to the capital of the Brigantes at Aldborough (North Yorkshire), but their queen, Cartimandua, had made a treaty with the Romans and duly handed him over as a captive. Over the next few years the Romans were engaged in suppressing uprisings among factions of the Brigantes opposed to Cartimandua, and it was probably at this time that forts were built on the River Don at Templeborough and in the Hope Valley at Brough (known by the Romans as *Navio*), with a network of military roads in between. In 2016, excavations at Whirlow Hall Farm uncovered the foundations of a Roman observation and signal tower that is likely to have been one of a series along the southern border of the Brigantes. Located at a high point on the edge of what is now Sheffield, this would have been in direct line of sight with the fort at Templeborough near Rotherham.

Archaeologists refer to the inhabitants of lowland Britain at this time as the Romano-British. In most cases they would have been indigenous people living under Roman rule. However, in one instance we know that a settler in the area had been part of the invading army. A thin bronze plate found in a field in Stannington in 1761, itself dating to 124 CE, records the grant of citizenship to a former infantry soldier following twenty-five years' service in the military units of the Emperor Hadrian. It was probably lost on the farm that had been given to him in reward for his service and therefore, remarkably, records the career of a man who was recruited to the imperial army in central Europe in the vicinity of the River Rhine, saw service at the military base at Caernarfon in North Wales, and retired in the Sheffield area. It is possible he was one of a group of legionaries who were given parcels of land in the locality at that time.

Remains that have been discovered close to North Lees Hall, near Hathersage, 14km south-west of Sheffield, give us an impression of what a Romano-British settlement would have looked like. The village was laid out on a series of terraces on a south-facing slope. Each terrace was about 20m long and 5m wide and was edged with low stone walls. On each terrace were one or two buildings constructed on square stone platforms, probably representing the house and associated outbuildings of a single family.

Nearer to Sheffield, excavations and landscape surveys that commenced in 2011 at Whirlow Hall Farm have revealed a substantial settlement that first developed during the late Iron Age and which continued in use through the Romano-British era. It was a large settlement of its type, with an enclosed area of over 70 sq m approached by an entrance causeway with evidence of a wooden gateway. Radiocarbon dating of organic remains suggests that the enclosure was built and first inhabited between 350 and 120 BCE.

Among the stone foundations, evidence of Roman occupation included pottery, iron nails and a fragment of blown glass. In all, more than seven distinct styles of Roman pottery were found, manufactured both locally and in various places on the Continent. The latest pottery evidence found on the site suggests that the houses were finally abandoned in the early fourth century CE. Evidence in the immediate vicinity of iron forging and the manufacture of objects made of pewter (an alloy of tin and lead) have been carbon-dated to the Roman period. As such, they represent some of the earliest evidence of metalworking in the immediate area of Sheffield.

Whirlow Hall Farm, a site that has been occupied since the Romano-British period.

Becoming the English

By the end of the fourth century CE, uprisings throughout their continental Empire prompted the Romans to withdraw from Britain. The archaeological record for the next three or four centuries in the Sheffield region, as elsewhere, is sparse and difficult to interpret. Following the Roman withdrawal, many units of local production, such as pottery kilns, went out of use, making habitation sites more difficult to date accurately. More generally, as the sophisticated monetary economy introduced by the Romans collapsed, people in the region who had grown used to storing surplus food in pottery vessels gradually went back to producing just enough for their families' immediate needs.

Despite the ambiguous archaeological evidence, it is clear that by the beginning of the first millennium CE, much of the layout of the settled landscape, in terms of networks of farms, villages and towns, had taken shape. This landscape was inhabited by a mixture of people, some of whose ancestors had been in the area for hundreds, if not thousands, of years, and some who had come to the region from parts of north-western Europe in an attempt to make a better living for themselves. Over the next few centuries, under increasingly centralised political control, these people were to become 'the English'.

The Angles

In terms of political organisation, the area found itself once again on a border, this time the southern boundary of the Celtic kingdom of Elmet, which arose during the late-Roman period from within the southern Brigantes and which exercised influence between the mid-fifth and early seventh centuries. Elmet may have existed as a significant tribal entity before the Brigantes made their peace with the Romans and then re-emerged following the end of the occupation.

The few surviving written records of the period do not make it possible to delineate the southern border of Elmet with any certainty. However, some historians have argued that it was marked by the River Sheaf (whose name derives from an Old English word for 'boundary'), a tributary of the Don that was in time to give its name to the settlement at Sheffield. It may also have incorporated the earthworks known as the 'Roman Rig' discussed earlier, and a structure thought to be of similar antiquity on Broomhead Moor to the north-west of Sheffield known as 'the Bar Dyke'.

The people who were to give their name to the country we know as England were a group of Germanic peoples who migrated from north-west Europe in

The Bar Dyke, probably once part of the southern border of the kingdom of Elmet.

the period immediately following the Roman withdrawal from Britain in the early fifth century. Over the next 200 years, Angles and Saxons settled throughout midland and northern England and formed independent kingdoms that included Deira to the north and Mercia to the south of the Sheffield region.

Like their predecessors, the first wave of Anglian settlers were buried in mounds, accompanied by choice items from their possessions, and in some cases reusing monuments that had first been constructed in the prehistoric past. One of the most spectacular discoveries of such a grave was at Benty Grange, 28km to the south-west of Sheffield, in which an apparently prominent individual was buried with equipment including a fine helmet incorporating both pagan and Christian symbols. A little to the south, at Wigber Low in the parish of Bradbourne, five Anglian burials were discovered within an earlier Bronze Age cairn. Nearer to Sheffield, there is place-name evidence suggesting the presence of large burial mounds, subsequently destroyed, in the vicinity of what is now Tinsley, where they must have been prominent features in the Lower Don Valley.

Towards the end of the sixth century, the Celtic British kingdom of Elmet came under increasing pressure from the expanding Anglo-Saxon tribes. Following the unification of the northern Angles into a greater Kingdom of

Stanage Edge, imposing frontier between the kingdoms of Mercia and Northumbria and subsequently forming part of the western boundary of Sheffield.

Northumbria in the early seventh century, Elmet was invaded and overrun, by which time Anglian domination of the area in the form of the rival kingdoms of Northumbria and Mercia was complete. Once again, the people of the Sheffield region found themselves on a major border between competing political groups. The border itself was marked by the River Sheaf, Meers Brook and Limb Brook, all names with Old English meanings associated with 'boundary' and 'division'. From the Limb Brook the frontier proceeded towards Whirlow, the name of which means 'mound on the boundary'. Perhaps the most dramatic stretch of the border is where it follows the line of Stanage Edge, which still forms the western boundary of Sheffield and from the craggy heights of which we can still imagine ourselves on the frontier between mighty kingdoms.

This borderland was subject to dispute for much of the Anglo-Saxon period until, in the year 828, King Ecgbert of Wessex, to whom Mercia then owed allegiance, led his army to the village of Dore (whose name had the meaning of 'gateway' or narrow pass between the two kingdoms) to receive the submission of King Eanred of Northumbria. By this action he established his sole power over the whole of England. The historical significance of what is now a commuter suburb of Sheffield is further highlighted by an entry in the *Anglo-Saxon Chronicle* for 942 when Edmund, son of Edward the Elder, King of England, was said to have conquered the Danes of Mercia 'as far as Dore divides'.

Linguistically, the Angles' influence on the landscape is evident from a number of place-names ending in *-field*, such as Bradfield, Dronfield, Ecclesfield and, of course, Sheffield itself, derived from the Old English *'feld'* denoting 'open country cleared from woodland'. In this, they were continuing a process that had commenced some thousands of years before their arrival. In general, their success in colonising the area is evidenced by the fact that the majority of place-names in the Sheffield region are of Anglian origin.

A significant transformation in Anglo-Saxon culture took place with their conversion to Christianity from the late sixth century. The existence of a church at Sheffield by at least the late ninth century is suggested by a carved stone cross of that date found in Sheffield Park 1,000 years later. This would almost certainly have originally stood in the near vicinity of Sheffield parish church (later the Anglican cathedral). In terms of political organisation, the Anglian period perhaps left its most lasting legacy through the division of the Northumbrian kingdom into a number of administrative territories or 'shires'. The most southerly of these was 'Hallamshire', which included a large area consisting of the ecclesiastical parish of Ecclesfield and its dependent chapelries of Bradfield and Sheffield. The origins of the name 'Hallamshire' are obscure. Alternative interpretations derived from the Celtic, Old English and Old Norse languages suggest meanings as varied as 'rocky place', 'hilly place', 'beautiful place' and 'land on the border', with the latter perhaps being the most likely given what we know of the strategic location of the region. Whatever the precise origin of its name, the existence of this ancient territory was to live on in the memory of the people of Sheffield, and in its institutions, to the present day.

Northmen

Raids on the coastline of the British Isles by warrior people from the near Continent, known as Danes or *Vikings*, had begun in about 800 CE. These early raiders are unlikely to have made much impression on the Sheffield region due to its distance from the coast and comparative isolation from a fully navigable river. However, in 865 the Vikings changed tactic and landed a large army in East Anglia with the intention of conquering all of Anglo-Saxon England, which at that time was divided into four kingdoms. After securing a base at Thetford in Norfolk, the 'Great Heathen Army' moved north and in 867 captured the Northumbrian capital at York. Within ten years the Danes had gained control over the kingdoms of East Anglia, Northumbria and Mercia, leaving only Wessex to be conquered.

There followed two years of intermittent war with Wessex, whose king, Alfred, managed in 878 to enforce peace in return for granting the Danes jurisdiction over most of the northern and eastern half of the country, divided along a border running roughly from the Mersey estuary in the north to that of the Thames in the south and marked by the course of the Roman road known in modern times as Watling Street. This huge area, which included all of Yorkshire and Derbyshire, in addition to thirteen other counties, became known as 'The Danelaw'. Over the next forty years the kings of Wessex gradually won back the territory to create a united English kingdom.

Due to the short-lived nature of the Danelaw, any lasting influence of the Vikings in the area was relatively limited but not without significance. It includes some place-name elements such as the ending -thorpe, meaning an outlying settlement, as in Grimesthorpe, Upperthorpe and Netherthorpe; isolated names such as Crookes from an Old Norse word for 'a corner of land'; and local topographical names such as Fargate, one of the main thoroughfares in the city centre, from the Old Norse word 'gata' meaning a street. However, one the most significant legacies of the Viking occupation is that at the time of the compilation of Domesday Book in 1086 by the Normans (or Norsemen, themselves of Viking origin) one of the major landholders of Sheffield was a Scandinavian earl by the name of Sven.

On the eve of the Norman Conquest and at the beginning of the period we call the Middle Ages, the population of the Sheffield region was therefore one of mixed origins. In one or two areas the earlier Celtic British people are likely to have kept themselves apart. In some cases, these communities have been commemorated by place-names such as Wales, from the Old English word for 'Britons'. In general, however, the broad scatter of place-names of British, Anglian and Scandinavian origin suggests a multi-ethnic population that was able to live together in conditions of relative peace and stability.

Conquest and Lordship

In 1086, twenty years after the Norman leader William the Conqueror won the Kingdom of England at the Battle of Hastings, comes the first historical record of the name 'Sheffield' (*Escafeld* in Old English) in the pages of his great tax survey known as Domesday Book. Meaning 'open country by the River Sheaf' (itself with a meaning of 'boundary'), the settlement had started to develop at the lower end of a spur of land descending from the upland moors known as Hallam Ridge, and was one of a number of villages within the historic administrative region of Hallamshire. It was most likely here that Waltheof, Earl of Northumberland and last of the Anglo-Saxon lords of Hallamshire, had his manorial base, or 'hall'. However, with substantial landholdings spread across the length and breadth of England, it is doubtful that he would have spent much time there.

At the time of the Conquest, Waltheof was one of three landholders with possessions in Sheffield, the others being Ulfac, Lord of Grimesthorpe, and the Viking descendant, Sven. Originally, Waltheof was such a close ally of the Norman leader that he had been permitted to marry William's niece, Judith. However, when rebellions broke out against the invaders, the earl found himself caught up in the intrigues and was executed for treason in 1076. To Victorian scholars, searching for the roots of English 'freedom', Waltheof became a hero in the struggle against Norman tyranny and is commemorated as such by a stained-glass window in Sheffield Cathedral.

Ulfac also disappears from the historical record at around this time, meaning that he probably fell out of favour with the new regime and was stripped of his possessions. As for Sven, though he was able to keep hold of a number of his lands, these did not include Sheffield itself. Waltheof's widow, Judith, retained the lordship of Hallamshire, though by the time of the Domesday survey she had leased it to Roger de Busli, lord of neighbouring Tickhill. The ancient territory was to remain a distinct entity, however, throughout the rest of the Middle Ages.

Like many of the entries in Domesday Book, that for Sheffield is relatively brief and difficult to interpret. In terms of its economic standing, we can say little more than that it was about half as productive as it had been at the time of the Conquest. Whether this means that the settlement was caught up in William's destructive revenge against rebellious landowners in this region known as the 'Harrying of the North', we may never know. However, what is

Surviving earthworks of the motte-and-bailey castle erected at Bradfield; Sheffield Castle is likely to have begun as a similar construction.

fairly clear is that Sheffield was at this time one of a number of fairly equally sized settlements in Hallamshire, among which Attercliffe and Grimesthorpe were specifically named, and which between them had sufficient resources to support a population of about 1,400 people. There is good reason to believe that the extent of Hallamshire (described as being 10 leagues by 8) was similar to the boundaries of modern Sheffield. The site of Waltheof's manor house within Hallamshire was not explicitly mentioned but was most likely on the site bounded by the confluence of the rivers Sheaf and Don chosen by the later builders of Sheffield Castle. The Norman lord of Sheffield, Roger de Busli, probably erected a motte-and-bailey earthwork fortification on the site, similar to his main base at Tickhill and that at Bradfield in the western portion of Hallamshire.

In about 1102 the lordship of Hallamshire passed from Roger de Busli to William de Lovetot, the grandson of one of the knights who had fought alongside William the Conqueror at the Battle of Hastings. One of de Lovetot's first actions on obtaining the lordship would have been to fortify the existing defensive earthworks between the Sheaf and Don, laying the foundations for a mighty castle that was to dominate the northern approach to Sheffield for the next 500 years. That approach was made by way of the bridge across the Don built by de Lovetot, which became known as Lady's Bridge in reference to the chapel in honour of the Virgin Mary that was established on its northern side. The thoroughfare continued up Spital Hill, the road taking its name from the leper hospital built by de Lovetot in the vicinity.

In surveying his new territory, de Lovetot had shrewdly calculated that this strategic crossing of the River Don, the point where upland and lowland converged, could form the focus of settlement and communications for the wider area. It is from his time that we see the emergence of Sheffield as the dominant settlement within the historic region of Hallamshire. The upper and lower ends of the Hallam Ridge on which the town grew are still known as Hallam Head and Nether Hallam respectively and the upland area is referred to as Hallam Moors.

William de Lovetot's development of the economy of Sheffield began with his construction of a corn mill at Millsands, of which he retained the monopoly, and most likely included the establishment of a regular market on land between his castle and the church that – almost certainly an Anglo-Saxon foundation – he had made a dependency of his monastery at Worksop. It was this sloping land between church and castle, with its market in between, that was to become the nucleus of the town of Sheffield.

Lady's Bridge, originally leading from Sheffield Castle (left) to the Wicker (right). Medieval stonework is clearly visible within the iron structure added following the Great Flood of 1864. On the east bank of the river was a chapel dedicated to Our Lady that gave the crossing its name.

As part of the process of bringing their estates together, the Norman lords of Hallamshire established a number of churches in the area. In addition to Sheffield itself, these were at Ecclesfield in the north, Handsworth in the east and Bradfield (next to their earthwork castle) in the west. Immediately after the Conquest it was Ecclesfield that was chosen to serve as the 'parish' of Hallamshire (perhaps continuing a pre-Conquest arrangement), with Bradfield and Sheffield as chapels to help serve a population spread out over a vast area. By the thirteenth century, Sheffield had become a parish in its own right and included a large area from Owlerton in the north to Heeley in the south, the sparsely populated area of Upper Hallam in the west and Attercliffe in the east. To help serve this area, chapels were established at Ecclesall and Attercliffe.

Also of contemporary significance to the economy of Sheffield was the foundation of the Premonstratensian monastery of Beauchief Abbey in the late twelfth century. This French religious order (named after the French village where they originated and usually known in England as the 'White Canons' in reference to the colour of their habits) was granted extensive agricultural interests in the Sheffield area, as well as a corn mill at Millhouses and a number

Beauchief Abbey, owner of some of the earliest ironworks in the Sheffield area.

of coal mines and iron smelting works across the wider region. Through its metalworking interests in particular, the monastery was closely bound to the emerging economic development of the Hallamshire district.

Within 100 years of the Conquest, the Anglo-Saxon manors of Hallam, Grimesthorpe, Attercliffe and Handsworth had all been consolidated into a single manor of Sheffield, dominant within Hallamshire and with its castle as the manorial base. Over the course of the next century, as extensive tracts of land within Hallamshire were granted by its lords to their retainers, dependent manors were created at Ecclesall, Shirecliffe, Darnall and Owlerton, though all were to remain subject to the chief manor at Sheffield.

The Early Development of the Town

If the details of the early foundation of the town are somewhat obscure, things become clearer during the lordship of the de Furnivals that followed the failure of the de Lovetot succession in the male line towards the end of the twelfth century. The original castle was badly damaged during the rebellion known as the Second Baron's War in 1266, but as reward for his loyalty during this period, King Henry III allowed Thomas de Furnival to build a new stronghold on the same site. From excavations that have taken place periodically since the 1920s, most recently from 2018, it is clear that this was a formidable edifice, comparable with some of the earlier castles built by King Edward I during his campaigns in North Wales.

In 1281, de Furnival's successor, also called Thomas, was asked by a royal inquisition by what right he claimed the lordship of Sheffield. His reply, that his rights had been enjoyed since time immemorial and included the privilege of holding a market and regulating the weight and price of bread, demonstrates that Sheffield's emergence as an economic entity can be traced back to at least the time of William de Lovetot. In 1296 these economic arrangements were formalised and given legal status by the grant of a charter by King Edward I, allowing the lords of Sheffield to hold a market every Tuesday and a fair for three days each year around the midsummer festival of Holy Trinity. An additional charter confirmed de Furnival's right to hunt deer in his park (in its contemporary meaning of an enclosed hunting ground) on what is still known as Park Hill, and in turn the lord himself granted a charter to his townsmen confirming their ancient privileges.

Although King Edward's charter did not grant Sheffield the full legal status of a borough that was a common arrangement in much of the country, it did

Castlegate Market, on the site where the lords of Sheffield held the first markets outside the walls of their fortress.

confer similar freedoms on the lord's tenants, who came to be known as 'burgesses' and were the body of men through whom Sheffield's lords administered the town. In his charters, Thomas de Furnival called them 'my free tenants of the town of Sheffield' and granted to them and their heirs 'all the tofts (houses), lands and holdings which they hold of me' at a fixed annual rent and without having to pay tolls (taxes) at the lord's market or anywhere else within Hallamshire. Therefore, while Sheffield did not enjoy the privileges of a fully fledged borough governed by a mayor and corporation (such as neighbouring Doncaster) it became what is known as a 'seigneurial borough', in which the lord retained his dominant position but the townspeople enjoyed a degree of independence.

The physical layout of the medieval town is clearly apparent in Ralph Gosling's map of Sheffield of 1736 and can still be traced on the ground today. Identically sized 'burgage plots' based on a measurement of twelve paces clustered around the market at the south side of the castle, uphill away from the river, and along the streets that stretched to the west and south-west. In the former direction, the limit of the medieval town was Fargate (meaning 'the far street') and in the latter West Bar (from a word meaning 'entrance'). While the northerly route into the town came via Spital Hill and

High Court, one of a number of narrow alleys in the city centre that preserve the town's medieval layout.

Lady's Bridge, that from the west proceeded via Western Bank, Brook Hill and Broad Lane to West Bar, at which there would have been a tollgate where taxes for both incoming and outgoing goods were collected. The main extent of the town was contained within the area between castle and church, and in the centre a maze of narrow 'courts', lanes and alleys was still evident on Gosling's map, and a number still survive to this day.

At the time of the grant of its town charter, Sheffield's population would have been around 2,000, in addition to a few hundred more who lived in the various outlying villages, hamlets and isolated farms of the wider Hallamshire region. Indications of some of the more important settlements and areas within Hallamshire at this time can be gleaned from additional details of the charter. For example, the inhabitants of Stannington and Fulwood, among others, were granted grazing rights 'throughout the whole of [the lord's] forest of Rivelin between Malin Bridge, Bell Hagg and Whiteley Wood on the one part and Stanage and the common way that leads towards Derwent on the other'. Rights of pasturage on the moors were granted to the inhabitants of the chapelry of Bradfield, and similar privileges to the people living in the vicinity of Loxley Chase.

Robin Hood – A Sheffield Hero?

The tales of an outlaw living in the forests and woods with his band of men, ambushing rich travellers and giving their money to the poor, first surfaced in England in the fifteenth century. Since then there have been numerous attempts to attach the legend to a real historical figure, and his exploits to a particular part of the country. The fact that the earliest versions of the tales were written in a northern dialect makes a Yorkshire setting quite plausible.

The first association of the mythical fugitive more specifically with the Sheffield area comes in the work of the great seventeenth-century antiquarian Roger Dodsworth, who wrote of a 'Robert Locksley, born in Bradfield parish, in Hallamshire, [who] wounded his stepfather to death at the plough, fled into the woods, and was relieved [supported] by his mother till he was discovered. Then he came to Clifton upon Calder, and came acquainted with Little John, that kept the kine [cattle]; which said John is buried at Hathershead [Hathersage] in Derbyshire, where he hath a fair tomb-stone with an inscription.'

While there is no clear indication of the source of Dodsworth's tale, it was enthusiastically taken up in the early nineteenth century by one of Sheffield's most famous sons, the renowned local historian and Keeper of the Public Records, Joseph Hunter. Hunter used his familiarity with the national archives to argue that the journey of 'Edward our comely king' mentioned in one of the earliest ballads, during which the king's baggage train was attacked by an outlaw band, could be identified with only one royal progress during the period, that made by King Edward II between April and November 1323. He then went on to point out that between the months of March and November in the following year a Robyn, or Robert, Hood appeared as a chamberlain in the royal service and that a man of the same name, together with his wife Matilda, had appeared in the court rolls of the manor of Wakefield in 1316 and 1317.

This Robyn Hood, so Hunter claimed (though without clear evidence), had been a supporter of Thomas of Lancaster, who was executed in 1322 for his leadership of a rebellion against Edward II, at which time Robyn had made peace with the king and entered his service. Subsequently, however, he had grown tired of his post and returned to his rebellious ways and had taken refuge in the woods of his native Yorkshire. All that remained was for Hunter to attach his Robyn Hood to the one referred to by Dodsworth. This he did in his famous *History of Hallamshire* of 1819, in which he mentioned that at Loxley, 3 miles to the north-west of Sheffield, were 'the remains of a house at which it was pretended he [Robin Hood] was born'. So, it is to Sheffield's most famous historian that the legend of Robin of Loxley, alias Robin Hood, owes its origin – though its facts have been disputed by historians, most notably the renowned medievalist J.C. Holt, himself a man of Yorkshire heritage.

The search for an historical foundation to the legends of Robin Hood continues to this day. One thing that can be said in favour of a basis in the Sheffield region is that its historical position on major boundaries, between competing jurisdictions (in which it would be easier for a fugitive to escape justice) and within a landscape where marginal upland wastes were once bordered by impenetrable forest, is just the kind of setting where historians would expect to see the emergence of legends of a heroic figure living on the edge of ordered society.

Even if we cannot securely attribute Sheffield's location on a number of prominent borders over some 3,000 years to the setting of an historical Robin Hood, there are good grounds for using it in our explanations of a people who for as long as Sheffield has existed have been noted for their powerful sense of opposition to central authority and an indomitable freedom of spirit.

From later maps and place-name evidence we can reconstruct something of the agricultural arrangements of these outlying villages, such as the ancient pattern of strips in the open fields at Crookes, which would have been allocated to individual peasant families, and which in many cases are still preserved in the nineteenth-century streets of terraced houses. In addition to arable land, the people of the villages would have enjoyed common grazing rights; for the people of Crookes these were the Crookesmoor, while the people of the hamlet known as Little Sheffield enjoyed rights of an area close to the town centre still known simply as 'The Moor'. Similar arrangements can still be inferred from names all around Sheffield, such as Shalesmoor and Batemoor.

A survey taken at the time of the death of Thomas de Furnival in 1332 gives a clear indication that within little more than a generation of its foundation, Sheffield was suffering from the effects of the climate change that adversely affected much of midland and northern Britain in the early fourteenth century. Some 240 acres (97 hectares) of arable land within the manor were unable to be cultivated in that year, probably due to the relentlessly wet conditions, and rents from grazing had declined by two-thirds. Soon after, in 1348, England was visited by the first outbreak of the devastating plague known as the Black

Death that, nationally, killed between one third and one half of the population. For Sheffield, the poll tax returns of 1379 record 354 households, half of which were of single people. This in itself gives an indication of the devastating effect of the epidemic, and even if we estimate that each household contained four children – which is on the generous side – we are looking at a total population of well under a thousand, about half of what it would have been at its medieval high point. That level of population was not to be attained again for another 300 years.

The Making of a Metalworking Town

The Town Finds a Trade

During the 400 years after the town was granted its market charter in 1296, Sheffield became established as one of the foremost metalworking centres in the country. One of the earliest references to metalworking in the area is the mention of four forges at Kimberworth on the border of Sheffield and Rotherham belonging to the monks of Kirkstead Abbey (Lincolnshire) in 1167 and which were to continue in operation for at least the next 200 years. The forges owned by Beauchief Abbey, mentioned above, were also established around this time.

These early furnaces were mostly of the type known as a 'bloomery', a type of stone-shaft furnace producing malleable lumps of iron ('wrought iron') suitable for working or forging. From the late fifteenth century, these were gradually superseded by larger furnaces able to draw in higher volumes of air – for which reason they became known as 'blast furnaces' – that allowed work at much higher temperatures, resulting in a higher-quality molten iron product that could be produced in larger quantities. Blast furnaces, the product of which was known as 'pig iron' (apparently from the way the molten metal ran off into channels that looked like the teats of a sow) became fairly common in Britain by the 1550s.

Of particular significance, given the importance of this occupation to the subsequent development of the town, is the first reference (in a tax record of 1297) to a Sheffield 'cutler', by which was meant a maker of knives and other edged tools. It was not long before the lords of Sheffield began to take a keen interest in the developing cutlery industry, and by 1322 they owned a number of forges (or 'smithies') in the vicinity of their deer park on Park Hill. By the late fourteenth century, tax returns show that in the Sheffield region there were already a large number of metalworkers, including forty smiths, three arrowsmiths, three cutlers, a locksmith and an ironmonger. Among those men described simply as 'smiths', many were likely to have been makers of knife blades, shears and other edged tools used in agriculture. In the early fifteenth century, one 'John of the smithy of Sheffield' was producing iron arrowheads in their hundreds for the English military operations against the Welsh prince Owain Glyndŵr.

There is no doubt that local topography and natural resources were key factors in enabling metalworking to flourish in the Sheffield region. Deep wooded valleys with rapid streams provided charcoal for smelting, fuel for forges and waterpower for hammers and grindstones. Local sandstones made excellent material for the grinding wheels themselves, instrumental in turning worked metal into knives. There were also good local sources of ironstone, the sedimentary rock that was the local source of iron ore, the industry's prime raw material. By the seventeenth century, however, this was found to be of insufficient quality, and imported ore would be required to produce the sharp-edged implements and tools for which the region was to become famous.

Sheffield's topography is characterised by numerous fast-flowing streams in narrow, wooded and rocky valleys, such as here at Wyming Brook.

Until the mid-eighteenth century, the main fuel used in metalworking was charcoal, a high-carbon product made by heating wood in the absence of air. Charcoal had the advantage over wood of being free of water and other volatile components, meaning that it could be burned at a higher temperature and gave off little smoke. Charcoal burners, commonly known as 'colliers', worked on a significant scale at sites around Sheffield such as Ecclesall Woods. Here they lived alone in small huts to tend their wood piles covered with damp clay. Management of the woods by coppicing ensured a continuing supply, though over time this resource came close to exhaustion and alternative sources of fuel were needed. These included the coal that was obtained from local seams. Early coal mines were often small, family-run enterprises known from their appearance as 'bell-pits' or, locally, as 'adits' dug into the valley sides. These gradually supplemented the traditional charcoal resources and, later, provided the raw material for the coke that was to transform the metal industries in Britain and provide the main fuel for the Industrial Revolution.

The local industry that developed from the Middle Ages was given further impetus from the late sixteenth century when metalworkers from the south

Ecclesall Woods, former hunting ground of the lords of Ecclesall and source of fuel for local industry.

of England were encouraged by the lords of Sheffield to settle and construct forges, furnaces and water-powered hammers in the north of the manorial estate towards Rotherham. Nationally, iron production peaked around 1620, from which time it became more economic to use the higher-quality product available from Sweden, imported via the North Sea shipping lanes to Hull on the Yorkshire coast, and less frequently from Spain and Germany. From this time, the local iron trade was largely in the hands of gentry families, such as the Fells who managed the Attercliffe ironworks, using a combination of local and imported iron. At the smaller end of the scale, the back-street yards of Sheffield were littered with small iron furnaces that were to be characteristic of the early industrial development of the town.

Within less than 100 years of the historic first mention of a Sheffield cutler, the Hallamshire region had become nationally renowned for the production of knives. The multipurpose implements that were carried attached to the belts of men of rank throughout the Middle Ages, known as 'Sheffield whittles', were sufficiently well known for the poet Chaucer to refer to one in his 'Reeve's Tale' in the late fourteenth century. A similar description was used for a small knife listed as being in the possession of the king at the Tower of London in 1340. Excavations at the site of Sheffield Castle in the 1920s also revealed a knife of this type with a plain wooden handle dating to the fourteenth century. Manorial accounts from the mid-fifteenth century show that by that time a number of waterwheels had been constructed on Sheffield's rivers, used to power the revolving grindstones that gave an edge to the cutlery pieces produced in the local forges and smithies.

The increased level of industry was noticed by the antiquarian John Leland, who, travelling through the area in 1540, noted that 'Halamshire hath plenti of woode' and 'ther be many smithes and cutelars'. From this time, local quarries such as those at Brincliffe Edge were being fully exploited to produce an even-textured soft sandstone that made high-quality grindstones. Such was the level of demand, however, that within a few decades these sources had been worked out, and by the seventeenth century the majority of grindstones used in the Sheffield region came from quarries at some distance away, such as those at Wickersley near Rotherham.

The Occupational Structure of the Cutlery Trade

By the early seventeenth century three out of every five men in the region were working as cutlers, and no other town in England could boast such a specialist workforce. In 1637, local surveyor John Harrison referred to the profitability of waterwheels used in the cutlery trade, and by 1660 there were at least forty-nine of these operating on the Don, Sheaf, Porter, Loxley and Rivelin, used for grinding blades and other industrial purposes. By the end of the seventeenth century, most Sheffield families had at least one member working in the metal trades and many had several. Over the next 200 years, cutlery manufacture spread right across the Hallamshire region, so that metal wares were being produced in the outlying villages like Bradfield and Wadsley, and razors and knives were being turned out by farmers in Stannington in small sheds at the back of their houses, with finishing being done at water wheels on the Rivelin. A list drawn up in 1740 shows how extensive the industry had become by then, with at least ninety grinding sites operating on the area's rivers.

From the start, Sheffield's industry developed in crucially different ways from towns in other parts of the country. In general, capital investment was not on the scale of contemporary industrial enterprises such as the Lancashire cotton mills. In its absence, the great expansion of the Sheffield cutlery trade was built on favourable export terms offered by the merchants of Hull, the port from which the majority of produce left the region. While this small-scale business model was unable to create substantial material wealth for the town, it undoubtedly produced people of remarkable self-reliance who transmitted their skills to their families over generations.

The typical unit of production was the Freeman Cutler, commonly known in local dialect as the 'little mester', and his apprentice. In complete contrast to the neighbouring towns of Manchester and Leeds, where the factory boss reigned supreme, Sheffield craftsmen were generally in charge of their own production targets and became fiercely proud of their independence. Cutlers were able to set themselves up relatively easily and, while trade was good, they could arrange their working lives very much to their own convenience, and earn – for the time – quite substantial wages. The majority, however, preferred to make a comfortable living and take regular time off, in particular the 'St Monday' that became established as an opportunity for a whole day each week to be spent in the alehouse or pub. Not for them was the slavish obedience to the factory clock that was becoming the norm in the neighbouring northern textile towns.

Although some men continued to work for others as 'journeymen', once they had served their apprenticeship more typically they started their own small businesses in their backyards. The 1672 Hearth Tax returns show that, for example, one in three houses in Attercliffe had a smithy attached. These

Drinking house built into the corner of the Cornish Place cutlery works, a place where workers would traditionally have spent the whole of each Monday.

were built of either stone or brick, often in the form of a 'lean-to' at the rear of the house, or a separate outbuilding. At about 3 sq m, the typical smithy had just enough room for the little mester and his young apprentice to carry out their trade. In one corner was a charcoal hearth and a pair of bellows to keep the fuel at the required temperature, and in another, a 'coultrough' in which blades were dipped in a mixture of water and oil after forging to prevent them from warping. Taking pride of place in the centre of this cramped room, an anvil set on a stone base (known as a 'stithy and stock') was the main focus of their daily work.

Within the broader manufacture of cutlery, specialist trades started emerging from the seventeenth century. The first of these was file making, and by the early eighteenth century it was the third largest sector of the trade after the makers of knives and scissors. Over the following half-century, further specialisms developed such as table knife and razor grinders, fork makers, saw smiths, scissor smiths and shear smiths. Even within the main cutlery trade, the forging and grinding of blades were frequently kept as separate occupations and the principle of subdivision of labour was very rigorously applied. Not only was each area of the trade carried out by separate workers, but grinders would frequently work only on a particular type of blade, such as those for spring knives or table knives. By 1748 a sufficient body of men were engaged in grinding as a sole occupation that they formed their own mutual aid society, the Grinders' Sick Club. This was an association that was clearly needed, since by the 1760s it was well-known that the particular dangers of the job, in the form of lung-damaging dust and occasional exploding grindstones, made grinders the best-paid craftsmen in Sheffield. It was undoubtedly the fact that such a large proportion of the population worked in cutlery and its related trades, together with links formed through apprenticeship and marriage, that gave to the people of Hallamshire that strong sense of common identity whose distinctiveness was recognised throughout England as early as the sixteenth century. Similarly, Sheffield's future position as the foremost metalworking centre of the country, and arguably the world, had its origins in the skills handed down through families both in the town and wider area during these centuries. The celebrated Sheffield antiquarian Joseph Hunter, who himself started out apprenticed to a cutler in the late eighteenth century, was certain that:

> the peculiar employment of the cutler has no less contributed to the formation of a self-reliant character. The work was principally done by the master and his apprentices [who] not only work together in the shop, but they live together under the same roof, and the association between them is necessarily more familiar than can exist between the employer and his hired servant.

Development of the Town

The first firm evidence of the size of Sheffield's population, from the 1616 Poor Law census, recorded 2,207 people in the central township. This means that Sheffield was larger than most English market towns of the time, and the records of baptisms from 1561 to 1640 show that it was growing steadily, albeit based on immigration from a fairly limited area. From this period onwards, the population trend of both the central township and wider Hallamshire was upwards. The Hearth Tax returns of 1672 record 494 households in central Sheffield and by the end of the seventeenth century some 3,500 people were living in the town. Over the next 100 years numbers increased remarkably as dominance of the national cutlery industry was gradually secured. Most of the immigrants from the wider area settled in the town itself, but others built cottages on the edges of common land and wastes in outlying settlements such as Grenoside and Gleadless.

In the course of his tour through Britain, the writer Daniel Defoe commented in 1711 that 'the town of Sheffield is very populous and large, the streets narrow, and the houses darkened black, occasioned by the continued smoke of the forges, which are always at work'. This was a description that was to recur through the eyes of visitors many times for the next 200 years and more. By the 1720s, the topographer Thomas Cox could describe the town as 'exceedingly large, populous and flourishing' and by mid-century the population had risen to over 12,000 and the wider parish about 20,000. Remarkably, Sheffield's population had witnessed a fourfold increase in just over fifty years.

When Ralph Gosling drew the earliest surviving map of the town in 1736, the layout of the streets was clearly still that of the medieval town; indeed, the majority of thoroughfares such as High Street, Fargate, Marketplace and the Wicker are still familiar now. The earliest expansion of the town, towards the west, took place from the 1720s on the site of the Crofts, the agricultural origins of this area still revealing themselves through its network of winding lanes. In terms of the buildings themselves, during the seventeenth century, stone and brick had started to replace timber for the construction of houses, and the quarries that for centuries had produced grindstones, such as those on

The Old Queen's Head, Pond Hill – a medieval timber building formerly belonging to the lords of Sheffield and known as the 'Hall in the Ponds'.

Brincliffe Edge and Psalter Lane, continued in use for many years as sources of building stone.

As the town grew, it still contained a number of poor cottages, and compared to towns of a similar size it lacked buildings of any great quality or distinction. One reason for this was that as a town of self-made independent metalworkers, Sheffield lacked an affluent merchant class, like that of other regional centres such as Nottingham, Leeds, Doncaster and York, that advertised its affluence through grand public buildings. Again, unlike these towns, Sheffield had no Member of Parliament, was not a centre of local secular or ecclesiastical government and, apart from a few lawyers, had no professional class to speak of. Finally, nestled as it was on the edge of the southern Pennines, Sheffield was at some distance from the country's main communication routes, a problem that was to be a continuing challenge throughout its development.

As a consequence, the only buildings in the town of any real note were the Town Hall of 1700, and the second Cutlers' Hall of 1725, and both were functionary rather than distinguished. However, despite its lack of architectural pretension, by the early seventeenth century Sheffield had established itself as a market town of some significance, holding weekly markets on Tuesdays and Thursdays that attracted custom from a wide area of Derbyshire, Nottinghamshire and the West Riding of Yorkshire.

Governing Town and Trade

Local Government and Society

By the mid-sixteenth century, the lords of Sheffield – the earls of Shrewsbury and their successors the dukes of Norfolk – were largely taken up with affairs of the royal court in London and rarely visited their Hallamshire estates. The manor buildings gradually fell into disrepair and, once the deer had been removed, Sheffield Park was divided into fields and leased to tenant farmers. The absence of direct lordship and control over the following centuries was to have a profound effect, not just on how Sheffielders organised their work and time, but on their aspirations towards independence in the political and religious spheres. In terms of practical government, right through to the height of the industrial period, the absence of established authority meant that Sheffield depended for its administration on a number of institutions handed down from the time of its medieval lords.

The first of these, known as the Town Trust, had its origins in Thomas de Furnival's market charter of 1297 by which he granted Sheffield freeholders all the lands that they held from him in the town in return for an annual payment. The principal trustee was to be known as the Town Collector and was the closest Sheffield was to have to a mayor before incorporation of the town in 1843. Arrangements that followed from a Royal Commission in 1681 further provided for the nomination and appointment of successive trustees by the majority of Sheffield's inhabitants, though in practice this broad franchise was not generally exercised. The other significant local institution, the Church Burgesses, was founded on the funds and landed endowments that had been applied before the Reformation for supporting 'chantries', religious institutions that provided masses for the souls of the dead. These funds had been confiscated by Edward VI, the country's first Protestant king, under the Chantries Act of 1548, but as soon as he died five years later the people of Sheffield petitioned the Crown for their return.

Together these two bodies formed the basis of Sheffield's local government arrangements until the town's incorporation in 1843. As well as being in charge of repairs to the parish church, they made some provision towards poor relief in the town and the repair of its highways and bridges. Crucially, the fact that, unlike neighbouring towns like Chesterfield and Doncaster, the Town Trustees did not originally seek formal incorporation meant that Sheffield had to rely on these antiquated institutions for its governance rather than the mayor, aldermen and burgesses involved in the administration of a fully incorporated town. Remarkably however, anachronistic as they might have been, these institutions of local government managed to preserve law and order, provide for the poor, and maintain essential services in a surprisingly ordered way. Similarly, although the town had no resident magistrate, and responsibility for law and order was not clearly defined, the absence of a wealthy professional and business class produced a more harmonious society with fewer sources of tension and one that was notably free from serious crime. Looking back from the beginning of the industrial period, Joseph Hunter felt able to comment that:

the want of a due mixture of persons well-educated and of superior situation in life rendered Sheffield at this period less distinguished by the elegancies and refinements of social life than by feelings of independence and rugged honesty, by hospitality, and a rude and boisterous conviviality. There were no assemblies, there was no theatre – the principal amusements of the place were the sports at the castle bowling green, and social meetings at the taverns.

In terms of local identity, it was perhaps the relatively remote position of Hallamshire, and the fact that the metalworking communities straddled the county boundary with Derbyshire, that explain why Sheffield people in this period did not generally consider themselves as belonging to Yorkshire. The county town was far away, and Hallamshire was the district larger than the local community of township or village with which local people identified. To the people of Hallamshire, the prominent towns of Leeds, Wakefield and Halifax were part of a different world dominated not by metalworking but by the manufacture of cloth. Indeed, the evidence suggests that when the people of Hallamshire thought of the wider world they looked not to Wakefield, Leeds and York, but to the national capital in London.

The Cutlers' Company

In 1554 the lords of Hallamshire started to award the right to stamp symbols known as cutlers' marks onto products to identify the specialist craft of manufacturers in the region. Rules and regulations negotiated between 1565 and 1590 with the Earl of Shrewsbury, Lord of Sheffield, set out the organisation of the trade and its rules of apprenticeship for many years to come. In 1614, Gilbert, Earl of Shrewsbury, had allowed a 'jury' of sixteen cutlers to take over the issuing of marks and generally to control the finances of the trade. When he died in 1616, control of the cutlery trade by the lords of Sheffield came to an end, and following petitions by the manufacturers themselves, an Act of Parliament of 1624 made the cutlers of the Sheffield region a self-governing corporation formally known as the Company of Cutlers of Hallamshire, and popularly as the Cutlers' Company. Since the Act covered the region of Hallamshire and 6 miles around, from this time onwards the regional name of the ancient region became fixed in historical memory. The craftsmen of Sheffield celebrated their newly won independence with the building of the first Cutlers' Hall in 1638 and the inauguration of an annual feast. The regulations are evidence of a strong corporate spirit among the cutlers and the consolidation of a powerful local identity among the metalworkers of the Sheffield region.

From the time of its foundation, the Cutlers' Company gradually adopted some of the functions of local government. As such, it was the nearest Sheffield had to a trade guild and claimed general responsibility for the industrial regulation of the town. Indeed, within the first half-century of its formation it had already proved its worth by successfully petitioning against imposition of the new Hearth Tax on smithies as well as domestic dwellings. Its main role, however, was to regulate trade through the registration of individual cutlers' marks. By effectively restricting free trade in the production of cutlery, the company hoped to maintain a thriving local industry.

As well as the manufacturers of knives, membership of the Company included the makers of shears, sickles and numerous other articles made of iron and steel. From the later seventeenth century, further subdivisions within the trade emerged, the first of which had been file-making in the 1650s. In 1682 the Company accepted filesmiths and scythe-makers into full membership. By the early eighteenth century, scissor-makers had also emerged as a separate craft and a number of others were admitted to membership in the succeeding decades.

From its inception, the Company exercised tight control on the admittance of freemen through the apprenticeship system, with the aim of preserving the livelihoods of its members. However, by the 1720s the Company's officers had become enthusiastic advocates of greater expansion and reduced restrictions, by which they hoped to further dominate cutlery markets at the expense of the London merchants. This included the Company's enthusiastic promotion of schemes to enable the navigation of the River Don from a point closer upstream to Sheffield and thus avoiding the necessity of a 30km overland journey to the inland port at Bawtry.

An original navigation scheme of 1721 met with a good deal of opposition from local landowners, especially the Duke of Norfolk, who felt that it would have a negative impact on his estates to the immediate north of the town. The compromise gradually emerged of making the Don navigable to Tinsley, where there would be a wharf for the transfer of goods by road into Sheffield some 5km away, and these arrangements were confirmed by the River Don Navigation Act of 1726–27. By 1740 the Don was navigable as far as Rotherham, and the Tinsley scheme was completed in 1751, providing a major boost to the local economy. By that time, however, rapid industrial growth and expanding markets had brought increasing conflict between the Company and individual cutlers, many of whom equated the relaxation of regulations with a lack of protection for their livelihoods and freedoms. This was a conflict that was to have significant repercussions for the political development of Sheffield in the decades to come.

A Nonconformist Community

In a town with an absentee major landowner, and in the dukes of Norfolk one that was Roman Catholic, the independent spirit of the people of Sheffield made itself evident through opposition to the Anglican (Church of England) establishment. It was during the English Civil War of the 1640s that the nonconformity of the people of Sheffield in terms of religion and politics first clearly emerged. The town's geographical position, at a distance from major communication routes, meant that it was not of major strategic importance during the conflict and the lords of Hallamshire kept well away. In their absence, families such as the Jessops of Broomhall, who enjoyed the historic right of appointing two in every three vicars to the parish church in Sheffield, used this patronage to present men of anti-establishment leanings, known to contemporaries as Puritans, thereby sowing the seeds of religious nonconformity in the town for centuries to come.

The growing influence of this faction within the town meant that at the outbreak of the war between parliament and king, Sheffield declared its allegiance to the parliamentary side and was occupied by Cromwell's forces in October 1642. At the same time its castle was duly secured, though it was to be retaken without significant resistance by a royalist faction in the spring of the following year. During their periods of occupation, both sides requisitioned local ironworks for the manufacture of ordnance and munitions. Following the Battle of Marston Moor near York in August 1644, and a local siege, the town was retaken by the parliamentary Major General Crawford. At the end of hostilities, Parliament ordered all castles that had been fortified by royalists to be demolished, and between 1649 and 1650 the once mighty stronghold of Sheffield's manorial lords, and the last remaining symbol of external power in the town, was completely destroyed.

The significant puritan presence in Sheffield was to a significant extent a result of the large sprawling parish within which the town had developed since the early Middle Ages. This made it difficult for the Anglican authorities to exercise close control of peoples' religious opinions, and by the mid-1600s, puritan families dominated the positions of Church Burgess, Town Trustee and other public roles within the town. The vicar of Sheffield, James Fisher, was himself a puritan and he and his three assistants were removed from their posts in 1662 during the establishment's purging of the Anglican Church of nonconformist ministers known as the Great Ejection.

What marks Sheffield out as particularly unusual during this episode is that instead of falling back into the Anglican fold, the great majority of the town's parishioners followed their ejected ministers and formed the basis of some of the largest nonconformist congregations in the country. During the late seventeenth and early eighteenth centuries, the vitality of nonconformist meeting houses in and around Sheffield was in sharp contrast to the lack of vigour displayed by the Church of England. By 1676, one in ten people living in the parish were listed as dissenters, which was well above the national average, and relations between the developing nonconformist denominations were generally good. At the same time, 90 per cent of the population was recorded as rarely attending religious services at all.

The strength of religious nonconformity helped to consolidate the special character of the people of Hallamshire, and in the two centuries following the restoration of the monarchy in 1662 provided a sense of common identity in both the town and surrounding countryside. At the same time, it formed a powerful basis for opposition to the establishment, central government and the emerging class structure that was to be a significant aspect of Sheffield's political development right up to the present day.

Upper Chapel, founded by followers of the ejected vicar of Sheffield, James Fisher, in a clear rejection of the established Church of England.

A Metal Revolution

By the early eighteenth century, the Sheffield region had become firmly established nationally for metalworking in general, and the manufacture of cutlery in particular. Over the next 200 years it was to become the most famous place in the world for the production of steel. In addition to the skill of generations of local craftsmen, this remarkable transformation has its origins in the ingenuity of a single man. Benjamin Huntsman, whose painstaking experiments led to the discovery of Crucible steel, was responsible for one of the greatest technological achievements of the industrial age and for starting Sheffield on its road to becoming, in the words of Joseph Hunter, 'the great metropolis of steel'.

Traditional Steel Production

Steel, a high-strength alloy of iron and carbon, had been produced in Europe on a small scale from the sixteenth century, mainly for the manufacture of weapons and knives. In Sheffield it had been used in the cutlery trade from around the same time by heating iron in charcoal furnaces to a sufficient temperature for some carbonisation to occur. By the 1650s, larger furnaces using the so-called 'cementation' process were starting to be built in the region. Charles Tooker of Rotherham had established a steelworks just before the Civil War using the same high-quality Swedish bar iron that was being worked by the Sheffield cutlers, and within the next twenty years steelworks had been erected at a number of sites in the immediate vicinity of Sheffield, including Kimberworth, Treeton and Orgreave. By 1700, John Fell had built a steel furnace at Attercliffe, and in 1709 Samuel Shore, the son of a Sheffield mason, was the first to set up a steelworks in Sheffield itself. Thomas Parkin built a steel furnace at Balm Green in the town centre in 1716, and Thomas Oughtibridge's 'View of Sheffield' of 1737 shows the characteristic bottle-shaped cementation furnaces that Shore had constructed on what became known as Steelhouse Lane. However, compared to cutlery, steel-making was a relatively minor activity in the Hallamshire region before Huntsman began his experiments, and much of the steel used by the cutlers was brought in from Newcastle. As for larger products, for most of the eighteenth century iron was in much greater use than steel.

One of the drivers of the emerging steel industry was the development of a new fuel, coke, which was made by heating coal in the absence of air and could be used at much higher temperatures than the charcoal that was traditionally deployed. It also had the benefit of retaining its heat for longer. It was originally produced by burning heaps of coal on the ground but, as the technology improved, large 'beehive' ovens were developed, using coal from deeper mines that were starting to replace the older open pits. From the mid-eighteenth century, larger collieries were being worked on Attercliffe Common and in the parish of Handsworth. As both coal and coke became cheaper, the iron industry in the region, originally dominated by gentry families, was opened up to a wider range of entrepreneurs.

In the traditional method that developed in Sheffield, brick-built cementation furnaces, generally about 6m high, contained a coke fire that was brought up to a heat of between 1,050 and 1,100°C and kept at that temperature for up to a week. Into the fire were placed two large sandstone chests (known locally as 'coffins'), within which were placed wrought-iron bars separated by layers of charcoal and covered with sand. The chests were sealed, often with the oily compound ('swarf') that was left over after grinding knives, to keep out air from the iron and charcoal inside. Fine judgement in questions of timing and temperature was required to determine when to remove the chests. The furnace and its contents were then allowed to cool over a period of a week or more, by which time carbon from the charcoal had been absorbed

Sheffield's sole surviving cementation furnace at Doncaster Street, Shalesmoor. At the height of traditional steel-making more than 250 of these structures dominated the town's skyline.

by the iron. The finished product was known locally as 'blister steel' from the characteristic marks left on its surface during the carbonisation process.

In larger steelworks, up to 16 tonnes of iron were converted in each cycle. Following manufacture, the bars of blister steel could then be forge-welded together to make 'shear steel', apparently so-called because it was of a suitable quality for making the blades of agricultural cutting implements. Although blister steel could be forged into excellent knife blades, the imperfections that arose from the fact that it had not been reduced to the real melting point meant that it was not completely uniform and therefore lacked the consistency and reliability for use in engineering work. For fine work, wrought iron was used, but its production was slow and expensive and the material was not always suitable for working on a smaller scale.

Benjamin Huntsman and Crucible Steel

The challenge of manufacturing steel of consistently high quality for use in specialist engineering applications was one that Benjamin Huntsman was determined to resolve. Huntsman, a strict Quaker with a resolute work ethic, had been born in Lincolnshire in 1704 and by the 1730s was working as a clockmaker in Doncaster. A good practical chemist, with the desire to improve the durability of small watch components such as springs, Huntsman started to experiment with melting blister steel and sheer steel in clay pots (or 'crucibles') together with a flux in order to produce a steel that could be 'cast', that is, poured into iron moulds while in a molten state. In 1742 he moved to Handsworth on the outskirts of Sheffield to be close to an area that had years of knowledge of metalworking. It is also likely that he was attracted to the area to gain greater knowledge of the crucibles made from Bolsterstone clay that were in use in the glass furnace at nearby Catcliffe.

The problem that faced Huntsman and his contemporaries was getting the materials to a high enough temperature within containers that could withstand the intense heat required. While the adoption of coke as fuel met the challenge of achieving a high enough working temperature, it took a number of years of trial and error to get everything right. Much of Huntsman's experimentation was carried out in secret at night. His attempts often failed, the biggest challenge being to find the right composition of clay that could withstand periods of up to five hours in a coke furnace heated to 1,525°C necessary to reduce the steel to its molten state and burn off impurities.

Former Britannia Inn, Attercliffe, originally the home of Benjamin Huntsman and standing opposite his new crucible steelworks.

His perseverance paid off, however, and within ten years he had been able to produce a material of reliable consistency and a hardness suitable for a range of applications. Critically, the complete melting of the steel was found to produce a highly uniform crystal structure that upon cooling gave the metal increased tensile strength. Through his hard work, Huntsman had succeeded for the first time in history in melting steel so completely that the chemical changes took place throughout the finished product, and manufacturers had a material on which they could rely for the demanding applications of the industrial age.

Having achieved his goal, in 1751 Huntsman decided to give up his former trade and become a full-time steel maker, moving from Handsworth to Attercliffe, close to where the River Don Navigation canal had recently opened at Tinsley, allowing him even greater access to his raw materials. Notably, it was from 1751 that Huntsman dated the foundation of his business, which remained in Attercliffe until the very end of the nineteenth century. At first, he kept his invention secret and no real competitors emerged before the 1760s.

The Crucible Steel Method

The raw materials for the Huntsman method were bars of blister steel from the traditional cementation furnaces. Up to twelve clay crucibles were first placed in a coke-fired furnace capable of reaching temperatures of up to 1,600°C. At ground level, the furnaces appeared as simple holes in the floor about a metre deep. Crucible furnaces are immediately recognisable by their square blocks of chimneys, such as those at the Titanic Works in Netherthorpe.

Typical crucible chimney stack at the Titanic Works.

Each crucible could hold about 15kg of metal. The quality of the finished product depended on the selection of bars of good quality blister steel and then upon the skill of the 'melter' in the management of his furnace. When the crucibles were white hot, they were filled ('charged') with bars of blister steel and a flux that included manganese to help reduce impurities. After about three hours in the furnace the crucibles were removed, impurities skimmed off, and the molten steel poured into iron moulds to produce cast ingots. A contemporary description from the mid-nineteenth century gives a vivid impression of the moment of casting:

The lid of the furnace is removed, and the dazzled eye falls with a wavering glance on the glowing mass within, from which pours out a stream of intense heat. A workman – his legs protected with wet sacking – proceeds to the hole. He looks down with a non-shrinking gaze. Guided by quick and experienced hands, his huge iron pincers firmly grasp the crucible, and the liquid metal is carried to the moulds, which stand at a short distance. The crucible is turned on one side, and the molten steel runs out in a thin white stream, from which shoot out a number of brilliant coruscations. This process is very beautiful when performed at night.

But while there was an undoubted beauty in this work, the job was hard and dangerous and manufacturers knew that good crucible team members had to be introduced to the work when young and, to use the phrase common in the trade, 'brought up to it'. The skill required to make the highest-quality products, which included choosing the best bar iron based on an expert reading of its crystalline structure or 'temper', took years of experience.

After being cast into ingots, the crucible steel would be passed on to other works to undergo the processes of rolling, 'tilting' and hammering. The aim of rolling, by which men standing on either side of the machine passed the heated material repeatedly through the rollers, was to further improve its structure, or 'grain'. Different rollers were used depending on whether it was to be rolled flat to make into articles such as saws, or in rods for cutlery, wire, needles, and other applications.

Steel that was to be used for cutlery and razors was also subjected to 'tilting' or hammering, processes originally carried out by water-powered machinery, but which became more efficient with the introduction of steam power from the mid-nineteenth century. The skill in hammering was to move the metal carefully so that the blows were distributed evenly across the surface, thus ensuring even consistency. When required, a number of ingots could be welded together for extra strength.

Ironically, given the importance of crucible steel to the future development of Sheffield and perhaps due to the fact that its inventor was viewed as an outsider, the product's significance was not originally recognised among the town's steel makers and cutlery workers, and Huntsman was dependent on exports to France. However, its immediate success there soon piqued local interest, and by 1787 there were about eleven local firms using the technique. As Huntsman's method of making steel became widely adopted, it was found to produce an ideal material for cutlery as well as the mechanical applications that he originally had in mind.

An additional benefit that was to be of huge significance for Sheffield's future industrial development was that the method allowed other elements to be alloyed with the steel. Huntsman himself was the first to start experimenting with alloys when he introduced manganese into the production process at an early stage. The invention of crucible steel was thus not merely revolutionary in itself, but in the impetus it provided for Sheffield to become a world centre in high-quality and so-called 'special' steels.

Before the introduction of Huntsman's method, Sheffield was producing about 200 tonnes of steel a year from Swedish bar iron; 100 years later that had risen to 80,000 tonnes, and Sheffield was responsible for almost half of the total production of cast steel in Europe. In skilled hands, crucible steel, suitably forged and heat-treated, became a crucial raw material in Britain's rise as the first industrial nation and gave Sheffield a head start over its rivals. Before long, a steady stream of foreign industrialists were making the journey to South Yorkshire to try and work out the secrets of crucible production, though none with complete success. Lack of suitable raw materials and a comparably skilled workforce meant that only German manufacturers were able to offer serious competition to Sheffield throughout most of the industrial period.

Thomas Boulsover and Old Sheffield Plate

Coincidentally, the second great invention that helped to transform Sheffield's fortunes, the revolutionary silver-plating method developed by Thomas Boulsover, was also made in 1742. Boulsover was a Sheffield cutler who, while working on a particular repair problem, found that when silver and copper were fused together, they could be worked as a single metal that had the external experience of silver. Initially he used his discovery to set himself up as a button maker, but found that his method was a cheaper way of imitating solid silver than traditional plating methods, and soon Sheffield manufacturers were producing luxury items such as candlesticks at a competitive price. At the other end of the market, the use of silver-plated handles on cutlery soon became common.

When Boulsover's method was applied to increased scales of production, rolling was required, a process that was carried out either at water wheels or horse-powered mills. In the early 1760s, Tudor & Co. had a horse mill on

Norfolk Street in the town centre, on the site now known as Tudor Square. It was Boulsover's former apprentice, Joseph Hancock, who was responsible for developing the rolling method around 1750 and bringing the process into general use. Unlike the cutlery trade, silver plating required more substantial capital and had the potential to generate greater profits. Due to the significant initial financial outlay, commercial partnerships were often necessary and a number of these were formed from the 1760s, among the most prominent being John Hoyland & Co. and the firm of Tudor, Sherburn & Leader.

As a completely new trade to Sheffield, imported labour was also required, and workers were brought in on high wages from other towns such as London, York, Newcastle and Birmingham. This was the first significant wave of immigration from outside the immediate region in Sheffield's history. The Boulsover method went on to dominate both the home and export markets until the introduction of electroplating almost 100 years later in the 1840s. Official recognition of the significance of the new trade came in 1773, when Sheffield was permitted to open an assay office for assuring quality, putting so-called 'Old Sheffield Plate' on a similar level to solid silver.

Taken together, the technological innovations of Huntsman and Boulsover harnessed the skills and traditions of generations of Sheffielders to remarkable effect in transforming a small town of backyard smithies into an industrial centre that became known as 'the workshop of the world'. Over the next 100 years, developments in Sheffield were to reflect – and often to shape – momentous events on the international stage.

Chapter Two

FORGE: 1750–1860

Cutlery Capital of the World

The early reputation of Sheffield was for its cutlery wares, and this reputation it still maintains. [It] is well-known to those who are conversant with the facts, that Sheffield produces the best cutlery that is made. A Sheffield knife or razor, with the mark of a good firm upon it, will hold its ground against the world.

Illustrated Guide to Sheffield & Neighbourhood, 1868

In the first few centuries since its foundation, Sheffield had been one of a number of places making iron and steel goods. From the introduction of the crucible steel method in the 1740s, however, an increasing share of national production, of cutlery in particular, was concentrated in the town and its region. By the end of the eighteenth century, all of the 115 waterwheel sites that were to be established in the river valleys of Hallamshire were already occupied, and two out of every three were being used for grinding cutlery and edge tools. The River Don had an average of three water-powered sites per mile (1.6km), the Loxley and Sheaf four, the Porter five and the Rivelin six. Nowhere else in Britain was there such a concentrated use of water power. Sheffield cutlery wheels were a source of local pride to its most famous antiquarian, Joseph Hunter, who commented in 1819 that:

The many works which have been erected on the Porter are so constructed and disposed that they commonly present an agreeable and harmonised feature in the landscape, a feature almost peculiar to the neighbourhood of Sheffield, so different are the low and small buildings erected for the iron manufactures from the huge cotton mills with which some of the finest valleys of Yorkshire are deformed.

Shepherd Wheel on the River Porter, a typical water-powered cutlery grinding works, first recorded in use in the sixteenth century.

By 1750, some manufacturers of both cutlery and edge tools had agencies in London and abroad, most significantly in America. This transatlantic business was conducted mainly through London, Liverpool and, occasionally, Birmingham. At the same time, there was a growing presence in the town of continental merchants, especially from Germany. Having already seen off competition from London, by 1800 Sheffield dominated the world cutlery trade. Greaves's Sheaf Works of 1823 reflected the increased scale of cutlery production and the exploitation of the American market following the end of the economic blockades of the Napoleonic Wars. In occupational terms, by 1841, 60 per cent of the country's cutlery workers were employed in Sheffield, and at the end of the century that figure stood at 84 per cent. In terms of sales, Sheffield's command of world markets is evidenced by the number of cases of overseas competitors pirating its cutlery marks in an attempt to pass off their own wares as the renowned higher-quality product.

How did this small market town come to dominate national, and ultimately international markets for cutlery and other metal goods? A number of factors, including the local topography and a highly skilled workforce, were undoubtedly involved, but one of the main advantages came from the complex organisation of the Sheffield cutlery trade. The emergence of specialist subdivisions such as grinders, hafters and forgers, coupled with the inherent flexibility of the outworking system, meant that production was able to react quickly to changes in demand.

In terms of business structure, the lack of barriers to entry into the trade meant that from the 1760s some second-generation cutlery manufacturers were able to set themselves up as merchants and dealers, employing capital and conducting business with trading houses in continental Europe and America. Large warehouses began to be erected in the town and new, wider streets were constructed, as well as elegant villa residences for the new generation of business owners. As for the workers themselves, at this time there was no segregation between residential and industrial areas, and cutlery and toolmaking shops were widely distributed throughout the town. To many of the town's visitors, it seemed that every one of Sheffield's inhabitants was involved in the work of grindstone and forge.

Business Structure of the Cutlery Industry

By the middle of the nineteenth century, approximately 11,000 people, about half the male working population, were employed in the cutlery trade. The size of the average work unit remained small, typically containing a 'little mester', one or two contracted workers and one, or perhaps two, apprentices. The industry was also still largely dependent on the craft skills of thousands of outworkers in small workshops scattered around the Hallamshire area who manufactured goods for the larger manufacturers in town. Some aspects of the trade became highly localised, including a concentration of fork-making in Shiregreen, spring-knife manufacture in Wadsley, and razor- and scissor-making in Stannington. Workers in these villages remained generally isolated from the activity of the town centre, visiting it on occasions only to pick up and return work to the merchants and middlemen commonly known as 'factors'.

The small units of production centred on the 'little mester' worked well when trade was good. Cutlery workers were free to determine their own hours of work and levels of production, and were adequately housed and fed compared with artisans in other parts of the country. However, the fact that working hours and conditions were not regulated by parliamentary legislation as in many other trades could mean that at times of economic depression cutlers found themselves in a poor bargaining position with the factors and the owners of the larger works that emerged during the course of the nineteenth century. At times like this, despite his undoubted skills, the Sheffield cutler could become little more than another of the outworkers with little control over his own business affairs.

Throughout Sheffield's history, cutlery establishments that employed more than 500 workers remained the exception, and even the larger concerns still relied significantly on the outwork system. Nevertheless, larger companies did inevitably emerge during the nineteenth century even if they were rarely described as 'factories' in the usage that was common in the neighbouring textile centres of Manchester and Leeds. Not only did large firms coexist within the complex network of independent producers, but even in the establishments themselves, workers were rarely subject to the direct control of the firm, but were in the position of independent contractors renting space and buying power, usually in the form of a grinding wheel, from the company.

Many, even though they were legally recognised as employees of particular cutlery firms, nevertheless still paid rent for their working space. Most would provide their own tools, buy their raw materials and sell their finished goods to whichever manufacturers or merchants would buy them. Essentially, even the largest of the cutlery works were often little more than a collection of

Cornish Place, established by James Dixon & Sons in the 1820s. Converted to steam power between 1851 and 1854, it became the largest cutlery works in Sheffield.

semi-independent workshops. In many of them, cutlers, grinders and forgers, as well as workers in quite unrelated trades, could all be housed under the same roof.

While the upward trajectory of the Sheffield cutlery industry was undeniable, trade cycles in these days of early global capitalism could be unforgiving, with collapses in world markets occurring every few years. Sheffield firms took American orders on very long credit terms and many suffered as a result of the American financial crash of 1818 in particular. From the 1820s, the United States started to develop its own cutlery industry, in some cases using Sheffield cutlers who had emigrated to escape harsh conditions at home, and Swedish iron exported from Hull instead of being delivered to manufacturers in Sheffield. Further losses in the US market in the 1830s led to a prolonged period of difficulty for the industry in Sheffield. The depression from 1837 to 1843 was particularly severe, with unemployment affecting 3,000 working people.

However, on top of the profits built on the Bowie knife craze, the gold-prospecting booms in the American West and Australia from the mid-1840s brought some additional relief. The firm of George Wostenholm, in particular, made substantial sums from the supply of pocket knives at modest prices to the US market, and went on to become a household name on the other side of the Atlantic, on the back of which the firm's appropriately named Washington Works developed rapidly from 1848. Other Sheffield firms established trading links in distant markets including the West Indies, Chile and Brazil.

The Big Cutlery Firms

Throughout its history, Sheffield's cutlery industry generally remained a small-scale craft business based on a workforce that passed on skills through family units. Nevertheless, a small number of firms took advantage of developing markets, particularly in the United States, to become some of the biggest cutlery concerns in the world. The famous names that were identified with Sheffield cutlery, wherever in the world it was used, included the following:

James Dixon & Sons

Founded: 1805

Premises: Cornish Place Works, at its height the largest cutlery works in Sheffield

Main products: Plated and silver goods, cutlery.

George Wostenholm & Son

Founded: 1810

Premises: Washington Works

Main products: Spring-, hunting- and Bowie knives, razors. By the 1860s the company was trading as far west as San Francisco. The famous 'I*XL' trademark was registered in 1826.

Mappin Brothers

Founded: 1810

Premises: Queen's Cutlery Works; by the 1850s they also had multiple outlets in London

Main products: Knives, razors, silver-plated goods.

Needham, Veall & Tyzack

Founded: 1820

Premises: Eye Witness Works, Milton Street

Main products: Table and pocket knives, razors, scissors. The Eye Witness trademark, first registered in 1838, has been one of the longest-lasting in the trade.

John Walters & Co.

Founded: By 1841

Premises: The Globe Works, believed to have been the first integrated steel, tool and cutlery works in the world

Main products: Table- and spring-knives, razors, scissors, files.

Joseph Rodgers & Sons

Founded: 1862

Premises: Norfolk Street Works

Main products: Spring knives, table cutlery, silver and plated goods. The principal Sheffield cutlery firm in the second half of the nineteenth century and by 1870 the largest cutlery company in the world, with 1,200 employees and a number of overseas offices from Calcutta in the east to Toronto in the west.

Getting to Market

The topographical features that favoured the rapid industrial development of Sheffield as the centre of the metalworking district of the Hallamshire uplands conversely put it at a disadvantage as a regional centre compared with many other towns in the country. Hemmed in by hills on all sides, Sheffield's history has been shaped in large part by a continual struggle to get itself connected to supply lines and markets beyond its borders.

John Warburton's map of Yorkshire, published in 1720, shows the main road communications that existed at that time. Commercially, the most important was the road from Sheffield via Tinsley to Bawtry near Doncaster, where goods could be taken on the navigable River Idle to the Trent at East Stockwith and then on to the Humber estuary for export from Hull. To the south, the road from London came through Derby and Chesterfield and carried on northwards to Barnsley, Wakefield and Leeds. None of these routes were easy going, but the most notoriously difficult was that which headed westwards though the Peak District towards Manchester. Despite the challenges, raw materials were able to find their way in to Sheffield and finished goods to get out, but if the town was to maintain its competitive edge it was clear that communications would need to be improved. In Sheffield, improvements in communications made difficult by the terrain were further hampered by the frequent opposition of absentee landowners who sought to protect their own economic interests over those of the wider community.

From the early nineteenth century a number of new routes were created, the most ambitious of which was the so-called 'Snake Pass' – named after an inn along the route that used the sign of the main symbol of the Cavendish dukes of Norfolk – which opened in 1818 and provided reduced times to Manchester via Glossop. Improved communications with Manchester, and then by canal to Liverpool, were crucial to opening up Sheffield's lucrative trade with America.

In 1815 construction started on a canal from Sheffield to the wharf at Tinsley, which opened in 1819 and included a new canal basin near the confluence of the rivers Don and Sheaf (now known as Victoria Quays). The construction of Greaves's new Sheaf Works next to the canal basin was a sure sign of the commercial significance of Sheffield's canals, which in turn provided an important catalyst to the development of Sheffield's East End. Over the course of the next century, this was to become the beating heart of Sheffield's heavy industry.

From the 1830s, plans were developed for connecting Sheffield to other population centres and potential markets by the emerging railway system.

Former office building of the Sheaf Works of William Greaves & Sons, an integrated cutlery and steelworks established in the 1820s to take advantage of the marketing opportunities of the recently opened canal link to Tinsley.

The parliamentary bill promoted by the Town Trustees for a railway from Manchester to Whaley Bridge was seen as having the potential to greatly enhance the export route to Liverpool. However, although the bill attained parliamentary assent, the scheme was abandoned due to the engineering challenges of the High Peak area. Ultimately, engineering considerations meant that George Stephenson's line of 1840 went from Birmingham to Leeds and York via Derby and Rotherham.

Those who had petitioned for a direct service into Sheffield initially saw the connecting line to Rotherham starting at the Wicker, which opened in 1838, as small consolation. Even this line had experienced a difficult birth, being long-opposed by the Duke of Norfolk, the chief owner of coal mines in the region, for fear of its effect on coal prices. Despite these initial objections, however, it soon proved to be an even greater stimulus to the development of Sheffield's East End than the earlier canal, and one of the town's most impressive features during the industrial period was the long chain of steelworks that lined the rail route to the north-east until their demise in the later twentieth century.

In 1845, a line from Sheffield to Manchester via Woodhead Tunnel opened after years of engineering problems. When completed, it provided a direct link

Wicker arches viaduct, constructed in 1848 to bring the Manchester, Sheffield and Lincolnshire Railway to the new Victoria Station.

to Manchester and Liverpool, and via this port to the United States. As such, it provided a massive impetus to the town's industry from the US market. This convenience had come at a cost, however: during construction, thirty of the mainly Irish workers involved had been killed and 700 injured.

Other Metal Trades

In the 1840s, a new method of silver plating, known as the electro-plating process, was introduced to Sheffield by businessmen who had connections with Birmingham where it had been first developed. Nowadays known as electrolysis, the procedure consisted of a quantity of fine silver being dissolved in a solution of water and cyanide in a vat, in which two sheets of silver were suspended and between which the articles to be plated were placed. Electrodes connected to a battery were placed in the vat and under the influence of an electric current, silver particles from the sheets, together with those in the solution, were deposited on the target item. The company of Dixon and Sons refined the process by plating articles of nickel silver rather than copper. Meanwhile, the firm of Walker & Hall moved into the area of' electro-bronzing' using a solution of zinc and copper. This process was particularly suitable for ornamental metalwork such as stoves, fenders, chandeliers and ornamental sculpture.

The material, originally known as 'white metal' or 'Prince's metal', was invented by James Vickers around 1769 and within ten years of being introduced to the market had become generally known as 'Britannia metal'. It consisted of a pewter alloy with a typical content of 92 per cent tin, 6 per cent antimony and 2 per cent copper, which produced a silvery appearance with a smooth surface. As such, it became an acceptable alternative to pewter at the lower end of the market for household utensils. Following the introduction of electro-plating in the 1840s, Britannia metal was widely used as the base metal for silver-plated cutlery and other items.

A Town Transformed

During the course of the nineteenth century Sheffield developed dramatically. The growing commercial success of the cutlery industry attracted increasing numbers of immigrants from the surrounding area, and after the first quarter of the eighteenth century the population of Sheffield grew threefold. At the beginning of the nineteenth century there were around 46,000 people resident in the parish of Sheffield, of whom just over 30,000 lived in the central urban area. The growth in population over the years between 1821 and 1841, from 65,275 to 111,091, was greater than in any previous period in the town's history.

While it was true that every one of the country's industrial towns saw significant rises in population during this period, Sheffield's growth was particularly spectacular. Between 1801 and 1851, while the population of the country as a whole doubled, that of Sheffield trebled. Over the course of 100 years, the town was transformed from the principal market of Hallamshire to one of the most important industrial centres in the world.

Growth of the Town
In contrast to towns such as Leeds and Nottingham, Sheffield still lacked a wealthy corporation that could redesign the layout in the face of a fast-growing population. The closest Sheffield got to town planning in this period was the grid-iron street plan laid out between 1776 and 1793 on the Duke of Norfolk's former estate of Alsop fields to the south of the town centre. However, this did not attract the level of interest among middle-class residents that had been expected, and within fifty years was largely taken over by industrial premises.

At around the same time, the building of Paradise Square commenced on land called Hicks Style Field, leased by the banker Thomas Broadbent since the 1760s. The layout of the square was evidence of the growing links between Sheffield and London at this time, and is an impressive, though rare, local example of Georgian town planning. The majority of housing in the late eighteenth and early nineteenth century was piecemeal, and dependent on economic fluctuations and sporadic leasing by principal freeholders the Duke of Norfolk, the Town Trustees and the Church Burgesses. The period between 1755 and 1796 saw a threefold increase in the size of the housing stock, characterised in particular by urban infilling like that of Hicks Style Field and at Little Sheffield Moor that, from the time of its enclosure and development, has been known simply as 'The Moor'.

By the 1760s, Sheffield's markets were struggling for space to keep up with the demands of an expanding population. In 1784 an Act of Parliament was obtained to reorder the market facilities, and the arrangements at Sheffield were considered a model of their time. More than 100 shops occupied the old marketplace and a slightly smaller number of stalls were strung out along the adjacent streets. The older shops, stalls and butchers' shambles were removed, the streets were widened and property frontages were straightened. In 1830

Paradise Square, commenced in the 1760s and modelled on examples in London.

Sheffield's Town Hall of 1808, a reflection of the rapid development of the town in the early nineteenth century.

a new Corn Exchange was opened by the Duke of Norfolk. Further evidence of the rapid growth of Sheffield came in the dismantling of the original, somewhat unimpressive, town hall and the construction of a replacement in the Haymarket in 1808. Ten years later the Sheffield Improvement Act set up a board of commissioners, which included the Town Trustees and members of the Cutlers' Company, to take over policing, lighting and street cleaning.

By the 1820s the town was expanding north-west across the former Shalesmoor, and both housing and industry started to spread along the Don Valley in that direction. The other main characteristic of the early decades of the nineteenth century was westward expansion. This was partly as a result of the construction of the Sheffield to Glossop turnpike (toll) road, which led to the development of West Street and Glossop Road, and partly from the desire of business owners to separate their residences from their places of work.

On the north bank of the River Don, the early settlements of the Wicker and Bridgehouses virtually joined to make a single large working-class district, while nearby Pitsmoor remained for some time as a distinct hilltop village by the side of the Barnsley turnpike road. In the opposite direction, by the 1830s, the area known as Little Sheffield to the immediate south-west of the town centre grew along London Road as far as Highfield, and by the mid-nineteenth century, the area around Bramall Lane had been fully developed in the form of densely packed terraces of working-class housing. Up until the late eighteenth century, the main building material had been sandstone quarried at Brincliffe Edge and other outcrops around town. After that, Sheffield followed the other prominent towns of the Yorkshire West Riding in choosing brick, in contrast to the smaller towns on the edge of the Pennines. However, more prosperous residents preferred stone, which was increasingly equated with high status.

Outside Perceptions of Sheffield

The sheer speed at which Sheffield developed had a marked effect on how it was perceived. So also did the fact that in the absence of a significant middle class, it was a town that was associated with 'ordinary working people'. A visitor in 1768 set the tone for much of the commentary of the following 200 years:

the town of Sheffield is very large and populous, but exceedingly dirty and ill-paved. What makes it more disagreeable is the excessive smoke from the great multitude of forges which the town is crowded with.

In 1795, the Scottish antiquarian William MacRitchie, during a tour of Great Britain, was probably the first to describe Sheffield as an unpleasant place set in an agreeable landscape, which became typical of subsequent commentators:

Adieu to Sheffield. It is a dirty, monotonous town, but surrounded with one of the finest countries in England: romantic dales, sweetly rising hills, plantations, enclosures, and neat gentlemen's seats of every size.

Six years later, passing through Sheffield on her way to the family seat of Wortley Hall on the town's northern upland fringe, Lady Caroline Stuart-Wortley gave no pretence of subtlety, saying of Sheffield: 'I was never in so stinking, dirty and savage place'. The 1867 edition of John Murray's *Handbook for Travellers in Yorkshire* took up this theme enthusiastically, informing its readers that:

Sheffield, with the exception of Leeds, the largest and most important town of Yorkshire, is beyond all question the blackest, dirtiest and least agreeable. It is indeed impossible to walk through the streets without suffering from the dense clouds of smoke constantly pouring from great open furnaces in and around the town.

In his report on the condition of the town in 1841, the Rev. J.C. Symons had identified topography as contributing to Sheffield's pollution problems but also noted that not everyone thought the smoky atmosphere was an altogether bad thing:

one of the dirtiest and most smoky towns I ever saw. There are a quantity of small forges without high chimneys. The town is also very hilly and the smoke descends to the streets instead of leaving them … One cannot be long in the town without experiencing the necessary inhalation of soot … There are, however, a number of persons who think the smoke healthy.

Working-Class Living Conditions

The debate as to whether, even in its poorest areas, Sheffield was healthier and better provided for than neighbouring industrial towns such as Manchester was to endure for the best part of another 100 years. In the early nineteenth century, most Sheffield workers lived in brick-built cottages with slate roofs typically built by speculators who, compared with other towns, had only the modest means to put up a few houses at a time for rent.

As in other industrial towns, these houses consisted of a single room on the ground and first floors, a cellar and a small attic room. Unlike in other towns, notably Manchester and Liverpool, the cellars were rarely used as a living space. The ground-floor room served as kitchen, dining and living room, as well as the place for bathing in a tin bath in front of the fire. Floors were stone-flagged, and cooking was typically done on an old grindstone placed in front of the fire. The husband and wife slept in the upstairs room with younger children, while older siblings, or a lodger, slept in the attic. Such humble dwellings were known as 'back-to-backs', with one facing the street and the other attached to it behind and facing into an unpaved yard, known in Sheffield as a 'court', where there was a communal water pump and privies (toilets).

Living conditions in some of these houses were undoubtedly unhealthy. Government commissioners reporting into the state of early working-class housing, from the vantage point of the 1840s, were particularly critical of

Part of a surviving row of workers' cottages in Gell Street, typical of Sheffield housing in the early nineteenth century.

conditions in the poorly drained part of the town immediately south of the River Don, known as the Ponds:

> their houses, if such they can be called, are miserable cabins, small, low, close, dark and dirty, where unpolluted air seldom enters – here a father, mother, and their children often reside in one room, and often sleep in one bed, or if they happen to be possessed of two, they are generally of such a wretched quality as to be fit only to generate filth, vermin and disease.

From the 1830s, in an attempt to improve their housing conditions, some workers combined to form co-operative building societies that allowed them to buy rather than rent their accommodation. The most successful of these constructed well-built cottages on the high ground of Walkley, Crookes and Heeley. The writers of a directory of Sheffield in the second half of the nineteenth century were full of praise for the initiative involved in such schemes:

> Even more pleasing [than the western middle-class suburbs] in a moral point of view, is the spectacle presented at Walkley and other of the out-districts. There are several

localities where estates have been purchased and partitioned out by means of the freehold land societies; but Walkley is particularly the region for these allotments. The hillsides are dotted in every direction with houses, almost all of them obtained by working men through the instrumentality of freehold land or building societies. Nothing can furnish a more striking and demonstrative illustration of the thrift of at least a considerable part of the Sheffield artisans.

By this time, when compared with many other towns, Sheffield appears to have been adequately supplied with housing for its workers, and in 1833 Sheffield's newly elected first MP, John Parker, welcomed the fact that the town did not have large numbers of cramped cellar dwellings that were the blight of the poorer inhabitants of towns such as Manchester and Liverpool. Ten years later, a report into working-class housing in Sheffield concluded that population density was generally lower than other towns. A local building regulation of 1864 was to outlaw the construction of any more back-to-backs, though by that time thousands had been erected and they were the main form of accommodation in the poorer, more crowded areas, which became known as 'slums'.

Segregated Living

During the first period of its expansion in the eighteenth century, Sheffield's newly emerging industrialists still lived in the centre of town. However, from the 1820s, as conditions there became more crowded and polluted, the middle classes started to move out to the western suburbs. The initial impetus was the construction of the Sheffield to Glossop turnpike that at the Sheffield end was laid out as West Street and its continuation as Glossop Road. Here, business owners started to build impressive villa residences in a deliberate attempt to separate themselves from their places of work. As in the other large towns of the country, the West End, taking advantage of prevailing winds, developed as the prime middle-class housing area, largely free of the heavy smoke pollution that blighted the industrial East End.

One of the first to make the move was Francis Newton, who owned cutlery works in Portobello, to the immediate west of the town centre. As this area became crowded with workshops and the poor houses of the cutlers and grinders who worked in them, Newton commissioned the building of Broombank House, a handsome late Georgian villa with extensive gardens overlooking the Porter Valley. Over the next twenty years, numerous other industrialists

Broombank House, built by Francis Newton, one of the first Sheffield industrialists to move into the western suburbs.

followed his lead and sought-after middle-class suburbs such as Broomhill, Ranmoor and Fulwood came into existence.

The preference among the middle classes was for detached and semi-detached houses with rooms for domestic servants, in most cases built with reference to standard pattern books rather than being designed by individual architects, although the company of William Flockton had a hand in many of the more ambitious designs. These included the Mount at Broomhill that, despite initial scepticism (his neo-Georgian terrace was disparaged in some circles as 'Flockton's folly'), proved itself to be attractive to Sheffield's small professional class. Broomhill itself developed from the 1820s as the first deliberately constructed residential suburb, on land that had belonged to the Broom Hall estate of the Rev. James Wilkinson, vicar and magistrate of Sheffield.

This was soon followed by the exclusive Broomhall Park laid out in the 1840s. With its lodges, gates and Sheffield's first crescent, this was a clear demonstration of middle-class aspiration and 'respectability'. A similar expression of class values was evident in cutlery manufacturer George Wostenholm's Nether Edge Estate, which he developed from 1835 and which included his own mansion of Kenwood, completed in 1844. Both the estate itself and the name of

The Mount, the most impressive survival of neo-classical domestic architecture in Sheffield.

Lodge at the corner of Wharncliffe Road and Broomhall Road, from which a barrier extended to restrict entry to the Broomhall Park estate. Constructed from the 1840s, it was one of the world's first exclusively middle-class 'gated communities'.

Wostenholm's own house were inspired by model towns he had come across on his business travels in the New England region of the United States. From the 1850s onwards, the first generation of steel barons were to build houses for themselves on an even grander scale, with notable examples being John Brown's grand Italianate mansion of Endcliffe Hall, Mark Firth's Oakbrook, and Thornbury, designed for Sir Frederick Thorpe Mappin by another celebrated local architect, M.E. Hadfield.

Public Health and Utilities

As Sheffield grew rapidly as an industrial town, the natural springs and public wells on which it depended for its water supply soon proved inadequate. From the early fifteenth century, Barker's Pool in the centre of town had become the town's first reservoir, and from the 1690s, various schemes were considered for supplementing the natural water supply. In the early eighteenth century, the Duke of Norfolk and the Town Trust allowed a private business to pipe water from the springs near a local landmark known as the White House in Upperthorpe to a holding pool near Townhead Cross, and in 1737 a new reservoir was built at the White House itself. From the 1780s, by which time a number of dams had been built on the outskirts of town at Crookes Moor and Hillsborough, the earlier pipe system fed by freshwater springs was largely abandoned. In 1782, upon completion of the enclosure of the common land, a system of reservoirs was built at Crookes Moor; the building constructed as the offices of the water company at that time still survives as 'Dam House'.

However, despite all this combined effort, by the early nineteenth century piped water could only be provided three times a week for two hours at a time, so the residents had to rely on tubs full of standing water for a considerable while. In 1829 the Sheffield Water Works Company was formed to purchase all the existing infrastructure and construct new reservoirs. These included two at Redmires that took the surplus waters of the Wyming Brook, a tributary of the Rivelin, and connected with the old works at Crookes Moor. Between 1830 and 1838, some 20km of old wooden piping was replaced with cast iron. Several of the smaller dams at Crookes Moor were filled up in 1839 and the ground let for cottage gardens. Two large reservoirs in the Rivelin Valley were completed in 1848.

Throughout the first half of the nineteenth century, the quantity and quality of the water supply, together with the inadequacy of drainage, were recognised as major causes of ill health. Indeed, the improvement of Sheffield's water

Former reservoir and water company offices, Crookes Valley Park.

supply was to remain an almost intractable problem that was to come to a head with fatal consequences in the first cholera epidemic of 1832. In total, 1,347 local people were infected, of whom 402 died, including the Master Cutler John Blake, whose memorial is prominent among the common graves of his fellow townspeople at the top of Park Hill. In response to the public health crisis, the Sheffield Public Hospital and Dispensary was opened later that year in Tudor Street, moving to West Street soon afterwards.

In 1836, at a time when the incidence of cholera was largely ascribed to lack of cleanliness among the urban poor, the town authorities opened Turkish baths on Glossop Road, and four years later, in 1840, a Fever Hospital was established that was eventually incorporated into the General Infirmary. When cholera came to Sheffield again in 1849, the authorities were better prepared and, in that year, only one in a hundred cases proved fatal, compared with one in three in 1832.

With the establishment of the Sheffield Gaslight Company in 1818, the town became one of the first in the country to adopt gas lighting. Gasworks were erected at Shude Hill in 1819 and over the following twenty years mains were laid in the principal streets and gradually extended. However, as with water, there were constant complaints about the quality of the supply, leading to the formation of a competing concern, the Sheffield New Gas Company, in 1834, which constructed a new works in Effingham Street.

Between 1835 and 1843 there was intense competition between the rival companies until their amalgamation in 1844 as the Sheffield United Gas Company. A year earlier, however, the town council had established the Gas Consumer Society but a protracted legal battle taken against it by its competitors, which went to the highest courts in the land, ultimately forced the two companies to combine in a second United Gas Company in 1855. This went on to become remarkably successful, remaining in private hands right through to the nationalisation of the country's gas supplies in 1948.

A Community of Workers

The Emergence of a Working-Class Identity

In 1851, Sheffield had a greater proportion of its population working in industry than any other town in the country, with 52 per cent of its working men, and 17 per cent of women, employed directly in the metal trades. There is no doubt that the occupational structure of the cutlery industry and the related light trades were instrumental in forming the special character of working-class people in Sheffield, and there is also good evidence that people working in the emerging steel industry took on many of the features of this established class. Whereas the textile industries of Lancashire and the West Riding of Yorkshire prospered on the back of a working population crowded into vast, capital-intensive factories controlled by a single master, the traditional crafts of Sheffield were characterised by low capital requirements and the typical worker, while renting both room and power, made his own decisions about how long he would work and, in many cases, for whom.

Similarly, in Sheffield, both masters and artisans came from the same social background and there was an absence of the rigid social distinction apparent in other industrial towns, particularly the factory-based centres such as Manchester and Leeds. Unlike the merchants of Liverpool, or the 'cotton kings' of Manchester, the masters in Sheffield had all at some time been apprentices and journeymen themselves, so that employers had far greater affinity with those they employed. In business terms, the difference between 'worker' and 'employer' was small, with 'little mesters' often employing outworkers on one contract and then being employed themselves on the next. While few people in the cutlery trade made large fortunes, nor were there many who were badly underpaid.

As for the job itself, it was in many ways the common experience of facing significant danger at work, whether at the grinding wheel or the colliery, that forged strong solidarities between the people of Sheffield. Individual and communal self-reliance was demonstrated most clearly in the large number of workers who contributed to sick clubs, which was significantly greater than in any other industrial town. Those established by the file makers, the edge tool grinders and Britannia metalsmiths, among others, all provided financial support and supplementary agricultural work for families forced to struggle during the all-too-frequent slumps that affected the manufacturing trades. In 1843 there were fifty-six such sick clubs, with an estimated membership of some 11,000 working people.

In general, there was a greater similarity of social and political values among the population of Sheffield than was noticeable almost anywhere else in the country. This situation was undoubtedly enhanced by the fact that so many of the inhabitants of Sheffield and its region gained their livelihood in the same way, through metalworking and the trades that supplied it. In the words of Sheffield MP John Parker, speaking in the 1830s:

> There is not that marked line of difference between the rich man and the poor man, which is becoming annually more observable in other places. The middle ranks are nearer both to the upper and the lower. The trade here is, as it ought to be, republican, and not an oligarchy – it is in their own [hands] and not in the hands of a few enormous capitalists.

Work, Drink, Celebrate

What emerged, then, in Sheffield during the eighteenth and nineteenth centuries was a distinctly working-class culture, in which the workshop and the public house were the centres of communal organisation and celebration. Significantly, for the majority of the working population, it was the working experience itself rather than, for example, religion that formed the bonds of community. The events that people looked forward to were the annual fairs, horse racing on Crookes Moor and celebrations of national events when

Mid-nineteenth-century terrace on Victoria Street, with a pub at the end. At this time, one in every six Sheffield houses was licensed to sell beer.

drink was provided free by the Town Trust. Major events in people's lives such as the beginning and end of apprenticeships, weddings and birthdays were all celebrated by time spent in the alehouse or home brewing followed by house-to-house visits to taste what had been produced and to dance and sing.

Remarkably, about one in every six of Sheffield's terraced houses was licensed to sell beer, and the census of 1831 records no fewer than 1,500 licensed premises, a greater concentration than in any other industrial town. As well as the alehouse, the focus of 'St Monday' free time included popular sports such as boxing and animal fighting that took place at locations on the edge of town such as Old Park Wood. This culture of communal drinking, singing and dancing found its most eloquent expression in the work of the 'alehouse poet' Joseph Mather and in the Sheffield dialect poets who succeeded him in following generations.

Joseph Mather, 'The Alehouse Poet'

Sheffield's emerging working-class culture found its most powerful expression in the work of Joseph Mather, widely known by both his devotees and detractors as 'The Alehouse Poet'. A passionate advocate of Thomas Paine's *Rights of Man*, Mather risked his freedom in promoting the cause of working people, particularly in the context of the government's response to the French Revolution, and specifically through its ban on 'seditious' writings in 1791.

Born around 1737 in Chelmorton near Buxton in Derbyshire, Mather was a file cutter by trade and came to Sheffield at the age of about 10 or 11 to take up an apprenticeship at a works near West Bar Green. It was undoubtedly his Methodist upbringing that gave him a familiarity with the Bible that comes across in much of his work. Mather first started writing satirical verse and songs while employed at the small works of Nicholas Jackson at Shemeld Croft in the Ponds area of town, and fellow workers soon persuaded him to perform his material in pubs to bring his attacks on employers and 'other persons deemed obnoxious' to a wider audience. Up until the 1820s, cheaply printed ballads and political broadsides were the most popular reading among the urban poor and helped educate working people about the impact of government policies on their communities.

Pamphlets would be read aloud in groups by literate individuals in the home, designated 'reading rooms' and, most commonly, during the 'St Mondays' spent in the pub away from work. Such readings, in which dramatic performance was highly valued, provided a significant impetus towards literacy among working people in the late eighteenth and early nineteenth centuries and helped inform growing political radicalism in Sheffield.

Mather himself was able to read but never learned to write, so his poems and songs were transcribed for publication by friends who attended his performances. In this context, Mather is significant not just for his evocation of working-class culture, but as an important expression of the oral tradition among the urban poor. The first of Mather's songs, in a volume published after his death, gives a flavour of his work with its themes of the pain of hard physical labour, poverty, hunger and debt (leading often to a comparison of working-class lives with slavery) and a call to revolution. The opening verse of 'The File-Hewer's Lamentation' runs:

Ordained I was a beggar
And have no cause to swagger
It pierces like a dagger
To think I'm thus forlorn
My trade or occupation
Was ground for lamentation
Which makes me curse my station
And wish I'd ne'er been born

His work uses chain rhyme, echoing the rhythm of hammer on metal, which would literally have resonated with his working audience, and which made it easy to commit to memory.

Joseph Mather died in 1804, at the end of Sheffield's first phase of working-class revolutionary expression, to which his work gave a voice, most powerfully in *The Battle of Norfolk Street* (see below).

Childhood and Youth

If the life the working people of Sheffield sought to ameliorate through pub culture was hard, this was especially true for children. In the metal trades it was common for boys to begin work at the age of 11, though some started as early as 6 or 7. Girls were occasionally employed as file cutters and more frequently in warehouses finishing, wrapping and packing goods. Before the 1847 Factories Act, which placed some restrictions on the employment of children, both boys and girls were often to be seen in the local coal mines moving loaded trucks and attending ventilation shafts. By their teenage years, the most common employment for girls was as domestic servants. The 1841 census shows that nearly three-quarters of Sheffield girls below the age of 20 were employed in this way.

In 1786, a Girls' Charity School had been established close to the parish church on St James Row, funded by voluntary subscription, to educate sixty poor girls between the ages of 8 and 16 and train them for domestic service. The building, with its stone inscription commemorating the foundation, still stands. Like the later 'House of Help for Women and Girls' in nearby Paradise Square, an implicit intention of such an establishment was to keep girls and women from falling into the economic necessity of sex work. As adults, an

Girls' Charity School, St James Row.

increasing number of women found 'legitimate' work as 'buffer girls', taking on the dirty work of polishing in the silver plate and cutlery trades.

Concern for the moral environment within which young people developed was one of the manifestations of middle-class attempts to exercise control over working-class life that became a feature of urban society in the nineteenth century. In 1841, Sheffield reformer Ebenezer Elliott told a public inquiry into the condition of young people employed in the Sheffield trades that religious observance was low and education provision had not kept pace with rapid population growth. Many young men and boys were alleged to spend their time playing pitch-penny and fighting bulldogs. The establishment view during this period was that the apprenticeship system gave too much freedom to young people, especially as compared to the strict regulation of children's lives in the textile factories of Lancashire and the West Riding. And unlike those children, who were under close watch in factory dormitories, young Sheffield apprentices in boarding houses away from their families were perceived to be out of control.

'Children are their own masters before fourteen years of age,' complained one middle-class contributor to a government inquiry. Fathers spent entire evenings in the pub rather than exercising patriarchal discipline, and parents seemed to attach low importance to education. In the case of the poorest members of society, submissions to the inquiry demonstrate that often this was because mothers were reluctant to let their children go to school dressed in rags for fear of being shamed in the face of a growing working-class 'respectability' informed by nonconformist religion and in opposition to the rough life of 'the street'.

Writing in 1845 in his investigation into the condition of the working-class in England, Friedrich Engels was particularly vivid in his description of this independent culture, as viewed from a middle-class perspective and inasmuch as it played out among Sheffield's youth:

> Immorality among young people seems to be more prevalent in Sheffield than any-where else. The younger generation spend the whole of Sunday lying in the street tossing coins or dog-fighting, and go regularly to the gin palace, where they sit with their sweethearts till late at night, when they take walks in solitary couples. In an ale-house which the commissioner visited, there sat forty to fifty young people of both sexes, nearly all under seventeen years of age, and each lad beside his lass. Here and there cards were played, at other places dancing was going on, and every-where drinking. Among the company were openly avowed professional prostitutes. No wonder then that, as all witnesses testify, unbridled sexual intercourse, youthful prostitution, beginning with persons of fourteen to fifteen years, is extraordinarily frequent in Sheffield.

This was a form of society that, though it clearly emerged from the inequalities produced by capitalist industrialisation, evidently perplexed and offended contemporary middle-class commentators. According to one historian of class formation in Victorian England, this was because it was one from which they felt excluded and over which they were able to exercise only limited control. This very much reflects the view of one of Victorian Sheffield's most prominent middle-class citizens, Dr Arnold Knight, who spoke of the futility of trying to 'improve' the emerging working class if it was not to be done by 'adapting our efforts to their taste'.

A Compact with the Devil

As with working-class society more generally, what undoubtedly precipitated the behaviour noted disapprovingly by Engels and others was that life for many of Sheffield's working people was hard and short. The relatively high wages that could be earned in the cutlery industry, that many in the middle class saw as the actual cause of perceived immorality, were in large part due to the dangers inherent in the job. Tellingly, it was often workers themselves who resisted efforts to improve working conditions and safety because they knew instinctively that this would make the trades more generally accessible and drive down wages. In the contemporary industrial world, the grinders of Sheffield were seen to have made a very pact with the devil, trading a short life for relative material gain.

The greatest danger was from 'grinders' asthma' caused by long hours spent crouched over wheels inhaling the dust produced from the friction between metal and stone. This situation only got worse with the introduction of steam power, which meant that men would spend even longer at the wheels. In 1830, the celebrated local physician Dr Arnold Knight was of the opinion that among 2,500 grinders, fewer than thirty-five made it to the age of 50. In 1845, Engels included a case study of the Sheffield grinders in his investigation into the condition of the working class in England, which noted that:

> By far the most unwholesome work is the grinding of knife-blades and forks, which, especially when done with a dry stone, entails certain early death. The unwholesomeness of this work lies in part in the bent posture, in which chest and stomach are cramped; but especially in the quantity of sharp-edged metal dust particles freed in the cutting which fill the atmosphere and are necessarily inhaled. The dry-grinders' average life is hardly thirty-five years; the wet-grinders' rarely exceeds forty-five.

The first serious attempts at improving workshop conditions were not made until the 1860s with the introduction of fans designed to draw the particle-ridden air away from the workplace and through a flue connected to the outside. But, despite the relative low cost of such modifications, one observer of the contemporary cutlery industry noted sadly that 'it is with much difficulty that the grinders can be induced to use the apparatus'.

Quite apart from chronic lung conditions, which included silicosis and pneumoconiosis, basic working conditions for grinders continued to be dangerous right up to the end of the nineteenth century and beyond. Men were not uncommonly killed when hit by bits of fractured grindstones. In the days before health and safety legislation, even where there was evidence that suggested machinery had not been well maintained, men were described as having been 'accidentally killed'. Again, moves to make grinding safer by putting chains around the stones to minimise the catastrophic effects of fracture were actually resisted by the men themselves on the grounds that a safer occupation would command lower wages. It was not until 1908 that significant improvements in the working conditions of grinders were introduced.

More generally, in a town that compared to any other in the country can be said to have been genuinely 'working class', where two-thirds of the population were employed directly in the metal trades by the 1870s, hardship and disease were rife among Sheffield's rapidly expanding population. At the time of the census in 1841, after making allowance for high infant mortality, the average age of death in Sheffield was 51 years.

However, by comparison this was still better than in many other industrial towns, in particular neighbouring Manchester. Similarly, deaths from typhus were only one tenth of those in Liverpool and one fifth of the count in Birmingham. In part, this was due to lower rates of immigration of poor people from other parts of the British Isles, particularly Ireland from the 1840s, and associated overcrowded living conditions that were much more common in towns such as Manchester and Leeds. The main differences were the comparatively better housing conditions in Sheffield and the advantages of working in smaller workshops compared with large, crowded factories. In truth, working-class life in the country's industrial towns and cities was universally hard, but when they came together to sing and dance in the alehouse and at public celebrations, the people of Sheffield perhaps had more reasons to be grateful than most.

'A Damned Bad Place'

In a story widely circulated at the time, England's King George III was at his favourite seaside resort of Weymouth in 1800 when, on his daily stroll, he came across some children playing on the beach under the charge of a nurse. 'And whose children are these?' asked the King, by way of making conversation. On being told that their father was a gentleman from Norton, near Sheffield, the King is said to have replied, 'Ah, Sheffield, Sheffield! Damned bad place, Sheffield.'

The King's derogatory remark reflected the general opinion at that time that Sheffield was the most politically radical town in the country and a potential catalyst for the revolutionary fervour that had neighbouring France in its grip. According to Joseph Hunter, who had been a young boy during this turbulent era, 'Sheffield lay for some time under the most vehement suspicions of being infected with principles decidedly revolutionary.'

Throughout the period from the late eighteenth to the mid-nineteenth centuries, popular politics in Sheffield were completely at odds with the nationwide mood of popular support for the establishment that manifested itself in towns including London and Birmingham as 'Church and King' demonstrations, and occasionally, riots. One of the most marked characteristics of Sheffield right through to the mid-nineteenth century – and beyond – was the persistence of a radical, and occasionally revolutionary, popular political tradition. At its height, this conflict between people and the establishment meant that Sheffield helped to bring the entire country close to revolution.

The Origins of Sheffield's Political Radicalism

Increasingly in a town dominated by the cutlery and associated trades, the freedom and independence that emerged from the occupational structure of Sheffield's artisans began to find expression in both the political and religious spheres, and through open conflict between working people and the establishment. The industrial structure of the town, based on small units of production and independent masters, together with growing tensions between artisans and the Cutlers' Company, fostered an individualistic ethos that provided workers with self-confidence and the impetus for radical organisation. One of the more remarkable aspects of Sheffield's emerging radical politics was that until the second half of the nineteenth century there was little discernible division between middle-class and working-class aspirations and sentiment, again promoted to a large extent by the egalitarian industrial structure, the relative weakness of the Anglican establishment, the absenteeism of the town's principal landowners and the prominence of working-class nonconformist businessmen in the town's administration.

This social and political egalitarianism meant that the town's political tradition took much of its energy from the anti-slavery (otherwise known as 'abolitionist') movement. In 1789 no fewer than 800 Sheffield metalworkers submitted a petition to Parliament calling for abolition of the slave trade. To what extent this was driven by a conscious recognition that much of the equipment used in the plantation system, such as mattocks, spades and hoes, were made in Sheffield we will probably never know. Either way, at the time, this was a markedly unpopular position to take, and one that was generally perceived as going hand-in-hand with the sort of revolutionary passions that had led to the loss of England's most valuable colony and the creation of the United States of America. Significant leaders of this movement, such as the radical newspaper editors James Montgomery and Joseph Gales, went on to provide momentum for the general struggle for social justice. Importantly, reformers such as these in Sheffield did not rely exclusively on the support of the middle classes as in other towns, but built on the prominence of men such as the 'alehouse poet' Joseph Mather to help construct a nationally pioneering working-class movement.

The growth of radicalism in Sheffield also owed much to the unsuccessful campaigns fought by freemen in the cutlery industry in the 1780s to persuade the Cutlers' Company to offer them protection by tighter regulation of entry into their craft. For its part, the Company made its position clear in 1814 when it declined to protest against Parliament passing legislation to strip it of its legal powers of trade regulation. These events had a profound impact on working-class opinion, highlighting the need for the representation of working people in Parliament that would form a recurring political theme of the first half of the nineteenth century.

The first signs of significant unrest in Sheffield occurred in 1756 when poor townspeople protested against high corn prices, during which stores of flour at the Pond Mill were destroyed. This was the first indication that the authorities might not be able to control popular protest. The same period saw demonstrations directed against the Duke of Norfolk's attempts to build a wooden railway to bring coal from his estates into the town to undercut prices, and matters escalated during the 1780s with fierce resistance to the enclosure of Crookes Moor, the site of popular horse-racing meetings that were one of the main social events for the working people of the town.

The fact that populous manufacturing towns like Sheffield had no representation in Parliament, and that the mass of the population was therefore disenfranchised, was an injustice that was cast into stark relief during the celebrations of the centenary of the so-called Glorious Revolution of 1688, when the country had thrown off the shackles of absolute monarchy and apparently set itself on the path to freedom. In the history of Sheffield radicalism, 1788 has particular significance, for that year Samuel Shore, a Sheffielder, was elected as vice-president of the London-based Society for Constitutional Information, founded with the aim of achieving parliamentary reform. From this time onwards, Sheffield was at the forefront of the country's revolutionary politics, playing a greater role than even the capital itself.

Sheffield and the French Revolution

It is in this context that between 1789 and 1792, the early stages of the French Revolution were greeted by wild celebrations in Sheffield right across the social spectrum, in marked contrast to more socially conservative industrial towns such as Birmingham. Sheffield antiquarian Joseph Hunter draws a vivid picture of even the most ardent Christian ministers, including his adoptive father the Rev. Joseph Evans, being heavily influenced by Thomas Paine's revolutionary tract *The Rights of Man* and attracted to revolutionary ideas to the extent that 'the atrocities of the Robespierre period scarcely changed his feeling ... in these political sentiments he was by no means peculiar'.

In November 1789, Dr Richard Price, an economist and leader in the Unitarian religious movement, delivered a sermon in London welcoming the advent of democracy in France that provoked the political theorist Edmund Burke's infamous response dismissing the working people as the 'swinish multitude'. On 27 November 1790, a rally was organised in the centre of Sheffield to mark the anniversary of Price's sermon and to celebrate the victories of the French revolutionary armies. At the centre of the procession was a roast pig on which an effigy of Burke was placed, lampooning his attitude towards the working class.

Local calls for reform were not long in coming, and in 1791 the Sheffield Society for Constitutional Information (SSCI) was formed, one of the earliest specifically working-class political organisations in Britain, and by far the largest outside London. With a democratic organisational structure based on the representation of cells of ten people (called 'tythings'), it gained 2,000 members in its first year, and similar organisations in London and Leeds were soon imitating the Sheffield system.

The political temperature reached boiling point in the summer of 1791 during the parliamentary enclosure of common lands in the Upper and Nether Hallam areas, which was completed against a backdrop of mass popular demonstrations only with the assistance of the military. In July of that year workers attacked Broom Hall, home of Sheffield's vicar and magistrate James Wilkinson, the member of the West Riding bench of magistrates who lived closest to town. On the same night there was an attack on the Duke of Norfolk's agent's house in Fargate, and on the town prison, during which inmates were released. Order was restored on the part of the establishment by the arrival of a military detachment from Nottingham and additional forces from York. Five of the alleged instigators of the actions, all aged under 19, were taken to York for trial, where one of them, John Bennett, who appears to have suffered from a learning disability, was found guilty of arson and hanged. In June 1792, the government in London reacted to growing support for the French Revolution in Sheffield by building a barracks in Shalesmoor on the edge of town. From this time onwards there was a permanent military presence in Sheffield and the authorities' response to popular protest was to be by resort to armed force.

In April 1793, radical newspaper editor Joseph Gales, whose *Sheffield Register* had been launched six years earlier, stepped up the pro-French campaign despite its growing association among the establishment with treason. The same month he chaired a meeting on Castle Hill to launch a petition for parliamentary reform that would gain 8,000 signatures but which was ultimately rejected by the House of Commons on the grounds of 'disrespectful language'. Amid rumours circulating in London that Sheffield forges were being used to manufacture arms for a forthcoming revolution, the authorities took increasingly direct countermeasures at the local level. Following the Castle Hill meeting, the mixed-race abolitionist campaigner Henry Redhead Yorke, himself the son of a freed slave, was arrested and imprisoned for conspiracy, prompting Gales to flee and take refuge in newly liberated America.

Broom Hall, home of Vicar of Sheffield and local magistrate James Wilkinson, was attacked in 1791 by Sheffield people angry at the enclosure of common lands.

In April 1794, the authorities established a volunteer corps of infantry in Sheffield consisting of 490 men, and a regiment of cavalry formed shortly afterwards attracted a number of members of the gentry class from the surrounding area. A year later, on 4 August 1795, fighting that broke out following a military parade in the centre of the town prompted Colonel Athorpe, commanding officer of the volunteer regiment and a prominent West Riding magistrate, to ride into the crowd brandishing his sabre. At his order, soldiers fired on the crowd, leading to two people being killed and a number wounded.

Athorpe's subsequent acquittal for any wrongdoing led to widespread public criticism, and a bitter attack in a song published by Joseph Mather commemorating what was to become known among Sheffield's working people as the 'Battle of Norfolk Street'. The song's lyrics left no doubt as to the popular interpretation of events and their aftermath:

> Corruption tells me homicide
> Is wilful murder justified
> A striking precedent was tried
> In August 'ninety-five.

Norfolk Street, where a crowd of protesters was fired on in August 1795.

When arm'd assassins dress'd in blue
Most wantonly their townsmen slew
And magistrates and juries too
At murder did connive.

Due to his great popularity, the authorities decided not to prosecute Mather, but instead arrested James Montgomery for publication of the events in his radical newspaper the *Iris*. At the same time, public meetings of the SSCI were prohibited.

The Post-War Period

Despite the economic hardship that followed the end of the Napoleonic Wars, the Tory government was determined on pursuing a policy of repression rather than reform. This served to drive the revolutionary movement underground for a number of months, so people began to meet in secret in outdoor spaces on the edge of town. In response, the government developed a network of spies, often drawn from former and current soldiers, including the notorious *agent provocateur* 'Oliver', who was operating in the area in 1816.

However, such was the strength of feeling in Sheffield that the reform movement did not stay hidden for long; indeed, the scale of popular protest grew dramatically in this period. In October 1816 a petition put before Parliament for the redress of economic grievances was signed by an astonishing 20,000 townspeople, and a subsequent mass meeting, one of many to be held in Paradise Square in the centre of town, attracted a crowd reported to have been of the same number. If accurate, this was almost half of Sheffield's adult population. Following this meeting, some felt the call to more direct action. In December, the militant working-class leader John Blackwell, who in 1812 had led a raid on the barracks to steal weapons, was arrested in the town centre for allegedly inciting revolution. The following May, a group of revolutionaries met at a grinding wheel on one of the Sheffield rivers to plan another attack on the barracks and other local targets including an arms depot at Doncaster. This attempted action was probably part of the wider revolutionary movements of the time that included Brandreth's Rising at Pentrich (Derbyshire) on 10 June that year.

Across the country, more and more people came together to demand reform, and as they did so the government's attempts to silence them became more severe. In August 1819 there was widespread revulsion when armed cavalry were used to break up a mass demonstration at St Peter's Field, Manchester, leading to the deaths of seventeen people and the wounding of hundreds more. Some of the demonstrators on that day were veterans of the last battle of the Napoleonic wars and likened the carnage to what they had seen at Waterloo. A demonstration held later in the month in Sheffield to protest at the events of what became known as the Peterloo Massacre was one of the largest ever held in the town, with an estimated 40,000 to 50,000 people in attendance, at a time when the entire population of the town was about 75,000. The people were united in their call for a public inquiry into the massacre, something that was continually resisted by the authorities. The remarkable class unity that prevailed in Sheffield at the time was apparent when Viscount Milton, son of the Whig Party leader and local landowner Earl Fitzwilliam, took to the stage and added his voice to the call for justice. The earl himself was subsequently removed from his post as Lord Lieutenant of Ireland by the Tory government for his part in calling for a public enquiry.

In addition to these mass gatherings, in February 1820 a meeting of 130 prominent Yorkshire citizens on the Fitzwilliam estate at Wentworth, near Rotherham, put its seal to a 6,000-signature petition expressing support for the earl following his dismissal as Lord Lieutenant, a significant demonstration of unity between Whigs and Radicals quite uncommon for the age. At the popular level, on 11 April 1820 the veteran revolutionary John Blackwell, recently released from prison in York, led a group of 200 well-trained Sheffielders as part of an alleged 'general rising' in the north of England. Significantly, this action gained considerable support among the people of the town. When Blackwell hesitated until the next day to attack the barracks, the plot was intercepted and its leader sentenced to another period of imprisonment in York. This popular Sheffield working-class hero was to die in the town's workhouse in 1839.

In 1822, a second large petition was sent to Parliament and when it, too, was rejected, Sheffield reformers looked to new ways of organising opposition to a government that refused to listen to the people. One was the formation of the Sheffield Political Union (SPU) in 1830. At its first meeting in January 1831, members called for reform of the House of Commons to ensure 'a real and effectual representation of the lower and middle classes'. Other aims included progressive taxation so that the working class was not unduly burdened. Originally a grass-roots working-class movement, its leadership was regrettably taken over by moderate businessmen and professionals, headed by T.A. Ward and including Robert Leader, Isaac Ironside, and the prominent Roman Catholic Dr Arnold Knight, and became a mouthpiece for middle-class reformism.

Meanwhile, anger at the government's repeated rejection of calls for a more democratic electoral system continued, and when the Second Reform Bill was rejected by the House of Lords in 1831, the country was close to revolution. There was rioting in a number of towns, but noticeably not Sheffield, where anger was channelled through the SPU and mass meetings aimed at gathering large numbers of signatures for further petitions. At the same time, the people of Sheffield expressed their anger at a public demonstration on 15 October targeting Lord Wharncliffe of Wortley Hall, who had moved the Tory motion against the bill; an effigy of the baron with a placard bearing the inscription 'The Dragon of Wortley: the enemy of King and people' around its neck was burned in protest.

Attempts by the House of Lords to make major changes to the Third Reform Bill in May 1832 drew widespread popular criticism in Sheffield. The council of the SPU went into permanent session and recruited a remarkable 15,000 new members. During the summer, two mass meetings were scheduled for every week; one, called for Paradise Square at only two hours' notice, once again attracted 20,000 people. At the first meeting, Edward Bramley, president of the SPU, told the crowd he would rather 'lay [his] head on the block than submit longer to the odious tyranny of a factious, unprincipled oligarchy' and affirmed his belief that the days when 'twenty-four million [would] bow down in the dust before 150 lords' were over. With a call for 'three groans for the King' in place of the traditional cheers he brought the meeting to an end, and with it, the first chapter in Sheffield's revolutionary story.

Reform or Revolution?

The Great Reform Act and its Aftermath

With growing calls for democratic change, and the Lords in Parliament realising that a third rejection of the Reform Bill would threaten the constitution, the Representation of the People Act was finally passed in 1832, but with compromises designed to appease its aristocratic and middle-class opponents. Gone were the 'rotten boroughs' in which wealthy landowners could gain parliamentary representation with a handful of votes, and in came representation for the new industrial towns, small landowners, tenant farmers and the majority of the middle class. Explicitly barred from voting, however, were people with property worth less than £10 – effectively the majority of working people – and all women. Hailed by middle-class reformers as a great triumph, in reality the Act was a betrayal of the legitimate aspirations of ordinary people who had fought and died for the right to vote over the previous fifty years. Crucially, too, it meant that large-scale support for democratic reform among the middle class was over and from now on working people were on their own.

Even with the extension of the franchise, Sheffield was only enabled to elect two Members of Parliament to represent a population of over 90,000, and of that, only 3,504 males were eligible to vote. Working people who felt they had been sold down the river by the commercial and professional class that had worked hard to gain control of the reform movement made their feelings clear at another mass gathering in Paradise Square, which called on Parliament 'to execute their undoubted privilege of withholding supplies until a redress of grievances is obtained' and made a direct petition to the King to 'recall his late ministers to his counsels, and by an immediate creation of peers, enable them to secure the success of a constitutional reform'.

The first election of 1834 was not a secret ballot and ultimately the popular favourites were beaten by establishment law-and-order candidate John Parker, son of a magistrate and representative of the county elite. Amid widespread protest, ninety soldiers of the 18th Irish Foot Regiment were brought from

Hillsborough Barracks: the power of the British establishment set against the people of Sheffield and their call for democracy.

Rotherham to put down any potential unrest. In the event, when the military met the gathering crowds in the centre of town, five people were shot dead and a large number injured. The subsequent coroner's inquest returned a verdict of 'justifiable homicide', and as ever, the authorities moved quickly to cover up events and silence any discussion in Parliament.

From this time on, a unit of the First Royal Dragoons under the command of Colonel Martin was permanently stationed at the old cavalry barracks at Shalesmoor. Not for the first time, the authorities were making an open admission that they felt unable to counter the calls for democratic reform among the working people of Sheffield except by means of a significant local military presence. In 1850, a massive new barracks was built at Hillsborough that, more than anything, symbolised the military might deemed necessary to suppress the call for democracy among the people of Sheffield.

The Chartist Movement and the
Sheffield Working Men's Association

The Chartist movement that emerged nationally following the disappointment of the 1832 Reform Act soon gathered significant support in Sheffield, where working people felt particularly betrayed. The movement took its name from the charters, or lists of demands, that its members drew up to present to Parliament, along with massive lists of signatures calling for electoral reform. In Sheffield the lists of demands always started with universal adult suffrage.

In the first ten weeks of 1836, a strike among filesmiths attached to larger firms demonstrated the strength of popular anger at the general economic distress together with the inadequacies of the Reform Act, and it was from this time, in the words of Joseph Hunter (himself a significant apologist for the establishment in spite of his background as a working-class cutler) that Chartism 'became rampant'. Once again, in contrast to other parts of the country, the roots of the movement in Sheffield were planted in working-class soil with the formation of the Sheffield Working Men's Association (SWMA), which soon found itself in conflict with middle-class liberals. The new organisation proved itself to be more effective at mobilising working people than the more middle-class SPU and its demands for, among other reforms, universal suffrage and the secret ballot, were very popular.

On 25 September 1838, the SWMA organised another mass demonstration in Paradise Square, which also attracted people from the surrounding villages, the neighbouring town of Rotherham, and from as far away as Manchester and

Birmingham. Speakers included the social reformers Ebenezer Elliott and Isaac Ironside, the latter accusing parliamentary reformers of betraying the people. The meeting called for national regeneration, including 'a thoroughly efficient system of education [since] democracy to be successful must be intelligent'.

A similar gathering was held in May the following year, jointly organised by the Sheffield and Rotherham branches of the SWMA and chaired by the veteran reformer John Wostenholme, who had been jailed in 1817 for his part in the Grinding Wheel Conspiracy. In July, Sheffield magistrates ruled that large assemblies were henceforth illegal, but the Chartists responded by holding meetings away from Paradise Square before returning soon afterwards in defiance of the ban. In practice, the authorities tended to tolerate large meetings, as long as they were deemed to be peaceful, but subsequently prosecuted speakers for sedition or attendance at an unlawful meeting.

Paradise Square and Popular Politics

For half a century, from the French Revolutionary period through to the end of the Chartists, Sheffield's fine Georgian square in the centre of town was the main arena for the expression of popular political feeling. Modern visitors to the square may be surprised to learn that during this period crowds of up to 20,000 citizens regularly packed tightly into this makeshift cobbled amphitheatre. Its steep-sloping aspect, which afforded good views of the speakers' platform on the northern, downhill side made it a natural venue for mass gatherings. The realities of such huge crowds in a relatively confined space are hard for us to grasp. Happily, we have an excellent description of this makeshift arena left by Sheffield's famous antiquarian writer Joseph Hunter, which is included in his *History of Hallamshire*:

> Before proceeding to give any details of the successive elections consequent upon the Reform Bill, it may be well to describe the battleground on which have been fought so many hard contests, political, municipal and social. The famous site is Paradise Square, the *Campus Martius* of Sheffield, where brain rather than muscle has been so often incited to its utmost efforts.
>
> It is a large square in the centre of the town and is admirably adapted to the purpose of public popular assembly. It slopes from the south to the north, on which side a broad flight of steps, descending from the first storey of a large building, forms excellent standing ground or hustings for the orators; and owing to the

descent of the pavement towards this rostrum, all persons in every part of the square can both see and hear what is going on.

It is, in short, to compare small things with great, what Palace Yard was (but with far greater advantages of gradient elevation) to Westminster; what the Pynx is said to have been to the Athenian democracy and the Forum was to Rome. Nor were the hearers unworthy of the place; for nowhere is sense, if rude, more muscular; and wit, if homely, more sharp; or the power of repartee or interruption more original and intelligent than at Sheffield: on no stage, therefore, is it more incumbent on the orator to put his best foot forward and to neglect none of the graces of his art; and nowhere is he more rewarded with the applause of his auditory if he succeeds in gaining their confidence and disarming their suspicions.

Looking back towards the end of his life, there is a hint of regret in Hunter's recognition that this phase in Sheffield's public political life had come to an end:

In giving this little sketch of the old square, we are bound to add that, of late years, either from change of habits among the middle and working classes, from want of adequate public objects, or – may we not say? – from the general contentedness of the people in their amended institutions, political meetings have been much less frequent than was the case some years ago.

It is thought by some that the change is, in some degree, attributable to the penny press, which brings home to everyone the intelligence he wants. But, be the cause what it may, Paradise Square is no longer (much, perhaps, to the satisfaction of its inhabitants) the anarchical and stormy theatre it used to be when the fierce struggle for Free Trade and Parliamentary Reform brought thousands and tens of thousands of the middle class, operatives and artisans, as in the Flemish cities in the Middle Ages, to hear and support their orators.

The Call to Direct Action

From the autumn of 1838, rumours began to circulate that the Chartists were meeting on the moors on the edge of Sheffield to test explosives, and that a fire-bomb attack was planned on St Mary's Church, Bramall Lane. Joseph Hunter, busy at that time compiling his acclaimed *History of Hallamshire*, caught the mood, writing that 'in the month of August 1839, great efforts were made by the leading Chartists to obtain a general rising of the people'.

The concerns of the local authorities had been evident three years earlier, when, in addition to the military presence, the Sheffield police were organised into a uniformed force that was increasingly unpopular with the ordinary people of Sheffield. During the summer months of 1839, armed police patrols were operating in Sheffield town centre alongside the military, specialising in ambushing suspected Chartists in narrow lanes where the cavalry could not operate. Together, the police and military moved to suppress rallies held on 12 and 13 August in Paradise Square, made more than seventy arrests (or in Hunter's words, took a number of 'prisoners') and sent those apprehended for trial.

It was at this point that divisions became evident between the trade union movement, still in its infancy, and the Chartists over the use of direct action, with the trade societies generally attempting to uphold a non-political position. On the national scale, adherents of the Chartist movement divided between those advocating 'moral force' (led in Sheffield by Ebenezer Elliott) and the 'physical force' proponents, who in Sheffield started to hold torchlight meetings on Skye Edge. The night-time meetings only came to an end when rumours started to circulate that the military were arming and making ready to suppress all signs of dissent. In their place, in September 1839 the Chartists commenced an effective strategy of 'churchgoings' at Anglican places of worship by which they attempted to take up seats that had been privatised and thus demonstrate passive resistance at the heart of the establishment. The response of the authorities was to employ armed police at the church gates to refuse entry.

The so-called Newport Rising of 4 November 1839, at which twenty-two Chartists among a large crowd gathering in the southern Welsh town were killed by the military, gave renewed impetus to the 'physical force' faction and in Sheffield saw the emergence of 21-year-old former soldier Samuel Holberry, who was among those who had taken part in demonstrations at the parish church. For their part, the authorities in Sheffield as elsewhere increased their use of surveillance and the number of arrests of potential agitators rose dramatically, prompting the Chartist leadership to become increasingly concerned with maintaining secrecy.

In January 1840 county magistrates, police and three military units all remained stationed in Sheffield to deal with potential disorder. On the 10th, intelligence allegedly reached Colonel Martin of an imminent uprising. Samuel Holberry was identified as the ringleader of a plot to take possession of the Town Hall and one or two other public buildings by force, and was arrested at his house on Eyre Lane at midnight on the 11th, the alleged day of the uprising. To make their case, magistrates subsequently displayed a cache of weapons apparently found at his house that included 'arms of all kinds, including bombshells, hand grenades, fireballs and *cats* [spiked blocks] for injuring the horse's feet'. Following the arrest, by the Chief Constable of Rotherham and two officers, it was further alleged at the subsequent trial that Holberry's plan had been to trigger concurrent insurrections in other towns of the West Riding of Yorkshire in order to bring about a national revolution.

In accordance with contemporary procedure, Holberry was barred from speaking in his own defence. At the York Assizes, the trial judge made the case that on the basis of the evidence, a conviction of 'levying war' and thus high treason against the Queen was warranted, but instead he sentenced Holberry to four years in prison for seditious conspiracy on the grounds that he had been arrested before any actual violence had taken place. In the event, Holberry died two years into his prison sentence as a direct result of his harsh treatment. He was just 26 years old.

Officially, the town of Sheffield gave thanks to the West Riding Yeomanry and the police, with a huge increase in the salary of the Chief Constable and a piece of silverware to Colonel Martin for their parts in suppressing the rebellion. More tellingly however, on 27 June 1842, when Holberry's body was

The grave of Samuel Holberry in Sheffield General Cemetery. According to the inscription he had been imprisoned 'for advocating what to him appeared to be the true interest of the people of England'.

returned to Sheffield, an estimated 50,000 people lined the route to his funeral at the General Cemetery. By way of comparison, this was more people than turned out for the funeral of any member of a royal family at the time anywhere in Europe. Even Joseph Hunter, who was no friend of the Chartists, conceded that Holberry was commemorated 'with much popular ceremony'. Indeed, the mood in Sheffield had been apparent two months after the alleged uprising was due to take place, when, on 13 March 1840, Isaac Ironside, the local spokesman for the 'moral forcers', addressed a huge crowd in Paradise Square who had gathered to express solidarity with the French revolutionaries of that year.

'Samuel Holberry's Uprising'

Visitors to Sheffield are often struck by the fact that, unlike most British towns and cities, it has very few statues of monarchs or establishment figures. In contrast, in addition to a number of representations of social reformers, its main public space is dedicated to the memory of a man who apparently attempted to seize the city by armed force. And it is clear that to the great majority of the people of Sheffield at the time, as much as to the Labour councillors who were instrumental in the naming of the Holberry Cascades in the city's main square the Peace Gardens, the 26-year-old former soldier was a hero.

Yet how much do we know about the circumstances of the plot ascribed to him, his trial and subsequent imprisonment? Contemporary writers have tended to view Holberry, in the words of the historian Catherine Lewis, 'either as a somewhat deluded violent Chartist who damaged the cause by encouraging the use of physical force; or … as a radical freedom fighter who should take his place alongside the likes of Wat Tyler and William Wallace'. She goes on to make the point that all commentators, whatever their views of Holberry, have accepted his guilt. There is much about his trial, however, that suggests we should not take this at face value.

First, it is clear to anyone who pursues Holberry's story that the details of the plot are suspiciously weak and there are very few references to this would-be revolutionary in reports about the Sheffield Chartists prior to January 1840. According to the official report, when police arrived at Holberry's house, his wife, on opening the door, did not call out any warning, and Samuel himself did not resist arrest when found in an upstairs bedroom. It is all the more curious that the leader of an armed insurrection planned for that night was found in bed, albeit apparently with his clothes on, only two hours before the alleged revolution was due to start. According to police, when arrested, Holberry told the officers he was 'for physical force' and would 'kill for the charter', yet it seems unlikely that anyone involved in the movement at this time would make such a frank disclosure.

The main prosecution witness at the trial was one Samuel Thompson, a Chartist who claimed to have been actively involved in the conspiracy. In fact, it appears that he turned Queen's evidence on 13 January because his father had been arrested and he wanted to protect him. In contrast to the detailed evidence taken from Thompson, once Holberry and two other alleged co-conspirators had been arrested, they were kept in isolation and offered neither legal advice nor assistance of any kind.

Thompson's evidence is almost too convincing, with much detail about plotting but little that would explain the practicalities. The obvious question is how they were going to tackle the significant military and police presence in Sheffield at the time, which was probably greater than in any other town in the country. As well as a troop of the First Dragoons, an infantry squadron and a number of police at the Town Hall, there was another military detachment stationed at the Tontine Inn, as well as reserves on active duty at the barracks just a mile from the town centre. To say the very least, any successful action against forces such as these would entail meticulous planning and substantial numbers of men. Yet according to Thompson, the plot was simply that to avoid suspicion the insurgents would advance in ones and twos on the Town Hall and at 2 a.m. 'rush in and kill every policeman and watchman' they found. This is extremely unconvincing. Furthermore, the only witness who made a statement to the authorities against the assertion that Holberry had organised an armed insurrection was not called at the trial.

It is also telling that it was forces from Rotherham, rather than from Sheffield itself, that played the main role in uncovering the alleged plot. The Chief Constable of Rotherham had recruited a local publican and would-be Chartist James Allen as an informer and later encouraged him to act as an *agent provocateur* to uncover details of the plans. Significantly, Allen's role was kept secret throughout the investigation and he did not appear at the trial. There is a strong suggestion that the authorities believed that the use of an informer would have severely strained relations with the people of Sheffield, who were already hostile towards the actions of the local police.

Finally, it seems strange that the apparent leader of a revolution against the state was committed to four years in prison rather than receiving a more severe sentence. Rather than apprehend him beforehand, given the size of the military and police force available in the town, why did the authorities not arrest Holberry during the course of the action and have him executed for high treason to get him out of the way completely? If the establishment's intention was not to produce a martyr, given his mass popularity at the time of his death, not to mention his subsequent local fame, it clearly failed. It is, of course, itself curious that Sheffielders turned out in such numbers for the funeral of an apparently hot-headed young outsider who had tried to take their town by force.

However, in the national context, the mere suggestion by the authorities that an armed insurrection had been planned in a large English town was probably sufficient to turn the tide of public opinion against the Chartists, who hitherto had enjoyed significant popular support. According to new research by Catherine Lewis, the evidence suggests that Holberry's conviction, rather than being the end of a period of conspiracy, was 'an insidious part of the state's

Memorial plaque in the Peace Gardens.

armoury for the *furtherance* of its dispute with the Chartists'. On the balance of evidence, it would appear that Samuel Holberry, up to that point a relatively obscure member of the Chartist movement, did not plan a 'Sheffield Rising' on 12 January 1840, but the authorities used the rules of criminal procedure and evidence in a clearly one-sided way to secure a conviction in the town where they most feared that a potential 'British Revolution' might begin.

Sheffield Incorporated

Whatever advantages Sheffield had gained to its national reputation by obtaining a degree of parliamentary representation, locally, as an unincorporated borough, the town's capacity for self-government was severely limited. Despite its remarkable growth in terms of population and industrialisation in the early decades of the nineteenth century, Joseph Hunter was quite uncompromising in his summary of the status of his home town in terms of self-government:

> … the local government was still only that of a village, with county magistrates to administer justice and a constable and night-watchman to protect property and life

… [but] excepting the office of Master Cutler (now largely ceremonial) there was scarcely a public office open to which local ambition could aspire, beyond becoming a Church Burgess or a Town Trustee, churchwarden or overseer of the poor. In the administration of justice, and even in the banking establishments of the town, the manufacturers had no participation. The place was accounted only rustic and had only village privileges.

By the mid-nineteenth century it was clear that the majority of local administrative units, many founded in the Middle Ages, could no longer cope with the demands of industrial expansion and rapid population growth. The Town Trustees came under increasing criticism for being a virtually closed corporation; only forty-five new trustees had been elected in the century up to 1843. An election of 1811 had been abandoned when several non-freeholders claimed their right to vote, and in response, a decision in Chancery in 1816 found in favour of a freehold-only franchise. The Town Trust acted effectively like an unreformed borough corporation and drew similar popular criticism for its closed nature and inability to solve the pressing social and political problems at hand.

The story of the Cutlers' Company in the eighteenth and early nineteenth centuries was similar to that of the Town Trustees: an ancient institution trying to keep pace with industrial and social change and becoming increasingly moribund, only to emerge in the second half of the nineteenth century with a more active, if largely symbolic, role. The new Cutlers' Hall, built in 1833, remains one of the city's more notable buildings, but at the time of construction was more a symbol of past glories than contemporary influence.

At the same time, the inadequacies of the 1818 Improvement Act for properly administering the town were becoming increasingly apparent. The 1832 Reform Act had created an anomaly in that the middle class, represented by the '£10 freeholders', had a say in national government but was still excluded from government locally. The reform of local government thus became a natural sequel to parliamentary reform, and it seemed increasingly inevitable to Sheffield's administrators that the town should follow the lead of Birmingham and Manchester in seeking formal incorporation as a fully self-governing borough.

Incorporation

The clamour for administrative reform was not universal, however, as a number of the more substantial ratepayers were put off by the possibility of raised costs in return for relatively small gains and, indeed, a counter-petition was submitted, with the Privy Council originally deciding against the grant of a charter. In the end, what brought people together was the attempt by the West Riding Constabulary in 1842 to extend its jurisdiction over the unincorporated industrial towns of the region, which led to thousands of people gathering in Paradise Square to petition for a new charter.

Sheffield criminal jurisdiction lay outside the town in the hands of the Justices of the Peace of the West Riding bench, drawn from a rural gentry whose remit extended to the unincorporated urban areas. They represented a class that was largely alien to the majority of Sheffield's inhabitants, and like the other administrations, their jurisdiction came to seem increasingly inappropriate, not helped by the fact that none of the JPs were resident in the town. Lord Wharncliffe's attempts to apply the 1839 County Constabularies Act to the unincorporated urban areas of the West Riding led the citizens of Sheffield to redouble their efforts to obtain incorporation. In this sense, Sheffield's moves towards incorporation were not so much the product of positive civic aspiration as a defensive reaction to defend local autonomy.

A charter of incorporation was finally granted on 31 August and inaugural elections to the new borough council were held on 1 November 1843. Among the first complement of fifty-six members of the council, thirty-four described themselves as manufacturers, of whom a dozen were engaged in various aspects of the metal trades. In effect, the administration of the town by a small number of magistrates drawn from the Anglican gentry class, often outsiders, had been replaced by Sheffield's first generation of nonconformist, formally uneducated steel makers. In its own way, this was to be a revolution of no small significance.

If anything, Sheffield's elevation to borough status made its inadequacies in terms of civic institutions even more glaring. The Town Hall, erected by the Town Trustees on the corner of Castle Street and Waingate in 1808, was enlarged in 1833 and included courtroom facilities for holding quarter and petty sessions, police offices and prison cells. In terms of local administration, however, so inadequate had it become to the needs of its rapidly growing community that by the mid-nineteenth century it was rarely used for significant meetings. These were generally held instead in the hall on Townhead Street that had been built by the Temperance Society in 1856. The town council also occasionally used a building in Norfolk Street, originally erected in 1762 for use as assembly rooms, as a council chamber. As for the Town Hall's judiciary function, the underground prison cells were cramped and unhealthy to such an extent that prisoners held there for any length of time frequently made petition to the magistrates to allow them to be moved to the house of correction in the county capital of Wakefield instead.

Inevitably, given the significance of Sheffield's traditional industry to its subsequent rapid development, the new Cutlers' Hall completed in 1833, with its decorated dining room in which the annual Cutlers' Feast was held, was the most impressive public building. More surprising, perhaps, is the fact that, with the exception of a marble bust of the poet and social reformer James Montgomery, the majority of the artwork that adorned the building – including portraits of the Duke of Wellington, Lord Wharncliffe, the Duke of Norfolk, Earl Fitzwilliam and the Rev. James Wilkinson – characterised it as a shrine to the establishment. In the middle of the most politically radical town in the country, this served only to highlight the growing rift between the Company and its ordinary members that had taken place over the course of the previous century.

Schools

With Sheffield's incorporation came the possibility that inadequacies in the town's education provision could finally be addressed. The management of the town Grammar School, founded in 1604 in Townhead Street, had long been one of the functions of the Church Burgesses. The school's charter opened it to boys from all religious denominations and required it to teach about thirty boys at half the ordinary fees. Boys' and girls' charity schools had been built in 1710 and 1786 respectively on either side of the parish church. The boys' school was rebuilt in 1826 and provided support and education for 100 poor boys from funds derived from various endowments and subscriptions. By the mid-nineteenth century the girls' school was making similar provision for about sixty poor girls.

From 1785, a number of Sunday schools were introduced to Sheffield as part of the nonconformist campaign for greater awareness of the Bible, and by 1790, with more than 750 children attending, the Sunday School movement was a significant factor in education provision that prompted a gradual improvement in the scope and standard of primary education. In 1812 a Sunday School union was formed, inspired by evangelical Christian principles and with James Montgomery as its first secretary. By 1820, some 3,000 children were receiving a minimum of education at thirteen Sunday schools supported by the authorities, as well as another 8,000 in schools attached to nonconformist chapels. On behalf of the establishment, a Church of England Sunday School union was subsequently formed that by the mid-nineteenth century governed the education of 5,500 children in twenty-one schools with 485 teachers. The majority of

Sunday Schools subscribed to the 'Lancasterian' or 'Madras' system by which older pupils were used to assist a small number of teachers in a monitoring capacity. The movement's founder, Joseph Lancaster, had visited Sheffield in 1809 and founded the first school, taking in nearly 320 boys under the supervision of a single master in a former rolling mill at West Bar Green, and a similar establishment for girls was founded six years later.

On the establishment side, one of the most significant charitable developments was the National Schools movement, and in 1812 Carver Street National School became the first of its type in Sheffield, with auxiliary premises opening in Garden Street soon after, educating 500 boys and a similar number of girls. Government inspectors placed Sheffield 'at the head of all the large towns of Yorkshire for its number of first-class national schools' in which, in the words of a contemporary directory, 'large numbers of children are receiving a sound education adapted to their position in life'.

In 1823 the Grammar School moved from its old site in Townhead Street to larger premises in St George's Square. By this time the Anglican authorities were becoming increasingly concerned at the growing involvement of the nonconformist communities in education. A significant part of their response

Former National School, Carver Street.

Former Sheffield Collegiate School, now part of Sheffield Hallam University.

was the establishment of the Sheffield Collegiate School in 1836 to impart a classical, and to a limited extent scientific, education together with moral and religious instruction 'according to the principles of the Church of England', specifically to the sons of the 'respectable' middle classes.

In turn, Methodists from Sheffield and the wider region pooled considerable resources to establish the Wesleyan Proprietary Grammar School of 1838 to provide classical education and religious training in the principles of Methodism at a time when entry to higher education by nonconformists was still proscribed. The scale of the school buildings, which are undoubtedly the most impressive example of neoclassical architecture to have been erected in the city, are a testament to the strength of Methodism in Sheffield and the influence it exercised on its civic development.

However, both of these prominent Sheffield schools were clearly aimed at the children of the relatively small Sheffield middle class. A survey taken around the time of their opening by the Rev. Thomas Sutton, Vicar of Sheffield, estimated that only one third of the working-class children of Sheffield received any meaningful education, and five years later government schools inspector J.C. Symons reported that 'two thirds of the working class children ... are growing up in a state of ignorance and are unable to read'. To many middle-class commentators the fault was with the apprenticeship system in the cutlery and related trades and its effect on parental control and child development. Writing in the 1850s, for example, the Sheffield-born mathematician Samuel Earnshaw pointed to the potential high earnings available to young people that promoted a desire for independence, to be free from schooling, and to 'become men'.

In response to the surveys into the education of the poor that were conducted in 1841, the Ragged Schools movement was established, starting in London in 1844, in which volunteer teachers could instruct destitute children (frequently rejected by the Sunday schools because of their unkempt appearance) in basic reading, writing and arithmetic. A Ragged School was set up among the slums of Pea Croft in Sheffield in 1848, and within twenty years 600 children were attending daily, the majority combining schooling with their daily work. On one evening a week a teacher from the school of art held a class in elementary drawing on a voluntary basis. While bread was distributed to the children without charge, clothing was supplied 'at a cheap rate'.

In 1854 the Duke of Norfolk invited the sisters of Notre Dame from Namur, Belgium, to set up a school for Roman Catholic girls on the Moor. The sisters subsequently moved to Springfield Place to establish a convent at what became Convent Walk and in 1854 Notre Dame School moved to Sheaf Gardens. With 800 girls on the roster, transcending traditional class boundaries, it was one of the biggest schools in Sheffield.

At around the same time, a Girls' Industrial School was founded under the auspices of the Church of England with premises rented at Broadfield, Heeley. The school was administered as a charity that took in girls from the age of 12 and through a weekly payment of 2s 6d provided for their maintenance. In the words of the founders, 'nothing which can be of use to them, either as domestic servants, or in their own homes should they become wives, is neglected'. This included the teaching of washing, cooking, baking, sewing and house cleaning. The aim was that each girl should be 'brought up in habits of saving, by having small sums of money allowed her for marks of good conduct'. The school's prospectus ended with the explanation that 'this school is not to be looked upon in the light of a reformatory, as its object is not to reclaim the vicious, but to qualify virtuous, well-conducted girls for respectable situations'. In Victorian Sheffield it was increasingly through the agency of education that the middle classes attempted to exert at least some influence on the culture and aspirations of the majority working-class population.

Poor Relief and Public Health

In common with other fast-growing industrial towns, Sheffield struggled with the challenge of helping its citizens through periods of unemployment and poverty within state structures that had been created for a long-lost agrarian world. The Elizabethan Poor Laws divided the disadvantaged into those unable to work and those whose unemployment was ascribed to idleness. By the eighteenth century, the primary mechanism for dealing with the latter was the workhouse. Sheffield's first workhouse had opened in 1628 at West Bar Green. A new facility was built following the passing of the Workhouse Test Act of 1723 that empowered Overseers of the Poor to refuse assistance to anyone who was not prepared to live within the workhouse and undertake prescribed tasks. This building was in turn enlarged in 1759, and a new workhouse converted from the former Kelham Island cotton mill opened in 1829. By this time, workhouses had also been established at Pitsmoor and Attercliffe.

Mutual support among the working men and women of Sheffield emerged as a consistent theme as the industrial town increased rapidly in size. The development of a strong tradition of communal self-reliance is reflected in the high numbers of workers who contributed to sick clubs compared with other parts of the country. The first of these had been established in 1728 by the scissor-smiths, and by 1820 no fewer than fifty had been set up in the town. By the early 1840s they took care of more than 11,000 members. Working alongside these mutual aid societies were local charities such as the Society for Bettering the Condition of the Poor, which had been set up by Quakers in the early 1800s to encourage the working poor to make small savings and establish funds for the provision of the sick.

In spite of the positive steps that were made at local level, the government's Poor Law Amendment Act of 1834, in attempting to deal with the growing problem of poverty in the industrial towns and cities, set down even harsher conditions for those forced into poverty. By insisting that the workhouse should become the default 'solution' to even occasional poverty, the 1834 Act sought to change the tone of legislation more overtly towards 'punishment'. To implement the new policy, the earlier arrangements were replaced by unions of parishes or townships that were responsible for the poor within their jurisdiction. In Sheffield, two such administrative units were formed: the Sheffield Union (which included the town itself, Brightside, Attercliffe and Handsworth) and Ecclesall Union (Upper and Nether Hallam, Norton, Totley, Dore and Beauchief).

Nether Edge workhouse: the architecture of state intimidation.

The emphasis on virtual incarceration in the workhouse that came with the 1834 Act was opposed strongly in Sheffield, where there was widespread horror at the prospect of the poor being forced into vast new buildings with the appearance of prisons, such as that opened at Nether Edge in 1844. In response to perceived governmental heavy handedness, the local philanthropist Samuel Roberts launched a pamphlet campaign against the changes, and in 1838 a petition against the new Poor Law Unions was signed by no fewer than 16,000 Sheffield people.

The short-term cyclical nature of the cutlery trade meant that the enforced provisions of the workhouse system were ill-suited to Sheffield. In general, periods of poverty were too brief to justify breaking up family homes, which in many cases were also their workshops. During the depression of the 1840s, for example, large numbers of workers were on low wages and 6,500 out of the town's workforce of 25,000 were unemployed, of whom 2,000 were receiving parish relief. Sheffield's year of incorporation, 1843, coincided with the deepest point of the recession that had started in 1837, and the town's population was hit particularly badly. Surveying the long queues that built up in town centre soup kitchens that year, a local doctor estimated that many of the deaths that occurred among the poor, in what should have been a year of celebration for Sheffield, were attributable to starvation. The bitter conflict that developed between the local administration in Sheffield and the government in Westminster over the town's reluctance to break up families in the interests of national policy was a glimpse of struggles between centre and locality that were to become a recurring feature in the town's history up to the end of the twentieth century.

Public health measures at the civic level began in 1797 with the building of the General Infirmary, deliberately established at some distance from the town's main manufacturing centre at Shalesmoor. Erected by public subscription, it was significantly enlarged in 1841, by which time it could accommodate 150 patients within the institution itself, in addition to 650 outpatients. In 1829 the Medical Institution, later the Sheffield Medical School, was established by Dr Arnold Knight in Surrey Street. Knight himself had come to Sheffield to investigate potential remedies for the devastating effects of 'grinders' asthma'.

In 1832 a public hospital and dispensary was opened on West Street. Following the cholera outbreaks of the 1830s and '40s it became apparent that the town would require increased patient care facilities, so the hospital was enlarged to provide fifty beds that proved particularly useful for accident and emergency provision nearer to the town centre and its hundreds of industrial workshops. By the 1860s, the North of England Institute for the Blind had also opened on West Street as a facility that was partly self-supporting and partly maintained by

Buildings of the former General Infirmary, Sheffield's first civic hospital, opened in 1791.

The General Cemetery, opened in 1836 to ease pressure on town centre burial grounds.

subscription. The twenty or so people in its care were taught crafts such as the making of baskets and mats that were sold in a shop attached to the premises. Public health measures of the mid-nineteenth century also included the opening of the commercially operated General Cemetery in attractively landscaped grounds in 1836, followed by a civic cemetery on City Road coinciding with the closing of the town's churchyards by council order in 1853.

Civic Politics and the Rise of the Democrats

The background to local politics in the ten years following incorporation in 1843 was high unemployment and the associated poverty, malnutrition and starvation that accompanied the economic depression of the 1830s and '40s. In Sheffield, the final years of the Chartist movement were characterised by active former members such as Isaac Ironside moving into council politics with the aim of effecting the greatest possible positive social change at local level. For the next ten years, the momentum for political and social change in Sheffield was maintained through a local evolution of the movement known as the Democrats. The party had been founded in 1848, the year of revolutionary movements across Europe, at a large assembly held on 16 April on Attercliffe Common that, as it moved into town, became the last of the mass meetings to be held in Paradise Square. There, in front of another massive gathering of

Sheffield's citizens, Ironside, the movement's emerging leader, called for the creation of a state based on principles of social justice, including free education, guaranteed jobs and provision for the sick and elderly, as well as for the federation of all the states of Europe into 'one free republic'.

In November 1846, Ironside, an accountant turned political radical (or 'debt collector and socialist' in the phrase often used by his detractors) was elected to the council. A skilled political organiser, he played a dominant role within the Democrats for the next seven years. Ironside's early political experience had been gained through the affairs of the Sheffield Political Union (SPU), which campaigned for parliamentary reform in the period leading up to the 1832 Reform Act.

By 1849 the Democrats had captured nearly half the seats on the new town council and had become the main opponents of the Liberals, who were working on behalf of the business-owning class and had dominated council affairs up to that point. The town council offered the reform movement a new arena of popular representation. The Democrats' success came on the back of the numerous artisans and small shopkeepers who had been drawn towards the egalitarianism of the Chartists since the late 1830s and was consolidated by meticulous organisation and mobilisation of the electorate by ensuring that as many people as possible were registered to vote. Party organisation was in the form of 'ward committees' that met regularly, carefully selecting candidates, promoting them and encouraging voter turnout, which rose from 39 per cent in 1847 to 54 per cent just two years later. To counter the well-financed campaigns of the local Liberal and Tory press, they launched their own newspaper, the *Sheffield Free Press*. In their contempt for centralising authority, they can be seen as a parallel movement to Sheffield Methodism and, indeed, in many ways a town that had long been a stronghold of religious nonconformity was now becoming a Methodist borough.

The Democrats stood on a platform of national political reform, the main aims of which were universal male suffrage, the removal of taxation of the print media, introduction of income tax and reform of the Poor Law. In Sheffield, they proved particularly successful at improving public health and conditions of the poor. In terms of council administration, they campaigned for sound economic principles and efficient government, opposed high salaries for council officials and openly criticised the unpopular local police. They also used the council as a means of promoting the wider aims of political radicalism through the official status it gave to petitions presented to Parliament in Westminster. The party's championing of local activism as a way of challenging reactionary government policies at national level set Sheffield on a course that was to continue right up to resistance to the policies of Margaret Thatcher's Conservative government in the 1980s and beyond.

Building a Civic Society

During the nineteenth century, Sheffield developed a distinct working-class identity, with a culture that appeared impenetrable to many middle-class observers both locally and nationally. Independent patterns of work and living made for a self-reliant and remarkably politically assertive community. The challenge over the course of the nineteenth and twentieth centuries was to harness these attributes in a way that forged a just and humane society in which all citizens were able to play a part. The extent to which Sheffield was able to achieve these aims in the absence of a prominent professional middle class and, by the twentieth century, provide a model of civic society for others to follow, was testimony to the communal spirit of its people.

Nonconformity in Religion and Politics

Those members of society who did not subscribe to the tenets of the Church of England faced a range of social and political restrictions. In response, the members of what were originally called 'dissenting' and later 'nonconformist' communities developed close bonds and effective networks for overcoming the barriers they faced. In Sheffield, the weakness of establishment institutions as expressed through the Church of England meant that nonconformists were able to exert an influence considerably greater than in most other large towns.

The most influential nonconformist grouping was the Methodists, whose congregations first grew in response to John Wesley's preaching visits to Sheffield, of which there were more than thirty between 1742 and 1788 and which regularly attracted large crowds. Between 1790 and 1850, nonconformity in general, and Methodism in particular, grew significantly and completely outnumbered those who participated in establishment religion. The Methodists' first large place of worship, Carver Street Chapel, opened in 1804. By the time Brunswick Chapel opened on the Moor thirty years later, the Wesleyan Methodists had been transformed from outsiders to 'respectable' pillars of local society.

This picture is complicated, however, since by that time Methodism itself had already split into different sects. While the Wesleyan Methodists remained the largest group, the New Connexion led by Alexander Kilham of Scotland Street Chapel in the heart of Sheffield's oldest cutlery district, which broke away in 1797, grew rapidly in the town, undoubtedly due to its close identification with the needs of the urban poor. Kilham's followers were also the most politically radical, known by their detractors as 'Tom Paine Methodists', since their opposition to the autocracy of the Wesleyan conference was influenced by the author of *Rights of Man*. The so-called Primitive Methodists formed their own organisation in 1812, and from 1849 Sheffield also became the centre of the new Wesleyan Reform movement.

Therefore, while at the macro level local politics in Sheffield played out in the opposition between the Anglican establishment and nonconformity, at the sharper end the distinctions were those expressed by the different Methodist groups. Increasingly, the Wesleyans gravitated towards Toryism, with Jabez Bunting, the group's national leader, declaring that 'Methodism hates democracy as much as it hates sin'. In stark contrast, the New Connexion Methodists embraced radical politics and exerted a powerful influence on the emerging trade societies and unions. However, from the time of the dissipation of the Chartist

Former Methodist Chapel, Carver Street. With room for a congregation of more than 2,000, a clear sign of the strength of nonconformity in Sheffield.

movement in the late 1840s, even the most radical nonconformist factions were moving in some degree towards the politics of the establishment, and there was certainly nothing overtly radical about the Firth family, the Sheffield industrialists who are perhaps the best-known members of the New Connexion.

If there was anything that prevented Methodism from becoming a truly radical force in Sheffield, it was simply that such a small proportion of the working population ever attended either church or chapel. At the national level, it has been argued that Methodism ultimately represented a counterrevolutionary influence, with the prominent French historian Elie Halevy arguing that 'Methodism was the antidote to Jacobitism' and that the popularity of the movement was the main reason Britain did not follow France down the road to revolution.

Nevertheless, in the first half of the nineteenth century the Anglican establishment was undoubtedly concerned about the revolutionary potential of the emerging industrial working class, no more so than in independent-minded Sheffield. At the national level, its most conspicuous response was the Church Building Acts of 1818 and 1824, which provided £1 million of state funding to construct new Anglican churches, predominantly in working-class industrial towns. Four of these – St George, St Philip, St Mary and Christchurch, Attercliffe – were built in Sheffield during the 1820s. Perhaps of greater significance was the fact that in the 1840s the sprawling ancient parish of Sheffield was finally divided up into twenty-five new ecclesiastical districts; this, it was hoped, would enable the Church of England to concentrate its influence – spiritually, socially and educationally – on local communities of working people.

Ultimately, however, these establishment attempts to influence the social and political culture of the working class were doomed by the simple fact that church attendance in Sheffield was even lower than the national average. The country's only ever national census of church attendance, taken in March 1851, revealed that well over half of the population of England and Wales attended neither church nor chapel on a regular basis. In Sheffield, the proportion was as high as 90 per cent, with the great majority of the population of this working-class town never attending any religious service, with the exception of the formal rites of passage of baptism, marriage and burial.

In terms of the town's administration, the transformation of local nonconformity into the bedrock of the establishment is evident in the large number of educated chapel members who became prominent in council affairs. The numerous Methodist, Congregationalist and Unitarian mayors, aldermen,

Masters Cutler and magistrates were drawn from that interconnected web of nonconformist families that dominated Sheffield's industrial and commercial life, among which the Firths, Coles, Bassetts, Wards and Osborns are just a few of the more famous names. Over the course of the nineteenth century, if such figures had a declining influence on the political aspirations of the workers in their companies, they became increasingly influential in promoting the notion of 'respectability' among the working class, with its emphasis on regular work patterns, thrift and temperate drinking.

Creating a Just Society

A notable feature of Sheffield's history is the prominence of individual and groups of social reformers whose campaigns helped to unite local and national concerns. In large measure it was the town's relative independence from the structures of established Church and State that encouraged women and men to campaign for social justice from a base in Sheffield. A few outstanding examples serve to highlight this important thread in Sheffield's story.

James Montgomery (1771–1854)

The most famous of the Sheffield reformers, Montgomery was born at Irvine in Ayrshire, Scotland, the son of a pastor and missionary in the Moravian Church. As a boy he was sent for training for the ministry at a school near Leeds while his parents travelled to undertake missionary work in the West Indies, where they both died within a year of each other. Montgomery did not settle at his education, and while still in his youth was apprenticed to a baker in Mirfield (West Yorkshire) at the end of which period, aged 21, he moved to Sheffield in response to an advert for an assistant to Joseph Gales, publisher of the *Sheffield Register*. When Gales fled to America following

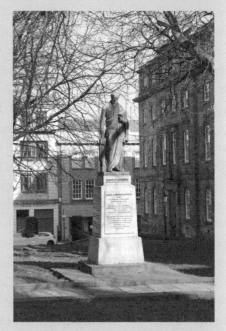

Memorial to James Montgomery, cathedral precinct.

his persecution by the authorities, Montgomery took over editorship of the newspaper himself and changed its name to the *Sheffield Iris* in an attempt to confuse the authorities. However, the young editor soon found himself persecuted by the establishment – first, in 1795, for printing a poem to celebrate the fall of the Bastille during the first phase of the French Revolution and again in 1796, for printing a criticism of the role of the magistrate Colonel Athorpe in the events of the Battle of Norfolk Street the previous year.

Montgomery first achieved fame as a poet in 1806 and simultaneously found his work attacked by the Tory establishment. Benefiting from the support of Lord Byron, he published a poem calling for the abolition of the slave trade in 1809, and in 1817 took up the cause against the use of boys as chimney sweeps. In 1780, Montgomery's mentor, Joseph Gales, had met the former slave and abolitionist Gustavus Equiano during his visit to Sheffield (where he had addressed an enthusiastic crowd) and published his autobiography in 1790.

In addition to his prominent political activities, over the course of a quarter of a century Montgomery met regularly with fellow social reformers Samuel Roberts, Roland Hodgson and George Bennett to discuss and promote philanthropic projects. He died on 30 April 1854 and was honoured by a public funeral and burial at the General Cemetery. In 1861 a monument was erected over his grave paid for by public subscription and moved to its current position at the east end of the cathedral in 1971.

Ebenezer Elliott (1781–1849)

Born the son of a Rotherham ironmaster, at the age of 6, Elliott contracted smallpox, which according to his biographer left him 'fearfully disfigured' and led him to suffer from illness and depression for much of the rest of his life. He hated school and attributed the poetic talent of his adult years to the long walks he took in the countryside around the town when he was playing truant. From the age of 16 he started working at his father's foundry. In his early 20s he married, but the family iron business went bankrupt, his father died and Elliott and his young family were made homeless and faced starvation. In the face of such adversity, he contemplated suicide. This experience led to a lifelong identification with the poor and oppressed.

In 1819 the family moved to Sheffield, where Elliott set up as an iron dealer, and within ten years he had become a successful iron merchant and steel maker. He soon became well-known in his adopted town for advocating

Memorial to Ebenezer Elliott, Weston Park.

reforms to improve the conditions of workers. In 1830 this included the formation of the first society in the country to call for the reform of the Corn Laws that had contributed to his own poverty, as well as that of thousands of working people across the country. He was active in the Chartist movement at both local and national levels, though he became less involved at the point that it split over the question of armed revolution.

The strength of his political convictions came out early in his poetry, earning him the nickname 'the Corn Law Rhymer' and making him internationally famous. His work was infused with a hatred of injustice and included the song 'The People's Anthem', which called on God to save the ordinary people rather than 'kings and lords'. Such an egalitarian sentiment led to it being banned in many churches.

Following his death in 1849, a commemorative statue, paid for largely by small subscriptions from working people, was erected in the marketplace in Sheffield and subsequently moved to a position in Weston Park where it remains today.

Mary Anne Rawson (1801–87)

Female political activism was a more prominent feature of the public life of Sheffield than perhaps any other town in England. More than anything, it was the anti-slavery (abolitionist) movement, through the challenge it presented to established structures of power and dominance, that gave birth to women's political activism and the campaign for female suffrage. In 1838, a Female Radical Association emerged within the Chartist movement, and in 1851 it was a group of Sheffield women who established the first organisation in the country to demand female suffrage.

The Sheffield Ladies' Anti-slavery Society was formed in 1825, and in contrast to many of its male counterparts, called for total and immediate abolition. The women sought to educate local people about slavery through the distribution of pamphlets, door-to-door campaigning, and increasingly, calling for the boycott of slave-produced goods, in particular sugar. As a town that was itself producing agricultural equipment used on slave plantations, Sheffield was an appropriate place for abolitionism to take hold.

Rawson was the daughter of Joseph Read, the wealthy owner of a gold and silver business whose family were prominent members of Queen Street Congregational Church. Following the early death of her husband, and her inheritance of the family estate at Wincobank Hall, she dedicated her life to the anti-slavery movement and associated causes. When the abolition of slavery in the British colonies was enacted in 1833, Rawson and other female activists continued the fight through the formation of the Sheffield Ladies' Association for the Universal Abolition of Slavery in 1837. Initially the association campaigned through the use of petitions, including one signed by a remarkable 25,000 Sheffield women, amounting to some three-quarters of the adult female population of the town.

Rawson herself was a prominent and vigorous promoter of the boycott movement and initiated the campaign against the imposition of a seven-year apprenticeship for former slaves, which meant they were forced to continue working for the same people who had owned them. In 1840 she attended the International Convention for the Universal Abolition of Slavery in London, an event

Memorial to Mary Ann Rawson, Wincobank.

that was fundamental to the formation of the female suffrage movement since, in common with the majority of public meetings at the time, women had not been allowed to speak. In 1846 Rawson met the American former slave and abolitionist campaigner Frederick Douglass at Wincobank Hall, and in her later years campaigned to raise funds for a training facility in Jamaica to prepare teachers for work throughout the former slave plantations in the West Indies. She died virtually penniless, having used all her resources in her campaigns for social justice, and was buried in the Congregationalist churchyard at Attercliffe, where her grave was restored by local campaigners in 2018.

The campaign against slavery ran in parallel with the struggle for female suffrage in which Sheffield women played a prominent part. The Sheffield Women's Political Association, formed in 1851, was the first campaign group of its type to be formed anywhere in the country and a prototype of similar organisations that carried on the struggle up to the present day.

The Struggle for an Educated Citizenry

An 1841 report into levels of education in Sheffield found that only two-thirds of the adult male population and about half of females had basic literacy. The fact that twenty years later Sheffield was above the national average, with only 27 per cent of the adult population completely illiterate, owed much to efforts in the sphere of adult education during this period. However, progress was not made without genuine struggle; just as was the case for children, educational provision for adults was adversely affected both by the middle-class perception of Sheffield as a town of manual labourers on whom intellectual development was wasted and, perhaps more seriously, by the aims of the Anglican establishment to keep working people 'in their place'.

The first of Sheffield's establishments for adult education, the Sheffield Literary and Philosophical Society (SLPS), was set up in 1822 by Dr Arnold Knight, a prominent Roman Catholic, and was clearly aimed at the middle classes. The first provision specifically for working men was the Mechanics' Library founded in 1824, from which developed the Mechanics' Institute eight years later. The Institute was established by members of the SLPS, including Knight and the social reformer James Montgomery, both of whom were keen to reassure their 'respectable' fellow members that it would not lead to subversion and revolution.

The library had its origin in the frustrations felt by reformers such as Montgomery that while many churches and chapels owned extensive book collections, they were intended solely for the use of their members. By 1842 the library had built up a stock of 5,628 volumes and had a membership of 643 readers. However, despite a philosophy of practical improvement, through such means as an ambitious programme of scientific instruction, within little more than five years of their foundation both the Mechanics' Library and Institute were under attack by the Anglican establishment. In the case of the library, this was for allegedly making available books that were likely to 'deprave the minds, injure the morals, and weaken, if not subvert, the religious faith of the great majority of readers'; in the case of the Institute, its education programme was deemed by a number of local Anglican clergy to be too overtly secular. In both cases, the attacks were clearly aimed at keeping the working class 'in their place'.

Following a visit to Sheffield by the philanthropic social reformer Robert Owen in 1833, an Owenite Hall of Science was opened six years later that went on to become the major educational expression of local radical politics among the working class. The Chartist leader Isaac Ironside, who had been ejected as secretary of the Mechanics' Library on the grounds of allowing readers access to works of 'a socialist leaning most dangerous to Christianity' – and to the works of William Shakespeare! – took on a similar role at this new institution. Under Ironside's direction, the Hall of Science encouraged open debate on controversial political issues. In 1841, for example, a series of lectures called 'The Principles of Socialism' was delivered, including one on 'the advantages and disadvantages of trade unions'. In general, Ironside was keen to put into practice his conviction that the broadest possible cultivation of working people's intellectual and critical faculties was an essential step towards political emancipation. Inevitably, under increasing censure on the part of the authorities, the Hall of Science closed in 1848, to be followed by the Mechanics Library in 1861.

It was in response to the opening of the Hall of Science that the Church of England Instruction Society, later to become the Church of England Educational Institute, was founded in 1840 and claimed by its supporters to be 'among the first of its kind in the country'. The intention of its founders was to provide a continuing education for graduates of the Sunday Schools and an alternative to the rough life of the street gangs for young apprentices. Its curriculum was heavily slanted towards religious indoctrination, and the strong support it received from the authorities enabled it to build impressive accommodation and thrive well into the nineteenth century, in contrast to the mixed fortunes of the secular and nonconformist foundations. By the 1860s, powerful establishment support meant that the Institute had nearly 100 teachers on its books, including seventeen members of the clergy.

Taking its cue from the Hall of Science, the People's College founded by local independent minister R.S. Bayley in 1842 aimed to deliver a sophisticated curriculum to both male and female working-class young people. As such, it was one of the first educational establishments in the country to admit women, and set a standard in equal female access to education in Sheffield that was to continue with the establishment of the town's university. Students were encouraged to debate issues arising from the history and science of politics in classes scheduled to fit around the working day. Once again, financial support from the wealthier sections of Sheffield society was almost completely lacking, and the College's continuing existence depended almost entirely on its students' fees. When Bayley left Sheffield in 1848, sixteen of the students took over the People's College and ran it as a self-governing institution supported by fees. Direct government involvement in the provision of adult education in Sheffield came in 1843 with the foundation of the School of Design, which by 1849 was a successful venture with 550 pupils, and was renamed the School of Art in 1857. Indeed, it was soon to become one of the most respected such institutions outside London, with prominent pupils including Godfrey Sykes and, later, C.S. Jagger.

The Development of Civic and Leisure Amenities

The fact that Sheffield developed predominantly as a working-class community during the industrial period is undoubtedly one of the reasons that there were fewer civic amenities than towns of comparable size. However, Sheffield's diminutive middle class started to exert some influence from the mid-eighteenth century with the foundation of the Sheffield Musical Society in 1750 and the opening of the Assembly Rooms with an attached theatre in Norfolk Street in 1762. Seven years later, the first music festival was held in the town and the Theatre Royal opened in 1773. A new music hall opened in 1822 for concerts, public meetings and art exhibitions. On the ground floor, in addition to rooms used by the SLPS, there was space for Sheffield's first subscription library, which had been established in the 1770s.

A good deal of middle-class resources went into the foundation of the Athenaeum in 1847 that, according to a contemporary description, and in contrast to the basic facilities provided for working people, included 'all the conveniences and attractions of a well-conducted club – well-furnished coffee, dining, smoking and chess rooms, a capacious, light and well-ventilated news room, an extensive and well-sorted library and a suite of rooms elegantly fitted up for the sole and especial use of ladies'. Pride of place in its social calendar was taken by a series of concerts provided annually 'exclusively for members'. By the early 1860s, exclusive facilities were further supplemented by the foundation of the Sheffield Club, 'an institution for social purposes, similar to the clubs of London ... supported by the elite of the town'.

In terms of outdoor amenities, there was a gradual recognition nationally that the cramped conditions of expanding industrial towns, characterised by high-density terraces of back-to-back houses, provided unhealthy living conditions. One response was the Report of the Select Committee on Public Walks in 1833, by which time there was an establishment perception that contact between the middle and working classes in public parks would foster competitive pride in appearance and an aspiration towards 'respectability', a cause that was enthusiastically promoted by Sheffield's nonconformist Christian social reformers.

In Sheffield, the first park in the modern sense to be created, the Botanical Gardens, which opened in 1836, was part of an ambitious neoclassical landscape scheme carried out by local architects William Flockton and Benjamin Broomhead Taylor that included the Mount and the General Cemetery on either side of the Porter Valley. For a number of years, admission was limited to members of the Sheffield Botanical Society. By the mid-nineteenth century the gardens were open to the general public in the form of promenades and music for wealthier inhabitants of the town, and a number of galas held in the course of every summer with a lower price of admission. These proved very popular and attracted crowds of up to 30,000 people.

Admission of the wider public to such facilities had been initiated in 1841 when the Duke of Norfolk provided general access to his Norfolk Park, one of the first such areas to be set aside for public recreation in the whole country. By the end of the nineteenth century, Sheffield had more than fifty public parks, and a city that was to many the epitome of dirt and squalor was to have the best provision of open green spaces of any industrial town in the country.

This was also the period that saw the beginnings of organised sport, with a Sheffield cricket team that formed the basis of the later Yorkshire County Cricket Club competing against Leeds in 1761. The Wednesday Cricket Club was founded in 1820 by skilled craftsmen who took the afternoon off from work to play. Sheffield United Cricket Club brought together a number of smaller

The Botanical Gardens, a private enterprise later opened to the public as one of Sheffield's first parks.

clubs in 1854 on grounds at Bramall Lane leased from the Duke of Norfolk. Cricket was also played on pitches at Hyde Park and Norfolk Park, and bowling greens were available by annual subscription at Broomgrove Road, Bramall Lane cricket ground and Pitsmoor.

The sport with which Sheffield was to become most closely associated was football. The first recorded football match in the town was staged in 1794, when a game was played between a town team and one from the Derbyshire village of Norton at Bents Green. This was played according to the tradition that had emerged in England in the Middle Ages where large teams of men from two sides attempted to take a ball cross-country to an agreed point on either side of the village. A contemporary report of the game noted that although several players were injured, no one had been killed. Sheffield Football Club, founded in 1857, is by general agreement the oldest organised club in the world and was instrumental in shaping the rules of the modern game. By the 1860s, in addition to a large number of smaller teams, there were also significant clubs at Pitsmoor and Hallam (based at Crosspool). Since December 1860, the Sheffield and Hallam clubs have played an annual fixture known as the 'Rules Derby' in recognition of the fact that it was originally played according to the Sheffield Rules. These regulations, which were drawn up by Sheffield FC between 1858 and

1877, included the introduction of corner kicks, free kicks for fouls and the separate field positions of goalkeeper and forward players. As such, they were formative in the development of the modern game.

Dawn of the Heavy Industrial Age

By the end of the eighteenth century, Sheffield was the centre of an industrial region, and an impressive but still comparatively small manufacturing base in steel and cutlery. In 1800, few would have imagined that it would become one of the most prominent industrial towns in the world. Nevertheless, by this time Benjamin Huntsman had already made Sheffield famous as a steel-making centre, and the skill of its workers was internationally renowned. Within fifty years of Huntsman's discovery of crucible steel, the Sheffield region was manufacturing 90 per cent of all the steel made in Britain and nearly half of that in Europe.

The Early Steel Industry

In 1774, one of the leading Sheffield trade directories named five 'manufacturers of steel'. Within another fifteen years this number had doubled, but until the second half of the nineteenth century, Sheffield steel was still manufactured by small firms. In many ways, the early steel industry mirrored that of cutlery; few firms could act entirely alone, and most were dependent on competitors for specialist operations known as 'hire-work'. Co-operation was as important as competition, with skills and knowledge being shared as necessary. Even the largest concerns did not always carry out their own tilting and rolling. As a result of these economies of scale, Sheffield firms quickly acquired a reputation nationally for innovation and adaptability.

At the same time, a small number of businesses were already self-contained units, making steel for their own cutlery and manufacturing tools on the same site. In the first half of the nineteenth century, Sheffield steel-making was still an industry heavily dependent on the handicraft skills of its workers, and progress in production techniques was made not through the application of scientific knowledge, but by traditional methods of trial and error, or what was generally called 'rule of thumb'. As had been demonstrated by Benjamin Huntsman himself, the trade was easy to enter and could be financed by small amounts of local capital. Steelmakers, prepared to take risks however humble their beginnings, were able to make a fortune.

Tilting machinery formerly belonging to W. Jessop & Sons, now on display at Abbeydale Industrial Hamlet.

Boiler house chimney at Cornish Place works. Steam power transformed Sheffield industry from the 1820s onwards, freeing enterprises from the necessity of being located next to fast-flowing water.

One of the main drivers of increased scales of production during this period was the introduction of steam power, which started to replace the traditional waterwheels on Sheffield's rivers from the 1820s. By 1846 there were 179 steam engines operating in the town. From this point onwards, manufacturing sites did not need to be built next to the rivers and streams but could take advantage of large, flat locations such as those on Milton Street that were developed in the 1850s. By 1868 it was estimated that more than 400 steam engines were employed in the town.

From around thirty-four in 1817, there were 224 steel manufacturers listed in the town in 1856. By the early 1840s, annual production of cementation steel had attained 20,000 tonnes, by which time, in the words of one contemporary commentator, Sheffield was a town 'as completely the metropolis of steel as Manchester is of cotton, or Leeds of woollens'. The crucible method had then become the dominant production process, and in addition to 206 cementation furnaces making blister steel, more than 2,000 'crucible holes' were producing almost 35,000 tonnes of high-quality cast steel each year. In employment terms, by 1850 more than 5,000 local people were working in the industry, though this was still relatively small compared with the 15,000 who found work in cutlery and the associated 'light trades'.

The Tool Trade

If steel was the newcomer, the tool trade, like cutlery, could trace its origins back to the early days of metalworking in the Hallamshire region. However, production levels generally were relatively small before the mid-eighteenth century and it took some time before Sheffield could compete in the wider market with the main centres of production in London and Birmingham. As with cutlery, it was the invention of crucible steel that allowed the tool trade to flourish on a larger scale. An example is the manufacture of saws, which from the mid-eighteenth century had been established as a separate trade and had started to develop in its own right. Following the introduction of Huntsman's technique, the trade began to expand rapidly, to the extent that by 1840, 80 per cent of English saw makers worked in the Sheffield area. For much of Sheffield's development, the main centres of local tool production were away from the town centre, such as the neighbouring village of Norton, which was already long-established as a centre for the production of scythes used in harvesting.

As world markets for tools expanded, it was again the quality of the products made in Sheffield that was able to give the town a competitive advantage. For example, in the market for edge tools – which included axes, chisels and planes – significant manufacturing bases had developed in Birmingham and further afield in Germany and the United States, but despite its relative size, Sheffield was able to hold its own throughout the nineteenth century.

By the mid-nineteenth century a number of large specialist tool firms had emerged. These included Spear & Jackson, who built their extensive Aetna Works beside the Midland Railway line in Savile Street; Moses, Eadon & Sons, whose President Works was built nearby; and William Hall of the Alma Works at Barker's Pool in the town centre. As the Industrial Revolution took hold, the specialist branch of engineering and machine tools developed rapidly, and once again the combination of access to high-quality raw materials and a skilled workforce began to give Sheffield a competitive advantage over the established centres such as Manchester and Leeds.

Other Metal Industries

Another significant branch of manufacture that developed in Sheffield alongside the cutlery and steel trades was the production of iron stoves, fenders and fireplaces. One of the leading manufacturers was Hoole & Co., which had operated at the Green Lane works near Kelham Island since 1795. By the mid-nineteenth century they were producing ironware that, according to a contemporary trade directory, constituted 'works of the highest order of art, as well as those of a more unpretentious class'. Meanwhile, the firm of Stewart & Smith was making pieces that gave 'great scope for the imagination and taste of the artist ... carried out with much skill'. A local brass-founding industry had also been established by the early nineteenth century that specialised in the production of miners' safety lamps among a number of other articles.

As the scale of engineering works increased during the nineteenth century, trade in the manufacture of steel wire and cable developed rapidly. Previously,

Elaborate frontage of the former Green Lane works at Kelham Island. Together with Cornish Place, this is the best example of Sheffield firms copying the architecture of country estates to legitimise their industrial endeavours.

such items had been made of iron, but crucible steel proved itself to have the advantages of comparative lightness, elasticity and durability. At the largest end of the scale, cables were being produced from six strands twisted together, each containing six pieces of wire. Such products were soon in great demand around the world in applications such as shipping and the construction of bridges.

The Emergence of the East End Giants

By the mid-nineteenth century, the scale of steel production in Sheffield was expanding rapidly, largely as a response to demand from the United States. The construction of the Midland Railway line to Rotherham along the Lower Don Valley was another stimulus to trade. By the 1820s, these expanding firms were starting to outgrow their restricted sites in the town centre. Both railway and canal drew the most ambitious manufacturers to the open lands to the east of Sheffield's historic core, and apart from the opportunity to expand, and the attraction of low rents, sites next to the railway allowed easy importation of coke and coal and export of finished products. The first of the new areas to develop was Savile Street, which led away from the long-established area known as the Wicker on the east side of the River Don. Once steam power had removed the need for industrial premises to be located near the upland streams, Sheffield expanded rapidly eastwards along the Don Valley towards Rotherham, with Attercliffe and Brightside becoming major centres of iron and steel production in the modern era.

In 1846, Charles Cammell established the first of the East End giants with the opening of his Cyclops Works on Savile Street, and by the mid-nineteenth century Sanderson Brothers & Co. had works in Attercliffe and Darnall, and Thomas Firth & Sons, which had been founded in 1842 with just six crucible holes and a few employees at their Norfolk Street works, relocated to Savile Street in the early 1850s. In 1856, John – later Sir John – Brown moved his operations from Furnival Street in the town centre to the East End and began to build his massive Atlas Works, which within a few years had spread north of the railway into Carlisle Street. By the 1860s all of these massive new enterprises were among the greatest steel producers in the world.

The large flat sites of the East End provided considerably more room for expansion than the earlier centres of production in the tributary valleys and the town centre. This extra space also meant that large-scale housing developments could be created right next to the factories to ensure a constant supply of labour. So just at the point when foreign competition was beginning to challenge

President Works (Savile Street) of Moses Eadon & Sons, *c.*1852, later absorbed into John Brown's massive Atlas Works.

the organisation of Sheffield's traditional light trades, the East End was rapidly colonised by modern, highly mechanised industry organised on a massive scale.

The Victorian Steel Barons

Many of the men who are synonymous with the Sheffield steel industry originated in the cutlery trade. They were mostly locally born and of relatively limited education, but to them is owed much of the achievement of bringing the name of Sheffield to the world stage. Following the example of an earlier generation of cutlery magnates, such as George Wostenholm, who developed his Kenwood Park estate in Sharrow from the 1830s, the leading industrialists all moved out to mansions in private parks on the south-western outskirts of Sheffield. These included Mark Firth, who having spent £60,000 on the construction of his Oakbrook residence in Ranmoor, hosted the Prince and Princess of Wales there for just under a week in 1875. A sign of the significance of the steel barons in regional and national society by that time can be glimpsed from the invitations to dinner on the first evening that included the Archbishop of York, the Duke of Norfolk, the Earl and Countess Fitzwilliam and Lord and Lady Manners. To pay for this opulence it should be remembered that even in the 1860s there were boys of 7 or 8 years of age regularly working twelve-hour night shifts in the new East End steelworks.

The leading steel pioneers included:

Charles Cammell (1810–79)

Cammell moved from Hull as a young man, and after gaining experience as a salesman for the Sheffield firm of Ibbotson Brothers, by 1837 he was a partner in a steel and file business in Furnival Street. He established the Cyclops Iron and Steel Works in the East End in 1846, specialising in heavy forgings, steel rails, railway springs and buffers, files and, later, armaments. On the proceeds of these enterprises, he bought Norton Hall on the southern outskirts of the town in 1852.

Edward Vickers (1804–97)

Two generations of his family had been corn millers at Millsands near the centre of Sheffield before Vickers started making steel on the same site. The River Don Works that he established on Brightside Lane in the 1860s became the largest crucible steelworks in the world. By the late nineteenth century his sons Tom and Albert had turned the firm into the country's biggest manufacturer of armaments. He served as mayor of Sheffield and was the first President of the Sheffield Chamber of Commerce.

Mark Firth (1819–80)

As a young man Firth joined the crucible steelworks of Sanderson Bros, where his father worked as head smelter, but he left in 1842 to set up his own steel business with his brother, Thomas Jr. By 1852, their father had joined them, and the firm of Thomas Firth & Sons had built the Norfolk Works in Savile Street, which boasted the largest rolling mill in Sheffield. By the later nineteenth century, the firm was one of the largest arms manufacturers in the world. Firth served as Master Cutler 1867–70, mayor of Sheffield in 1874 and chairman of Sheffield School Board in 1879. In 1867 he built Oakbrook in the western suburb of Ranmoor along with thirty-six almshouses nearby. In 1875 he donated a 14-hectare estate to the town of Sheffield as Firth Park. Firth College, which he founded in 1879, was a forerunner of the University of Sheffield. He is buried with his wife under a substantial monument in Sheffield General Cemetery surrounded by iron railings made at his Savile Street works.

Sir John Brown (1816–96)

The son of a Sheffield slater, Brown was apprenticed to a firm of merchants before setting up his own steel business in 1844. By the mid-nineteenth century Brown & Co. were specialising in the manufacture of files, railway springs and buffers. Their patented buffer ensured the commercial success of a firm that by the later nineteenth century had become one of the world's largest manufacturers of armour plate. Brown served as mayor of Sheffield in 1861–62, Master Cutler from 1865 to 1867 (in which year he was knighted) and first chairman of the Sheffield School Board in 1878. He built his impressive Italianate residence Endcliffe Hall in 1863–65.

Thomas Jessop (1804–87)

Jessop built up the family business with his father and sons and by the mid-nineteenth century the firm had branches in Manchester, Paris, Canada and six in American cities. He served as Master Cutler in 1863 and mayor of Sheffield in 1863–64. He bought his mansion at Endcliffe Grange from the Sanderson family in 1851 and founded Jessop Hospital for Women in 1877. He was buried in the cemetery at Ecclesall Church following a funeral procession that included 700 workers from his steelworks and carriages, including the mayor and Master Cutler.

From Railways to Industrial War

The construction of railways throughout the world from the 1840s greatly expanded the demand for crucible steel for the manufacture of locomotive parts, rolling stock, rails and the machines to make them. In 1848, John Brown invented and patented the conical steel buffer at his Rockingham Street Works and from that point on Sheffield firms responded quickly to satisfy the market. Big fortunes were made, and a number of Sheffield's most successful steel firms saw their first spectacular growth during this period.

But while much of world railway construction was directed towards quite benign purposes, it was the application of new materials to human destruction on a greater scale that was to provide the greatest impetus to the growth of Sheffield's industry from the mid-nineteenth century. Specifically, the Crimean War of 1853–56 prompted huge government contracts to supply armour-plating for the new 'ironclad' vessels of the Royal Navy, to the extent that leading local manufacturer Thomas Turton & Sons installed a massive Nasmyth steam hammer in its Hecla Works in 1855 to keep up with demand. Meanwhile, at his nearby Atlas Works, John Brown diverted much of his company's capacity to the production of rolled armour plate of up to 30cm thickness at a rate of 300 to 400 tonnes a week.

Responding to government demand, huge investment was made in plants and frequent visits were made to factories by government officials including the Prime Minister, Lord Palmerston, and heads of the armed forces. It was during the Crimean War, and its immediate aftermath, that Sheffield forged its strong links with central government and London as opposed to the more parochial connections of the cutlery age. Another effect of the massive increase in demand for steel products that came with the Crimean War was the merger of a number of big Sheffield steel firms that took the town's industrial base to another level. In general, almost all the steel used by British forces in the Crimea – everything from razors and mess kits to bayonets and projectiles – was made in Sheffield. The conflict was a foretaste of the 'industrial warfare' that was to characterise the first half of the following century, the dramatic impact it would have on the economic fortunes of Sheffield and the devastating toll this shift in the focus of steel production would take in human lives.

Making Steel for the Modern World

While there seemed no end to the number of products that could be made from crucible steel, it did have one significant limitation: a product that took more than two weeks to produce, and in relatively small quantities, was expensive and unable to meet the bulk demands of large-scale engineering work. For this reason, iron remained indispensable to the progress of the Industrial Revolution in Britain and beyond. However, the advent of crucible steel had shown up the weaknesses of wrought iron, particularly in terms of uniform strength and structure, and from the mid-1850s steel makers began the search for a material superior to iron but more affordable than cast steel.

At the same time that John Brown was looking for ways to increase his output of railway steel by modifying the furnaces at his Atlas Works, Henry Bessemer, an engineer and inventor from Hertfordshire, was experimenting with ways of bringing steel-making into the realm of mass production. In August 1856, Bessemer revealed his solution to the world: by blowing air into molten pig iron at intense heat of up to 3,000°C (twice that of a crucible melt) in a large, egg-shaped furnace, the oxygen in the blast rapidly combusted

A Bessemer converter at Kelham Island Industrial Museum.

carbon and other elements, leaving almost pure iron. Compared with traditional steel-making, which involved the firing of iron in a cementation furnace for about two weeks, followed by a further four hours to be converted to cast steel in a crucible furnace, the whole process took less than thirty minutes. Not only was the Bessemer Convertor faster, but it could produce large tonnages of the mild steel needed for the Industrial Revolution's heavy engineering applications at about a fifth of the price.

After various technical problems had been overcome, most significantly by the Scottish metallurgist Robert Mushet's fine tuning of the carbon balance in the converter, Bessemer himself moved to Sheffield and began operations at his own steelworks in Carlisle Street in the town's East End. His specific intention was to provide the stimulation for local manufacturers to follow his lead, and it was not long before even the most hardened supporters of the crucible method were adopting his system by taking out licences to install their own converters. The first to do so was John Brown, who built new forges, rolling mills and the converters demanded by the Bessemer process at his Atlas Works in 1858. The heyday of Sheffield steel-making by traditional methods was over: a little more than 100 years after Huntsman had perfected the crucible method, a new technique of mass production was set to revolutionise the steel industry and further consolidate Sheffield's position as steel capital of the world.

Chapter Three

FURNACE: 1860–1935

The End of 'Old Sheffield'

In the 1850s, Sheffield experienced another massive increase in population, at a rate almost double that of other industrial centres such as Birmingham. In a little over 100 years, the town had grown from a small settlement of cutlers to become the greatest centre of steel production in the world. Within Britain itself, by the end of the nineteenth century Sheffield had overtaken Leeds to become the largest population centre in the county of Yorkshire. The surge in population was a result of the expansion of steel-making and engineering, and the rapid growth in particular of the suburbs of Attercliffe and Brightside resulted from immigration of unskilled men from the surrounding villages, and further afield, to provide labour in this emerging sector.

The following decade witnessed the culmination of a lengthy period during which Sheffield's traditional metal trades, with their highly skilled workforce and dependence on local capital, expanded and dominated international markets in tools and cutlery. It was also a time when immigrant German steel manufacturers and toolmakers made a significant impression on the development of Sheffield industry. Finally, the opening up of deep coal mining through the exploitation of the 'Barnsley Seam' brought a new product to the Sheffield region, a fuel particularly well-suited to locomotive use and therefore in demand to drive the second phase of the Industrial Revolution. By 1870 there were more than 100 collieries in the South Yorkshire area employing over 60,000 miners, many of whom were resident in Sheffield.

By this time, Sheffield was the undisputed centre of world cutlery production, and 'Made in Sheffield' was one of the best-known manufacturing brands in the world. Pre-eminent in terms of quality and the craft skills of its artisans, Sheffield was able to keep ahead of new centres of the industry such as those in the eastern United States. Yet in hindsight, this was clearly the high point of

Sheffield's traditional trade, and the forty years between then and the start of the First World War marked the start of a lengthy period of decline that ended in the industry's near-extinction at the close of the twentieth century. The main contributor to this twilight period was the inexorable march of mechanisation in the new centres, particularly those in Germany and the United States. Cheap, well-finished cutlery made in bulk and marketed aggressively was always going to be a difficult rival for Sheffield to withstand, and all too often the town's ancient industry seemed just that – one that was entrenched in the hand-crafted ethos of a distant past.

Indeed, much of 'Old Sheffield' was changing. The second half of the nineteenth century saw a growing differentiation between the character of central Sheffield and the East End. The old township remained home to the myriad of small workshops typical of the cutlery industry, toolmaking and other 'light trades', while the emerging East End, on the flat lands of the lower Don Valley, witnessed the emergence of the monolithic factories associated with heavy steel.

The Great Sheffield Flood

The terrible event known as the Great Sheffield Flood can be seen as emblematic of the rapid transformation of Sheffield in the mid-nineteenth century from cutlery town to major industrial city. The rapid rise in population, from 45,755 in 1801 to 185,172 in 1861, led to a massive increase in demand for water. In response to a significant drought in 1851, the Sheffield Water Company, which had been formed twenty years earlier, started looking for sites in the Upper Loxley Valley at which to build new storage facilities. Work began on the Bradfield or 'Dale Dyke' reservoir five years later at a time when the company was striving to produce the best capital return for its investors while providing an adequate supply to residents and maintaining power to the waterwheels of the Rivelin and Loxley valleys.

On the stormy night of 11 March 1864, while it was being filled for the first time, the newly built Dale Dyke dam collapsed, sending a huge wall of water down the Loxley Valley, through Loxley village itself and onto Malin Bridge and Hillsborough, where the Loxley joined the River Don, before continuing into Sheffield centre and through Attercliffe towards Rotherham. The deluge destroyed everything in its way, including some 800 houses, fifteen bridges and a number of business premises, and took the lives of 240 of Sheffield's inhabitants. It remains Britain's worst man-made disaster. Sheffield's mayor, steel magnate Thomas Jessop, quickly set up a relief committee which raised over £45,000 from private donations.

Confluence of the rivers Loxley and Rivelin at Malin Bridge.

The immediate cause of the disaster was found to be a crack in the embankment, though the Water Company, denying any fault in the structure and design of the dam, argued that the adverse weather conditions had resulted in an unavoidable natural landslip. Despite its denials, local and national opinion was united in hostility towards the company and the behaviour of coroner John Webster, who was accused of bullying working-class witnesses at the subsequent inquest. After just two days, the jury found that 'there [had] not been that engineering skill and attention in the construction of the works which their magnitude and importance demanded', a verdict that seemed designed to absolve the Water Company from direct responsibility for the disaster.

By the end of the year, 650 claims for damages had been submitted and settled. The surviving records give a striking impression of the value that was given to property relative to human lives. Businesses and property owners that suffered damage were in most cases fully reimbursed, whereas little compensation was awarded to the relations of people killed where they had not been the main breadwinner. For example, Selina Dyson of Hillsborough, who lost her husband and six children, was granted only £60 of her claim for £500, and a Mrs Ryder, whose young son Robert was swept away as they both clung to a lamp post, received £20 compensation for the loss of his earnings of 4s 6d a week as a child worker. By contrast, William Howe, of Neepsend, was given £110 for the loss of furnishings in his house, which were listed as including his piano and music, a display of wax fruit and flowers, a *History of England* in four volumes and a mahogany card table.

For its part, the Water Company sought permission from Parliament to levy a 'moderate increase' in the water rates to meet its liability. In the event, and in the face of vociferous opposition from the town council, it was given approval to impose a staggering 25 per cent increase. In the long run, it was this struggle between the council and a large private company run by powerful citizens (which included the industrialist Sir Frederick Thorpe Mappin), that provided impetus for Sheffield's successful bid for the greater powers of city status that were granted in 1893.

Changing Employment Conditions

By the later nineteenth century, a few large cutlery firms were operating within the shrinking world of independent producers and outworkers that had been the foundation of Sheffield's traditional industry. Some of the larger establishments, such as the Cornish Place works of Joseph Rodgers & Sons, contained up to 2,000 individual rooms, occupied by small teams of 'little mesters' and one or more outworkers. Existing alongside them were unknown numbers of workers employed in the underworld of domestic production dependent on traditional hand tools.

For Sheffield's traditional cutlers, the advantages of maintaining their independent ways of working were diminishing. Gradually, there was a realisation that the industrial structure they had worked so long to maintain left them unprotected by emerging factory legislation and open to exploitation by the larger employers. Indeed, their independence was increasingly illusory, their status and remuneration continually declining in a world of big business. As mechanisation slowly took hold of the cutlery and tool sectors, growing numbers of men sought more lucrative employment in the emerging heavy industry of the East End. As a direct consequence, the number of women employed in the cutlery trade between 1870 and 1890 doubled, and on the eve of the First World War, one in five cutlery workers were women, though the majority of them were employed in the poorer branches of the industry and in areas such as warehouse work and packaging. Very few women broke into the heaviest forging and grinding trades, which continued to be dominated by men.

In the early twentieth century, women under the age of 20 made up the fastest-growing sector of the workforce. By this time, it had become common practice for the largest firms to employ girls straight from school at the age of 12 or 14, then dismiss them once they were married. The age distribution of cutlery workers at this time indicates that it was becoming low-paid, low-status and low-skilled work, with men over the age of 45 accounting for 30 per cent of the male workforce. Many of these men were on low wages, forced by poverty to work into their old age. Throughout this period, the wages of most cutlery workers were both failing to keep pace with those of heavy industry, and falling in real terms.

A visit to the town by parliamentary commissioners in 1899 exposed the full extent of the sweatshop system by then operating in much of the cutlery trade. Investigations revealed that some men worked more than sixty hours a week for a wage of less than 14s (70p) and that in general, overwork and underpay were commonplace. Attention was drawn to one particularly sad case of an elderly pocket-blade grinder who, though he worked all the hours he could, had died of malnutrition. The report concluded that the larger 'factors' were the main problem, not the traditional 'little mesters', who were generally at the mercy of the larger employers. In the knowledge that 'little mesters' and outworkers would be hard up when trade was depressed, factors were able to barter them down by refusing to take goods at previously acceptable prices and, in the words of the report's compilers, to 'cut one another's throats, and thereby bring the prices down so that they cannot live themselves nor the men who work for them'. This undercutting was at its worst during trade depressions, when only the largest firms continued to pay standard wages, until they too were forced to cut both wages and prices. This was all a far cry from the heyday of the proud, independent Sheffield cutlers.

Toolmaking

Among the light trades, the Sheffield tool industry generally fared better than cutlery in this period, and had grown from a modest scale in the mid-eighteenth century to world leadership by the late nineteenth. Toolmaking operations, which were commonly located away from the town centre and in the surrounding villages, were usually organised on a larger scale, sometimes on the basis of five or more men working together. A good idea of the

Former Abbeydale Works (now Abbeydale Industrial Hamlet) with the chimney stack of the crucible steel shop prominent in the centre.

arrangement of a toolmaking business can be gained from the surviving Abbeydale Works, where water wheels, tilt forge and grinders' shops were located together with the manager's house and workers' cottages. During its heyday in the early nineteenth century, Abbeydale was one of the largest water-powered sites on the River Sheaf.

Sheffield toolmakers had the advantage of ready access to supplies of crucible steel, and some of the most prominent toolmaking firms produced their own steel as well as often having an interest in the manufacture of cutlery. A typical example was Butcher Brothers, who inherited a cutlery business that could trace its origins back to 1725. Success in the US market allowed them to expand between 1830 and 1860, when they were manufacturing steel at the Philadelphia works, as well as a range of tools and cutlery at their large integrated works in Arundel Street known as Butcher's Wheel, which had a combined workforce about 1,000 strong.

By the 1870s there were more than 250 tool firms in Sheffield, mostly operating on a fairly small scale but including a number of larger companies employing between 200 and 400 men. File making was the single most important sector of the business. By the end of the nineteenth century the most famous tool firms included Spear & Jackson, who employed more than 800 workers at their Aetna Works on Savile Street, and Thomas Turton & Sons, who took over part of

Former Butcher's Wheel (now renovated as Butcher Works), one of the largest integrated manufacturing establishments in the town centre.

Greaves's Sheaf Works in 1850, by which time they were described as 'merchants and manufacturers of steel, files, saws, edge-tools, and every description of cutlery [as well as] locomotive and railway carriage springs'.

Workers United

A Collective Tradition

By 1870, Sheffield was the most solidly working-class town in the country, with some two-thirds of its adult population directly engaged in the metal trades. This was a town in which hard industrial labour was the common experience of the majority of the population, and it is therefore no surprise that it is in Sheffield that we see the first development of robust traditions for protecting the employment position of workers that at times spilled over into direct action.

During the second half of the eighteenth century, the craft unions emerged as one of a number of powerful expressions of a community organised around the workshop and the pub. From the start, these associations were highly specialised. By the mid-nineteenth century, for example, there were no fewer than ten separate grinders' unions, looking after the interests of 'jobbing grinders' as well as those who worked edge tools, files, fenders, forks, pen knives, pocket knives, saws, scythes and sickles.

Over time, relations between these specialist craftsmen and the Cutlers' Company had gradually soured, due largely to the fact that by the 1780s journeymen cutlers outnumbered the freemen who dominated the Company by ten to one. A parliamentary act of 1791 altered aspects of the constitution of the Company so that it lost its ancient right to control admission to the trade, thus effectively ending the apprenticeship system. In 1814, the main provisions of the Elizabethan Statute of Artificers were repealed, and entry to the cutlery trade became entirely free. From this point onwards, regulation of trade effectively shifted into the hands of the unions, who came to see themselves as the true heirs of the Cutlers' Company. In the fifty years following the end of the Napoleonic wars in 1815, the role of the trade unions would become the most hotly contested issue in Sheffield public life.

Emerging originally from the craft associations, a number of fully formed trade unions were founded between 1820 and 1860. These included the Sheffield Mechanical Trades Association (1822), the Trades General Union (1831), the Alliance of Organised Trades (1838) and the Committee of Trade Societies (1843). In 1845 the more ambitious National Association of United Trades for the Protection of Labour was founded by the secretary of the Razor Grinders' Union, John Drury. In 1858 an umbrella organisation, the Association of Organised Trades of Sheffield and Neighbourhood, was founded with seventeen branches and more than 3,000 members. By 1860 this had risen to thirty-five branches with 4,000 members and was the first of a virtually unbroken line of Sheffield trades councils that continued to the present day.

By this time Sheffield had become probably the most highly unionised industrial town in the country, with regular meetings being held, usually weekly gatherings in local pubs. Effective unionisation led to a Sheffield workforce that was particularly resistant to change, and opposition to mechanisation in particular was powerful among the craft unions, especially those associated with the file trades. In the 1850s and '60s, the craft unions increased their effectiveness at industrial bargaining, and there were many in the movement who even argued against traditional practices such as the maintenance of 'St Monday'.

In July 1866, the conference of the Association of Organised Trades was held in Sheffield and drew delegates from national, regional and local unions, as well as trades councils from as far away as Glasgow and representatives of the International Working Men's Association. The conference was recognised at the time as 'one of the largest ever held in the cause of labour' and put forward motions including mutual support against lockouts, shorter working hours, formation of councils of arbitration and conciliation, schemes for co-operation and the amendment of employment legislation.

But perhaps the most significant outcome of the conference was the formation of the United Kingdom Alliance of Organised Trades with its headquarters, appropriately, in Sheffield. Despite this organisational triumph, however, Sheffield unions were soon to become isolated both locally and nationally by the eventual collapse of the file makers' strike and the ramifications of the 'Hereford Street Outrage' of October 1866.

The Great File Makers' Strike, 1866

This famous action was an iconic moment on the path the traditional Sheffield industries were to take in the second half of the nineteenth century and into the twentieth. Starting on 24 February 1866 as a wage dispute, it increasingly became bound up with the issue of resistance to mechanisation. The file trade was a prominent part of that sector of Sheffield industry in which firms combined steel production with the manufacture of tools. Such firms employed a large number of skilled craftsmen both on and off site. Firms such as Turton's, J. Kenyon & Co., Spear & Jackson, Eadon & Sons and Ibbotson Brothers were at the centre of the conflict between local craft traditions and the developing practices of large-scale mechanised industry.

Nearly 4,000 filesmiths, file grinders and associated workers went on strike over a wage claim and faced a lockout by the employers, who were themselves organised in a File Manufacturers' Association within which Frederick Mappin, a later mayor of Sheffield, held a prominent position. A number of employers had installed file-cutting machines of a type recently introduced in Manchester but which had been outlawed by the unions. In response, the file unions organised a co-operative society to undertake file cutting by hand and joined the Association of Organised Trades (AOT).

A contemporary song sung by file cutters on the subject of a machine that had been unveiled by a Manchester firm gives eloquent testimony to the strength of feeling in the trade:

It's the wonder of wonders, is this mighty steam hammer
What folks say it will do, it would make anyone stammer
They say it will cut files as fast as three men and a lad
But two out of three, it's a fact, they are bad.

They say it will strike 300 strokes in a minute
If this is a fact there will be something serious in it
The tooth that is on them looks fine to the eye
But they're not worth a rush when fairly they're tried.

These Manchester cotton lords seem mighty keen
To take trade from old Sheffield with this cutting machine
They've a secret to learn – they know it's the truth –
The machine is naught like flesh and blood to raise up the tooth.

So unite well together by good moral means
Don't be intimidated by these infernal machines
Let them boast as they will – and though the press clamour,
After all, lads, there's nothing like wrist, chisel and hammer.

For more than fifteen weeks the unions paid out well over £1,000 per week in subsistence to their members. The AOT's attempt to arbitrate during March – including an open debate between both sides at the public house owned by William Broadhead, Secretary of the Saw Grinders' Union – failed when employers insisted upon unconditional acceptance of the new machinery by the unions.

By early June the file unions, popularly regarded as the strongest in Sheffield, were forced to send their men back to work on the new machines without any increase in wages. The most they were able to win, after further strikes over the following twelve months, was an agreement that employers should only put skilled men on the machines. Despite being ultimately unsuccessful, the strike had been a show of strength by one of Sheffield's biggest craft unions in a contest that was widely viewed at the time as a crucial test of the fitness of the emerging capitalist system itself.

Working Practices in the Light Metal Trades

In Sheffield, the line between employer and employee was blurred. While independent cutlers were sometimes employed at a manufacturer's works, at other times they might work on individual orders in a public workshop, known locally as a 'hull', where the owner charged rent and provided power. On such occasions they might employ one or more men or boys themselves to work alongside them. The majority of workers were tenants of larger works, paying a weekly rent and working to piece rates. Workers like these were in a position to determine the length of their working day and to supplement their income through subcontracting (or 'outworking'). In the same works there might be men who rented a room and power only occasionally and worked entirely on materials for outsiders. The idea of a self-contained factory, where each operation was controlled by a single owner or manager, would have been beyond the comprehension of a typical Sheffield cutlery worker. The entire industry operated on the basis of great numbers of outworkers exercising remarkable levels of control over the industrial processes themselves.

Within this flexible employment structure, the movement of single individuals between the position of wage labourer and manufacturer, and back, was surprisingly common. The more enterprising workers could buy their own raw materials or semi-finished goods, rent more than one workspace, and at the same time employ a number of apprentices on a short contract to complete a particular order. With relatively small capital, they could even go on to set up a trademark and rise to 'master' status, known locally as a 'little mester'. Problems occurred where such men operated unscrupulously, whether through embezzlement, underselling, false trademarking or the exploitation of child labour through operating fake apprenticeships. Such 'autonomous craftsmen' had the capacity to operate on a highly individualistic level and the scope for employment mobility could result in certain workers and business owners sharing mutual interests.

Yet this level of worker mobility was inherently unstable. Ultimately, the reality of the cutlery industry was increasingly of outworkers earning depressed wages, locked into relationships of dependency with manufacturers who controlled access to external markets. One way that manufacturers tackled decreasing prices was to offer financial inducement for craftsmen to work for a fixed rate over a number of years. Such a practice took advantage in particular of the desperation of little mesters and journeymen. An even worse practice was the so-called 'pawning' of workers. In times of price depression, manufacturers would keep rents high and workers were forced to agree to work off large debts. This often led to perpetual bondage to a single firm, restrained men from taking strike action and put a disproportionate burden of risk on workers themselves. During economic slumps, such contracts weakened unions' abilities to resist price cuts, while in boom years raising prices became more difficult due to the weight of existing contracts.

By the 1860s, a number of cutlery manufacturers were growing both in size and power. Particularly significant was the emergence of manufacturing firms that combined centralising tendencies with integration of sub-branches of the trades. Typical of this trend were Joseph Rodgers & Sons, whose Sycamore Street works grew from 500 workers in the 1840s to 1,200 in the 1870s; George Wolstenholme & Son, who expanded rapidly in the 1860s; and Mappin Bros, whose Queen's Cutlery Works was greatly enlarged during this period. These three firms were at the time the largest light metal manufacturers in the world.

At the same time, from the 1850s, highly mechanised 'heavy steel' firms based in the East End were booming. From 1860, industrial 'steel elites' took over the old Cutlers' Company, to the extent that between 1863 and 1873 only two actual cutlers rose to the position of Master Cutler. Men such as John Brown, Mark Firth and Thomas Vickers dominated this position, so that the role now reflected the growing economic power of large manufacturers, a long way from its origins in Sheffield's independent craftsmen.

Mechanisation first appeared in blade manufacturing in 1861 when James Drabble & Co. began producing machine-made knives to compete with those of American and German manufacturers. In saw making, Spear & Jackson introduced American grinding machines in 1851 and Thomas Turton & Sons introduced file-grinding machines in 1865. As international competition intensified, Sheffield manufacturers faced the choice as to whether they should follow the lead of the Germans and Americans and install machinery, or make a full commitment to higher-quality goods with a smaller market share. However, the issue with the new technology was not just depression of wages but also the creation of a whole new class of semi-skilled workers that would significantly affect established working practices.

Rattening

The strength of neighbourhood and occupational bonds that kept together families dependent upon a common means of earning their living was expressed in the widespread toleration of physical sanctions against anyone who disobeyed the norms of the community. A typical reason for sanctions being imposed was the infringement of union rules, for example on apprenticeship, payment of contributions, or the use of machinery, and these were directed against both workers and employers.

The most common sanction was 'rattening', the covert removal of the leather bands that connected the axles powered by the waterwheels or steam engines to an individual worker's grindstone, and the confiscation of his tools. The next day the victim would discover that 'the rats had been' and they might receive a threatening letter signed by 'Mary Ann'. In the words of Sheffield's most famous nineteenth-century historian, the former cutler Joseph Hunter, rattening was 'an ancient custom, probably as old as the grinding wheels on the streams which flow towards the town'. Joseph Thompson, secretary of the Scissor Forgers' Union, said the custom was looked upon as 'an ancient law' originating long before unions had come into being. In reality, employers generally turned a blind eye to the practice, while small unions co-operated among themselves to enforce it. A report in the *Sheffield Independent* in 1867 expressed the confident opinion that:

> to those who know the usages of the Sheffield trades, there will not appear to be anything more wonderful about [rattening] than in the executions put into force every week by the bailiffs of the County Court, except that the law of the land sanctions the one and forbids the other.

The 'Sheffield Outrages'

The tensions inherent in the shift of the Sheffield light trades towards a more capitalistic business structure came to a head in the middle decades of the nineteenth century. In response to the changing labour markets in the 1850s and '60s, in which independent workers increasingly saw the larger employers as enemies, Sheffield trade unions pursued increasingly extreme industrial relations strategies that took the intimidation of 'rattening' to its logical extreme. A number of incidents saw angry cutlers throw gunpowder down the chimney stacks and into the grinding troughs of men who broke the community rules. In 1854 a saw grinder was shot at, and a file grinder was the victim of an explosion in 1857. In 1859 a saw grinder was murdered, and a bystander was killed in a gunpowder attack on a workshop two years later.

These incidents soon came to the attention of a horrified national press and became known as the 'Sheffield Outrages'. However, despite the fact that the grinders' unions were deeply implicated in these acts of violence, they attracted surprisingly little local interest until the file makers' strike of 1866 put the trade unions into the national spotlight. Indeed, the feeling that such actions were expressions of a collective moral code is strongly supported by the sheer difficulty and obstructiveness that the authorities encountered when tracing offenders, and the failure to elicit information even following the offer of large rewards. The turning point was the so-called 'Hereford Street Outrage' of

The Globe Works of John Walters & Co. In one of the first acts of intimidation carried out by Sheffield tradesmen, two members of the Saw Grinders' Union threw a can of gunpowder down its chimneys in 1843 as a warning to non-union workers.

8 October 1866 in which a home-made bomb exploded at the house of a saw grinder who was in dispute with his union. On this occasion the Sheffield Chamber of Commerce called for an inquiry and was backed by the town council, the Cutlers' Company, the Manufacturers Protection Society, the Sheffield Association of Organised Trades (SAOT) and the Conservative *Sheffield Telegraph*.

In 1867, the government convened a Royal Commission on the trades unions following a wave of strikes nationally, and in light of the incidents in Sheffield. The inquiry lasted five weeks and in Sheffield implicated William Broadhead, secretary of the Saw Grinders' Union, treasurer of the Associated Trades of Sheffield and United Kingdom Alliance of Organised Trades and landlord of the Royal George on Carver Street. However, since witnesses had been examined under indemnity from prosecution, Broadhead was not charged and was able to travel to America in 1869.

The inquiry established that the most violent acts were carried out on behalf of the Saw Grinders' Union, which was attempting to maintain high wages by rigidly controlling entry into the trade and maintaining idle workers out of union funds. This was a system whereby the unions paid out doles known as 'box money' to a rotating surplus labour force, thus artificially maintaining labour scarcity and upholding wages. The victims of the outrages, apparently instigated by Broadhead, were saw grinders outside of the union seen as producing inferior goods at low prices and taking on apprentices who would be undertrained and who would flood the labour market.

The two individuals killed in the outrages, James Linley and Thomas Fearnehough, emerged in the inquiry as the type of worker characterised in local union circles as the 'unscrupulous little mester'. Linley had learned the trade of scissor grinder but moved into saw grinding because it was more profitable. He then took on several apprentices at a time, undercutting the union's prices with his cheaper wares. These poorly trained apprentices were then turned out onto the labour market and had to be immediately 'placed on the box', in other words, supported by union funds. Indeed, his murderers, Samuel Crookes and James Hallam, were both disaffected former apprentices. Fearnehough's case was similar, and he was described by his attackers as 'the type of man who takes bread out of another man's mouth – not because he himself wanted bread, but because he's got a tooth for lazy roast meat'. Defending the perpetrator, Henry Cutts – secretary of the Filesmiths Union – went further, describing such workers-turned-masters as 'receptacles for the filth of the trade'.

Yet despite the national outrage, the behaviour of Broadhead and his men was not generally perceived as deviant in the eyes of their peers, but in fact was generally condoned as displaying commitment to common values held by the majority of Sheffield working people. The hatred felt for non-union men was related to a perception of workers who had turned themselves into 'tyrannical masters'. Regulating such turncoats was generally seen in union circles as securing the group welfare of workers. This involved a rejection of the capitalist enticement for workers to become petty entrepreneurs, and sharpening the line between employer and employee. Rather than being a divide between 'the trade' and the 'unscrupulous little mester', the fault line was between the union and the 'tyrannical master'. Such men, blinded by greed, had misunderstood where their interests lay, and needed a sharp reminder.

These communal values help to explain why the victims of the incidents apparently had few friends in Sheffield; even the Tory *Sheffield Telegraph* was forced to admit 'that outside the immediate circle of roughs proper there are hundreds, and we very much fear, thousands who extenuate and palliate the dark deeds disclosed and who secretly, if not openly, sympathise with Broadhead'. Defending union actions in the course of the inquiry, Joseph Thompson, secretary of the Scissor-forgers Union, was asked whether he knew of any act of intimidation that had been carried out by masters. His response was straight to the point: 'I cannot bring any charge of intimidation against the masters, but I can bring this charge; that in the absence of trades unions, prices in our trade are reduced something like 40 or 50 per cent.' Former Democrats leader Isaac Ironside gave evidence to support this view and, indeed, asserted that the Outrages Inquiry itself was 'a great outcry to reduce wages ... to continental rates', and a 'conspiracy of the governing and employing classes to crush the liberties of the working men and their means of defence'.

In this context, the union-sponsored violence that broke out in this period can be seen as the outcome of contested power relations. Underlying the violence was an attempt to wrestle power away from manufacturers and towards the workforce. Unions went to whatever level they saw as necessary in an attempt to control the labour market and the process of production, including dramatic acts of violence at the point of production. In this sense, in the words of one historian of the Sheffield trade unions, 'they were making territorial claims over the workshop'. As such, the Sheffield Outrages can be seen as a final, existential struggle of Sheffield metalworkers to defend their centuries-old independence and freedom in the face of an emerging system of factory capitalism that, in its pursuit of profit, cared little for the communal welfare of workers.

Towards a Better Way of Living

Despite the structural changes that were taking place in the cutlery industry and associated light trades, the period from the 1860s to 1914 saw a significant rise in the real standard of living for the people of Sheffield and a general reduction in the number of hours worked. The same period saw a decline in infant mortality, growth in education and wider access to public facilities such as trams and parks, which all contributed to an improvement in the quality of life. A flourishing labour press, characterised by publications such as the *Sheffield Guardian*, and the formation of groups such as the Clarion Cyclists and Ramblers were signs of a growth in the aspirations of wage earners that was unimaginable in the first half of the nineteenth century.

Against this, cyclical fluctuations in trade resulted in periods of unemployment and real hardship. Pollution, disease and poverty still blighted the lives of too many of Sheffield's citizens. Throughout the second half of the nineteenth century, mortality rates in Sheffield from infectious disease were among the highest in the country. At the dawn of the twentieth century, the authorities had not yet responded adequately to the housing and public health challenges posed by explosive population growth, and tackling these challenges became one of the main issues that confronted those involved in local administration and politics.

Living Together

A national report of 1861 entitled *Condition of our Chief Towns* delivered a harsh assessment of Sheffield at a time when the rapid growth of the heavy steel industry was leading to an even more pronounced tendency towards residential segregation based on income and status. On the one hand, hundreds of poor people were still packed into the unsanitary 'courts' and slums of the town centre and increasing numbers of largely immigrant steelworkers crowded around the huge plants in the East End suburbs of Attercliffe and Brightside. On the other hand, white-collar professional and managerial families increasingly moved out into spacious villas on the uplands to the west and south-west of town.

This geographical segregation of communities was not unique to Sheffield and was mirrored in other British towns and cities during the period of rapid

'Blind back' houses in Canning Street. Built cheaply in the 1830s with no rear yards, by the mid-nineteenth century such dwellings were already becoming outdated.

industrialisation, most notably London and Glasgow. However, compared for example to the other great metalworking town of the period, Birmingham, the degree of social segregation in Sheffield was much more marked.

The western suburbs became increasingly accessible with the introduction of horse-drawn buses, and the steeper routes that had been unprofitable in a time when transport was dependent on horses became more viable with the laying of tramlines from the 1860s. In 1896, the corporation took over the horse-drawn tram system and electric trams were introduced at the very end of the century, the first running from the city boundary at Tinsley into the town centre. For all Sheffielders, trams provided cheap and efficient transport, which enabled both the working and middle classes to live away from their places of work and brought people into the town centre for shopping and entertainment.

At the end of the nineteenth century, nine-tenths of the housing in Sheffield was occupied by working-class families and standards of accommodation remained a challenge. The most common type of accommodation was in the form of back-to-back brick terraced houses. By 1864, when a corporation by-law prohibited the erection of further buildings of this type, Sheffield had 38,000 back-to-backs. Most were built in blocks of between ten and fifteen houses as speculative enterprises by local tradesmen. Landlords were more interested in getting a return for their capital than undertaking necessary maintenance work, let alone improvements, and the rapid development of the steel industry from the late nineteenth century led to the construction of much poor-quality housing.

Sporadic slum clearances commenced from 1890 and included a scheme to clear and rebuild the Crofts and Scotland Street areas that had long been associated with severe poverty, crime, and gang violence among the largely immigrant Irish population. Under the Liberal-controlled council, forced evictions began in 1898 from those dwellings deemed to be dangerous and which had tenants who were behind in rent payments. No attempt was made to rehouse those who were evicted, they were merely given notice to quit and left to fend for themselves.

Meanwhile, in the centre of town, the slum clearances in the vicinity of Campo Lane and Townhead Street were carried out on a somewhat more humane basis in that the substandard dwellings were replaced by council housing. Slum clearance on an even larger scale began in 1903, by which time the building of council houses had started to get under way. In general, however, the council's decisions during this period were increasingly directed towards a policy of economy and low rates, and as a result both the housing and educational needs of the city were neglected.

Former council houses erected in Hawley Street following slum clearances in the late nineteenth century.

More enlightened councillors supported what at the time was a very novel proposal, that of creating working-class housing estates in suburban areas. In 1899 the council voted to acquire land at High Storrs for corporation housing but the scheme faced problems from the start. The local government board in Westminster refused to sanction a loan on the grounds that the site was 'not suitable for houses for the working classes', since they would allegedly be too far from their place of work. This despite the fact that plans were already under way to extend the city's tram network in this direction.

There was opposition too from local residents, and in particular the Conservative councillor Muir Wilson, who lived at Whiteley Wood Hall about half a mile away from the proposed estate and claimed that the site was unsuitable, 'bleak and uninviting'. In the opinion of Liberal alderman John Wycliffe Wilson, local residents 'thought that High Storrs was too good a neighbourhood for working people' and there was also an argument that rents would be too high for the slum dwellers whose rehousing should take priority.

For their part, the trade unions and the Labour group on the council proposed a policy based on the 'garden city' and 'model cottage' movements, and in 1906 the council inaugurated a housing experiment at High Wincobank, purchasing forty-four exhibition cottages for rent at a range of values. Inevitably, the

Houses on the High Wincobank ('Flower') estate. When they were first built, between 1907 and 1914, they were considered by Conservative commentators to be 'too good' for the working classes.

Conservative *Sheffield Telegraph* denounced the scheme as 'blatant socialism' and its editorial expressed resentment at 'the provision of trim and dainty villas for well-paid artisans', arguing that former slum dwellers would not be able to afford the rents. By contrast, in 1907, the Wincobank estate was visited by representatives of the International Housing Congress, who were very impressed.

By 1914, 230 houses had been built on the Wincobank scheme, but in the absence of any subsidy from central government rents had to be set at the market rate, which was in reality too high for the majority of the people they were supposed to house. However, the scheme enabled more enlightened members of the council to make the case for a substantial commitment to council housing as the way forward, and between 1910 and 1914, Sheffield built more council houses than any local authority in the country and its schemes were seen as more ambitious than even those of London.

Public Health

The turning point in the provision of improved living conditions was the Public Health Act (1872). Over the next twenty years mains sewerage and drainage systems were installed, so that a reliable water supply for the town was at last obtained. However, the majority of houses were still dependent on basic sanitary provisions that were little more than open pits rather than water closets connected to this new sewerage system. In the more crowded working-class

Former Jessop Hospital for Women, now part of the University of Sheffield.

areas communal privies were shared by more than sixty people. Improvements to such arrangements went hand-in-hand with slum clearance schemes, but it was to be a slow and laborious process.

Aside from the impetus provided to the council, the 1872 Act also prompted the generosity of local philanthropists such as the steel baron Thomas Jessop, who built a new hospital for women in 1878. However, challenges such as high infant mortality among disadvantaged families continued to the end of the nineteenth century. Attempts to tackle its root cause, urban poverty, began in the 1880s with the work on behalf of his impoverished parishioners by the humanistic pastor of St Matthew's, Carver Street, Father George Ommanney, and the 'settlements' and related movements of the 1890s following this lead.

The Settlement Movement was an initiative of social reform that aimed to foster social contact between poorer and better-off inhabitants of industrial cities. This was put into effect by establishing 'settlement' centres in poor urban areas in which middle-class volunteers (known as settlement workers) would live and provide services such as education, hygiene and basic health-care. In Sheffield, the Rev. William Blackshaw, Minister of Queen Street Congregational Church, started working in the Crofts, one of the poorest areas of the city, in the 1880s. Blackshaw and his volunteer assistants established a base in a former chapel in Garden Street and in October 1902 the Lord Mayor opened the new Croft Settlement Hall. This included a boys' club, gymnasium, reading room, musical facilities and a Sunday School. Free breakfasts and soup

Croft Settlement Hall, still a focus of community support in the twenty-first century.

were provided throughout the year, and weekend summer camps in the Peak District were organised for men and boys as well as play facilities for younger children. Provision specifically aimed at women and girls was introduced later and included classes in parenting, sewing and basic hygiene.

In a metalworking town such as Sheffield, pollution was a growing problem. On many days of the year a dense smog spread across the city, which sunlight could barely break through. The first local by-laws to limit smoke emissions appeared in the mid-1850s and at national level, the 1875 Public Health Act included some limited attempts at environmental regulation. Later in the century the anti-pollution cause was taken up by the social reformer Edward Carpenter, but it was to be another 100 years after the first by-laws were enacted before this particular struggle was won.

Education for All

The tone for the development of educational arrangements in Sheffield was set in 1835 when an informal agreement between nonconformists and the Church of England allowed the former to take the lead in education on Sundays and the latter for weekdays. As a result, the Sunday School movement developed rapidly in the town, and by the 1860s the annual Whit Monday gathering of Sunday scholars in local parks was numbered in the thousands. As with much that was positive in the town, it was the educational initiatives of Isaac Ironside, leader of the Democrats on the council, that helped pave the way for Sheffield's impressive educational advances in the later nineteenth century.

Former Ebenezer Sunday School, Kelham Island, one of many nonconformist establishments that flourished from the mid-nineteenth to the mid-twentieth century.

The most significant development in education in the later nineteenth century, both nationally and locally, was the passing of the 1870 Education Act, which for the first time established a framework for the schooling of all children between the ages of 5 and 12 in England and Wales. This was carried out through the establishment of 'school boards' with members elected by local ratepayers. In many cases parents still had to pay fees for their children to attend school but the Act gave boards the power, widely adopted in Sheffield, to pay for places for poorer children. The weakness of opposition in Sheffield from the Church of England, which elsewhere in the country vigorously opposed the broadening of education outside its direct control, meant that the Sheffield School Board was established a lot more quickly than in many other towns.

The first Sheffield School Board was elected on 28 November 1870 with an initial aim of providing education for an additional 9,000 children, and set about this task with a level of energy and a sense of purpose unrivalled anywhere else in the country. Indeed, Sheffield's first Board School, Newhall, was the first to be built in England. Fourteen schools had been built by the end of 1874, and nineteen of Sheffield's eventual total of twenty-two Board Schools were completed between 1873 and 1881. They still stand as some of the city's finest buildings. Careful consideration was given to questions of classroom layout, lighting, ventilation and heating. Typical features of the new schools included separate access and playgrounds for girls, boys and infants, and provision of a single schoolroom for each age group.

The Sheffield School Board worked hard at consolidating Sheffield's hitherto haphazard education provision, and in the thirty-two years of its existence built or reconditioned a total of forty-seven schools. It is notable that a third of the members of the first school board were steel men, including Charles Doncaster, Sir John Brown and Mark Firth, Brown and Firth being elected successive chairmen in the late 1870s. The quality of the Board offices on Leopold Street are testament to the sense of civic pride that the creation of Sheffield's first education authority engendered in the town. In 1880, Sheffield Central School, one of the first higher-grade schools in the country, also opened on Leopold Street. The 1902 Education Act brought the Sheffield School Board to an end and transferred its powers to a new Sheffield Education Committee administered by the city council. One of its first acts was to bring about the amalgamation of the Royal Grammar School and Wesley College to form the new King Edward VII School, and in 1905 a teacher training college was established on the site of the former Collegiate School.

Subsequent council initiatives included a campaign to improve and extend primary education, the provision of school meals, a School Medical Service, and advanced classes for children staying beyond the school leaving age. Innovative schemes included the foundation of Whiteley Wood open-air school

Springfield Board School: Sheffield adopted the provisions of the 1870 Education Act with enthusiasm.

in 1909 for children above the age of 10 suffering from diseases and disabilities associated with poverty. In general, from the early decades of the twentieth century, Sheffield educationalists and architects were at the forefront of national moves towards better school provision for whole sections of the community that had been neglected during the rapid growth of industrial towns.

A University for Steel City

The last quarter of the nineteenth century was also an important period in the development of education beyond school level. In 1874 the Sheffield School Board started evening science classes for adults, and during the following year the University Extension Movement that had been established by Cambridge University in conjunction with the Church of England put on its first lectures in Sheffield. Among those who attended was the industrialist Mark Firth, who in 1879 was spurred on to the foundation of Firth College, at which subjects including mathematics, classics and history were taught based on the traditional Cambridge curriculum and aimed at preparing students to take degrees from the University of London.

Firth College (now part of the Leopold Hotel), a major contribution to continuing education in the town and a forerunner of the University of Sheffield.

Sheffield's progressive attitude in the sphere of education is demonstrated by the fact that as soon as it opened in 1879, Firth College admitted female students on an equal basis to men. Not long after its foundation, the College started collaboration with the existing Sheffield Medical School, which in 1888 moved into new premises on the other side of Leopold Street. Following the death of Mark Firth in 1880, just a year after the opening of the college that bore his name, fellow industrialists Sir Henry Stephenson and Sir Frederick Thorpe Mappin took steps to keep up the momentum in adult education. Stephenson devoted much of his later life to ensuring that Firth College was able to continue financially, and Mappin pursued his interest in the provision of advanced education in engineering and metallurgy, both to counter increasing competition in steel production from the United States and Germany and to promote a skilled labour force potentially free from the control of Sheffield's trade unions. Sheffield Technical School was established in 1884 and two years later opened in bespoke premises on the site of the former grammar school in St George's Square. By the late 1880s, it was providing a number of local steel firms with the results of the metallurgical research, supervised by its principal, J.O. Arnold, and Professor of Mechanical Engineering, William Ripper. Indeed, so close had the relationship between industry and technical research become that in the early years of the foundation of the new Sheffield University, Arnold was complaining of 'an attempt by a limited number of manufacturers to dictate to its professors'.

In 1890, by which time a number of former students of Firth College were working in the laboratories of leading steel firms, the town council took over the administration of the Technical School. From 1918, Ripper worked to establish links between the new University and local industry at all levels to promote serious study and open discussion on the technical challenges faced by practical steel-making. The result was the Trades Technical Societies movement, which gained widespread support among the region's industrialists and went on to influence best practice in other areas of the country.

In 1897 Sheffield Medical School merged with the Technical School and Firth College to form University College Sheffield, with degrees awarded by the University of London. Initially the new institution applied to join Victoria University, a federation of university colleges in Manchester, Liverpool and Leeds, but the application was refused on the grounds that Sheffield did not have enough academic staff. Victoria University itself disbanded in 1902, with Leeds University College being encouraged by the government to incorporate as

The premises of Sheffield Medical School from 1888. Originally founded in 1829, the school became one of the constituents of University College Sheffield in 1897.

Firth Court (1905), flagship building of the new University of Sheffield.

'Yorkshire University'. Confronted with the possibility of Leeds becoming the sole university city in the county, Sheffield made a late bid for a charter of its own. This was successful, and the city acquired a full university with the privilege of awarding its own degrees in 1905, although up to 1912 it was required to submit its statutes and ordinances to the three former Victoria universities for approval.

The University was partly endowed, in the sum of around £50,000, by public funds raised in the city to commemorate Queen Victoria's Diamond Jubilee in 1897. This was supplemented to a lesser extent by a second appeal under the slogan 'A University for Sheffield', which attracted small individual subscriptions from a generally enthusiastic public, including pennies collected from thousands of the city's working men and women. The new university was soon conducting front-line research in metallurgy in conjunction with the local steel industry, as well as providing much part-time teaching in technical subjects on behalf of the city council.

In Search of a Life with Value

In the 1870s, Sheffield's long tradition of an independent skilled workforce and strong trade unions proved fertile ground for testing new ideas of how society could be organised for the common good. A new wave of social reformers, led by John Ruskin and Edward Carpenter, were attracted to Sheffield to try out new forms of living.

John Ruskin (1819–1900) was one of the leading English art critics of the Victorian era, a philosopher and philanthropist whose work increasingly focused on social and political issues. From the 1860s, Ruskin increasingly attacked industrial capitalism and the utilitarian economic theories that underpinned it. Over time, his social views developed from concerns about the dignity of labour to issues of citizenship and concepts of the ideal community. He heavily criticised the capitalist system that led to the separation of the worker from the product of his labour as 'dehumanising', and argued that emerging economic theory failed to recognise the importance of the social bonds that hold communities together. Ultimately, Ruskin's ideas were to influence the foundation of the British Labour Party and the establishment of the welfare state.

In 1871, Ruskin began publishing his monthly *Letters to the Workmen and Labourers of Great Britain* in which he developed the principles underlying his ideal society that led to the foundation of his utopian society the 'Guild of St George'. This was intended as a communitarian protest against industrial capitalism, by which he aimed to show that people lived best in harmony with the environment and with the minimum of technological dependence. At the same time, he sought unashamedly to educate and enrich the lives of industrial workers by inspiring them through encounters with fine art, for which he set aside a personal donation of £7,000 to acquire land and a collection of objects.

Looking for the most suitable place in England to establish his project, Ruskin chose Sheffield as an archetypal industrial town, centrally situated within the country and within easy reach of beautiful countryside. Appalled by the grime and smoke of the town, he was nevertheless attracted by the handicraft skills of the Sheffield cutlers and by the wonderful views that could be obtained from former industrial sites such as the Bole Hills of Crookes. Within the cutlery industry he particularly admired the 'spirit of co-operation and discipline' that bound workers together and which he contrasted with the massive, faceless new industries like the heavy steel factories emerging in the Lower Don Valley.

In 1875, Ruskin turned his attention to a cottage high on a hill in Walkley where he opened his St George's Museum, filled with 'treasures to educate and inspire the working classes'. In a letter to *The Times*, he explained that 'the mountain home of the museum was originally chosen, not to keep the collection out of smoke, but expressly to beguile the artisan out of it'. The collection itself consisted not just of paintings, but minerals, books, medieval manuscripts, architectural casts, coins and other 'precious and beautiful objects'. With the help of this collection, Ruskin aimed to bring within reach of working people the sights and experiences otherwise reserved for the wealthy who could afford to make grand tours of the Continent and, in the words of Ruskin's friend, the artist and academic W.G. Collingwood, 'introduce higher aims into ordinary life'.

In 1876, Ruskin was introduced to a local group of communists that included secularists, Unitarians and Quakers, who had established a mutual help group in Sheffield's Hall of Science. The older members had their roots in Chartism and were part of the Sheffield Mutual Improvement Society, by which they aimed to encourage people to become independent of the prevailing capitalist system by mutually exchanging the products of their labour. Ruskin himself, despite some reservation towards the more extreme principles of communism, was happy to give encouragement to the group due to the strength of his feeling against what he perceived as the immorality and ruthlessness of capitalism. In 1889 his museum was taken over by Sheffield Corporation and moved to Meersbrook Hall, and the collection is now in the city's Millennium Gallery.

Edward Carpenter (1844–1929) defies conventional categories by the sheer breadth of his interests as poet, mystic, social theorist, mathematician, man of action, socialist pioneer and gay rights and animal rights activist. The basis for his social views was a firm rejection of Victorian middle-class values, which he described as:

... cant in religion, pure materialism in science, futility in social convention, the worship of stocks and shares, the starving of the human heart, the denial of the human
body and its needs, the huddling concealment of the body in clothes, the impure hush
on matters of sex, class division, contempt of manual labour, and the cruel barring of
women from every natural and useful expression of their lives.

Carpenter's socialism was born out of a visit to Paris in 1871, soon after the fall
of the Commune, and like a previous generation of Sheffield reformers, including Gales, Roebuck and Ironside, he was inspired by revolutionary France. On
his return from another visit to the country in 1874 he was struck by his life's
mission: 'it suddenly flashed on me, with a vibration through my whole body,
that I would, and must, somehow go and make my life with the mass of the
people and the manual workers'. The same year he moved to Leeds as part of
the University Extension Movement led by Cambridge academics who wanted
to introduce higher education to the working people of the industrial towns
and cities. Disillusioned when he found that the majority of his lectures were
attended by the middle classes, he moved to Sheffield, where he at last came
into contact with the manual workers he wished to inspire. Carpenter's attraction to Sheffield was immediate:

From the first I was taken with the Sheffield people. Rough in the extreme, twenty
or thirty years in date behind other towns, and very uneducated, there was a hearti-
ness about them, not without shrewdness, which attracted me. I felt more inclined
to take root here than in any of the northern towns where I had been.

In Sheffield, Carpenter's politics and social views became increasingly radical.
Influenced by the ideas of Henry Hyndman, a follower of Friedrich Engels,
he joined the Social Democratic Federation (SDF) in 1883 and attempted to
found a branch in the city. Instead, the group chose to remain independent
and went on to become the Sheffield Socialist Society. While living in the city
he worked on a number of projects with the aim of highlighting the poor living
conditions of industrial workers. In 1884, along with William Morris, he left the
SDF to join the Socialist League and his numerous disciples in the Sheffield
region did much to advance the fortunes of the nascent British Labour Party.

Increasingly, Carpenter was active in the movement against industrial pollution, and in an article in the *Sheffield Independent* in 1889 drew attention to the
'giant, thick cloud of smog rising out of Sheffield, like the smoke arising from

Judgement Day – the altar on which many thousands would be sacrificed'. In his view, 100,000 Sheffield adults and children were struggling to find even the basic necessities of sunlight and air and were enduring miserable lives, unable to breathe and dying of respiratory illnesses.

Carpenter eventually left Sheffield in 1890 to travel to India. On his return to England in 1891 he met George Merrill, a working-class man from Sheffield twenty-two years his junior. The two started living openly together from 1898 and remained as a couple until Carpenter's death. At a time when there was much public hysteria surrounding the trial of Oscar Wilde, the relationship between Carpenter and Merrill provided the inspiration both for E.M. Forster's gay novel *Maurice* and D.H. Lawrence's straight rendition, *Lady Chatterley's Lover*. In his latter days, Carpenter developed much of his thinking around the interconnections between gay rights and democracy, which inspired subsequent generations of English political activists and social reformers.

Big Steel

And now let me say something of that famous town, the very name of which is identified with steel. Steel in its crudeness; steel in its progress; steel in the multiple forms in which it traverses the globe; steel in the shaft and wheel of the ponderous locomotives; and steel in the pretty knife in a lady's dressing case.

Sheffield Independent, 4 January 1871

During the second half of the nineteenth century, steel outgrew cutlery as the major industry of Sheffield. In the age of railways and modern warfare, steel manufacturers were no longer primarily dependent on the cutlery industry to supply demand. In this new age, steel that was made in cementation and crucible furnaces in the centre of town was to be superseded by the massive output of Bessemer converters in Sheffield's East End. Sheffield's cementation and crucible steel industries had reached peak production of around 130,000 tonnes a year by about 1870, and twenty years later production had fallen by about two-thirds. Even the largest firms, however, such as Vickers and Brown's, maintained a profitable interest in the crucible method for specific applications such as railway buffers, but the general trend was clear.

These new developments enabled Sheffield to maintain the position of the world's primary centre of steel production that it had held ever since Benjamin

Huntsman had moved to Attercliffe with his perfected crucible technique 100 years earlier. By the end of the nineteenth century, new competitors had emerged, particularly mass producers in Germany and the United States, but for now, Sheffield's reputation for producing the best cast steel in the world remained unrivalled. Aided by the shift towards bulk production, the period from the late Victorian era to the end of the First World War can be seen as a golden age for Sheffield's steel industry and in the development of the city.

The Bulk Steel Revolution

The cause of this momentous change was the shift towards bulk steel production, particularly using the Bessemer method. Bessemer's invention provided the impetus to take forward the 'second industrial revolution' of the 1860s and 1870s characterised by an increase in the scale of engineering. Indeed, its commercial introduction marked the end of the first phase of that vast social, commercial and technological upheaval in which iron had played such a pivotal role. From now on, the process would be more adequately supported by the age of steel. During the four decades that the Bessemer process was a major part of the Sheffield steel-making scene, from the 1860s to 1900, the town rose from a cutlery and edge tool producer, through the nation's largest producer of steel rails, to become one of the world's largest centres of armaments and ordnance manufacture.

Together, the Sheffield industrialists who took up the first Bessemer licences were responsible for the emergence of a whole new branch of the local steel industry based largely on the production of steel railway materials. To take the example of John Brown: a man who had started business on his own just twenty-five years earlier, by 1864 was head of a company with a capital value of £1 million and whose massive East End production plant employed almost 3,000 people.

The significance of the rapid development of the heavy steel industry from the time of the introduction of the Bessemer process was marked symbolically by the 1860 Act of Parliament that allowed the Company of Cutlers to accept steel manufacturers to join their ranks. From this time also, the gravitational pull away from local concerns towards regional and national networks of commercial power and influence was increased by the transformation of a number of the leading steel firms into limited companies drawing on capital from outside Sheffield. This process strengthened the links of local manufacturers with financiers in other parts of the country, particularly Manchester, while the growing significance of central government arms contracts increasingly prompted Sheffield industrialists to look to London.

The Big Steel Firms

The adoption of the Bessemer process and the advent of big government arms contracts saw the consolidation of some of Sheffield's steel firms into giants of world industry. The growing influence of Sheffield's steel makers is reflected by the fact that they were admitted to membership of the Company of Cutlers from 1860 and a number of them went on to serve as Master Cutler, aldermen and mayor. The biggest steel companies in the Sheffield region at the outbreak of the First World War in 1914, in terms of numbers of employees, were as follows:

Vickers Ltd

Founded 1820s. Over 5,000 employees. River Don works constructed on Brightside Lane in 1863. In the top ten British firms in terms of capital. Main products included armour plate, guns, forgings and alloys.

John Brown & Co. Ltd

Founded 1837. Over 5,000 employees. Atlas Works established on Savile and Carlisle Streets from 1856. Main products included railway components and armour plate.

Cammell, Laird & Co. Ltd

Founded 1837. Over 5,000 employees. Cyclops Works established on Savile Street, 1846. Main products included railway components and armaments.

Hadfield's Ltd

Founded 1872. Over 5,000 employees. Constructed East Hecla Works at Tinsley in 1897. Main products included steel castings, projectiles and tool steel.

Firth & Co. Ltd

Founded 1842. Over 3,000 employees. Constructed Norfolk Works on Savile Street 1851–55. Main products included steel castings, guns and projectiles and tool steel.

William Jessop & Co. Ltd
Founded 1793. 2,000 employees. Established the Park, Soho and Brightside Works by the 1870s. Main products included cast, alloy and tool steel.

Samuel Fox (Stockbridge)
Founded 1842. 2,000 employees. Established his business in a disused corn mill in the village. Main products included umbrella frames, crinoline wire and railway components.

Steel, Peech & Tozer (Rotherham)
Founded 1871. 1,800 employees. Main products included railway components and forgings.

Jonas & Colver Ltd
Founded 1873. 1,500 employees. Main products included tool steel and tools.

Parkgate Iron & Steel (Rotherham)
Founded 1823. 1,500 employees. Main products included pig iron and bulk steel.

Samuel Osborn & Co.
Founded 1851. 1,000 employees. Established the Clyde Works on the Wicker in 1851. Main products included tool steels, alloys and castings.

Brown Bayley's Steel Works Ltd
Founded 1873. Over 800 employees. Established the Sheffield Steel and Iron Works by 1880. Main products included railway materials and alloys.

Edgar Allen & Co. Ltd
Founded 1868. Over 400 employees. Established the Imperial Steel Works, Tinsley, by 1880. Main products included steel castings, tool steels and tools.

As steel took over from wrought iron, the biggest industry to adopt the Bessemer process in its early days was railway engineering. Led by Brown's and Cammell's in 1860, entire Sheffield steelworks were turned over to the manufacture of steel rails to replace those made of iron, and the growth of this business meant that by 1875 there were eight massive Bessemer steel plants in Sheffield alone. For a number of years, John Brown was the biggest producer of steel rails in the world. In 1871 his nephew George founded Brown, Bayley & Dixon in Attercliffe for the exclusive manufacture of Bessemer steel and rails.

In practical tests, steel rails were found to be nearly as good as new after a year of heavy use, whereas iron rails had needed to be replaced on main-line railways about every three months. At first, because of the greater cost, steel rails were limited to use in stations and at busy junctions, but as economies of scale improved, they were adopted for general use. Due to its greater durability, steel came to be used in practically all railway applications, a major selling point being that, compared with the early days of steam locomotion, fatal accidents from breakages of wheels and couplings were significantly reduced. Between 1865 and 1874, Sheffield was the world's largest manufacturer of steel rails, with annual production of about a quarter of a million tonnes. The quality of the product exported from Sheffield to the United States in particular established its reputation and ensured the future of the process.

During the 1860s, a very lucrative addition to Sheffield's product range came from the fashion for crinolines, wide skirts supported by a light frame that through the use of steel wire became one of the world's first mass-produced items of clothing. From Sheffield it was exported, in the full range from raw steel to made-up skirts, to markets as far away as Canada and Australia. Firms

Premises of the Samuel Fox Steel and Iron Works, Stocksbridge.

such as Gray & Co. became world famous for their crinoline skirt production facilities, which attracted visitors from all over the world, incidentally providing some of the earliest industrial work for women in the assembly shops of their Pond Hill works, where up to 800 women were employed during periods of especially high demand. By the mid-1860s, Samuel Fox was using the Bessemer process to make both steel wire for railway components and crinoline skirts, as a result of which Stocksbridge became established as an important steel centre in its own right. Immigrants from both the region and further afield settled in the former village in large numbers; by the early 1880s there were 4,600 of them living in 895 new houses.

The boom in railway construction in Britain came to an end around 1873, and by 1876 the export trade to America had collapsed. More than at any other time in its industrial history, increased competition from other steel-making centres exposed Sheffield's weakness in relying on supplies of imported iron. Even within Britain, production centres with better access to raw materials fared better, so that by 1878 the biggest Bessemer plant in the country was Vickers' works at Barrow-in-Furness on the north Lancashire coast. American and German producers had also been quick to adopt the Bessemer process and by 1890 both had overtaken Britain in terms of total output.

By the late nineteenth century, in order to improve access to overseas markets, a number of Sheffield firms established depots overseas, with the United States being the most favoured base. Firth had the controlling interest in a joint steelworks in Pittsburgh from 1894 and Jessop acquired a base in the same city in 1901. Sanderson Bros opened a tool steel production facility in Syracuse, New York, in 1900 and Edgar Allen commenced alloy steel melting operations at Chicago Heights, Illinois, in 1910. Closer to home at around the same time, Samuel Fox started manufacturing steel from a works in France; Joseph Jonas opened a subsidiary in his native Germany; and Cammell's, Firth's and Saville's all set up factories in Russia.

Some of the larger Sheffield firms such as Cammell's, Brown's and Vickers, started to take on the character of multinationals, mainly as a result of their involvement in the arms trade. The top five Sheffield steel producers in 1914 – Vickers, Brown's, Cammell's, Hadfield's and Firth's – were all arms manufacturers that had witnessed significant growth in the period leading up to the First World War. By that time, none of these companies could still be seen primarily as steel makers, or even, realistically, as Sheffield firms. In addition to armaments, shipping increasingly attracted the attention of the big firms, with

Vickers' River Don Works, Brightside Lane. At its height in the years leading up to the First World War it was one of the largest steel, engineering and munitions factories in the world.

Brown's acquiring shipyards at Glasgow and Belfast, and Cammell's in Birkenhead. Indeed, as Cammell Laird, the latter was to develop in the twentieth century primarily as a shipbuilder.

After Bessemer: The Technology of Bulk Steel Production

The Siemens (Open-Hearth) Method

Further developments in the technology of bulk steel production continued with the open-hearth furnace introduced by German-born engineer Carl Wilhelm Siemens (who changed his name to William after settling in Britain) in 1870. This method originated in the inventor's attempts to use the waste heat from furnace exhaust gases, and involved the melting of material from blast furnaces, together with scrap metal, in an open hearth.

While it was slower than the Bessemer method (taking on average between four and twelve hours as opposed to thirty minutes) it had the significant advantage that molten steel could be analysed and modified during the melt. In addition, although the process was slower, it had the capacity to produce up to four times the amount of material in a single melt.

The Siemens method gradually became adopted as the preferred technology for the manufacture of guns, special forgings, power transmission and a number of other heavy engineering applications. Led by Vickers, open-hearth furnaces were operating in Sheffield by the early 1870s. Total production of steel by the Siemens process exceeded 20,000 tonnes by 1880, and global production surpassed that by the Bessemer method by the beginning of the twentieth century.

Electric Arc Melting

Developments in electrical engineering towards the end of the nineteenth century led metallurgists to believe that melting by means of electricity could be more efficient than the crucible, open-hearth and Bessemer methods. The first successful furnace was patented in Scotland in 1889, and further developments were made over the following fifteen years in France and the United States. The process works by melting scrap metal in a furnace heated by the creation of an electric arc between two electrodes while oxygen is injected.

The first furnaces in production were relatively small, with a maximum capacity of about 8 tonnes, and were employed predominantly for using up scrap metal. Over time, however, used in conjunction with high-quality raw materials, they came into use for the production of high-grade tool steels. The prime advantage of the electric arc furnace over previous methods was its adaptability to differing production requirements, being able to be scaled up or down as required.

In 1910, Edgar Allen & Co. conducted the first successful steel melt in Sheffield using an electric arc furnace, and within a few years Jessop, Firth and Kayser Ellison were also in production. The biggest electric melting operations in the Sheffield region took place at the Templeborough steelworks near Rotherham after six electric arc units were installed to replace ageing open-hearth furnaces in the 1950s. As a result, with an annual output of 1.8 million tonnes, Templeborough became the largest electric arc steelmaking plant in the world.

Special Steels

The sixty years between 1860 and 1920 were the great period of development of alloy or 'special' steels, and Robert Hadfield's discovery of manganese steel in 1882 can be said to rank with Huntsman's in creating a whole new branch of the Sheffield steel industry. During the twentieth century it was to be through the production of special steels, rather than in bulk steel production, that Sheffield was able to maintain its position as a world power. By the development of specialist materials such as silicon steel, with its myriad of applications in electrical technology, Sheffield can be said to have played a crucial role in the creation of the modern material world.

Most of the major alloy steels (that is, those products containing elements other than carbon) were discovered before the outbreak of the First World War. Before the introduction of the Bessemer method in the 1860s, developments in Sheffield steel-making had owed little to science and almost everything to trial and error. In the late nineteenth century, however, directors of the major firms increasingly saw research and development as crucial to commercial success. As early as 1864, Cammell's had appointed a company chemist, and six years later Vickers were carrying out experiments in their own laboratory.

Meanwhile, in the Forest of Dean on the Welsh border, Robert Mushet, son of a prominent Scottish ironmaster, was conducting experiments aimed at improving the performance of crucible tool steel. By 1868 Mushet had discovered that the addition to the steel melt of finely powdered tungsten produced a significantly more durable tool steel that retained its hardness in use, thus solving a perennial problem for machine shop engineers. Lacking the necessary finance to produce tungsten steel himself commercially, Mushet chose to license the technique to the Sheffield firm of Samuel Osborn, which from 1870 produced large quantities of 'Mushet's Special Steel' at its Clyde Iron and Steel Works on the Wicker. The impact of this new alloy on the engineering world was immediate, particularly in the field of railway manufacture both in Britain and abroad.

Robert Hadfield's pioneering work followed directly from Mushet's. The son of an Attercliffe steel maker, he joined the family business as soon as he left school and in his spare time carried out experiments with a small furnace that he had persuaded his father to install in the basement of their family home. He was only 24 when he discovered manganese steel, which actually hardened with use and was the first steel alloy to have universal application across the whole of engineering and industry.

Following Hadfield's discovery, the demand for more systematic research and training grew rapidly. In response, Sheffield Technical School was established in 1884 to give students the opportunity to work with steel within a theoretical framework informed by physics and chemistry. As for Hadfield himself, his skill as a metallurgist was matched by his business knowledge, and after becoming chairman of the family firm at his father's death, he developed the company into one of the largest and most successful manufacturers of armaments and other steel alloy applications in Britain.

Manganese steel was put to use quickly in a range of applications including crushing machinery, mining and dredging equipment and, even more widely, railway and tram track work. Close to home, Hadfield could point to the experience of Sheffield Corporation, which included manganese rails in one of its busiest tramway junctions in 1907 and found that they lasted for twelve years, compared with a few months in the case of carbon steel track. Other emerging markets included those for use in the developing bicycle and automobile industries.

From the early twentieth century, advances in alloy steel technology in Sheffield continued apace and the city acquired a worldwide reputation for its expertise both in production and anticipation of engineering problems and solutions. The first generation of special steels found their home mainly in the field of machine tools, where so-called high-speed steel (which hardened at ultra-high machining velocities) transformed engineering across the world and made previous tools and equipment obsolete overnight.

This new branch of the steel industry was widely regarded as a revolution, and Sheffield was at its forefront, not only developing the technology but also making the tools that the industrial world now demanded. Even more revolutionary was the discovery in Sheffield of another new alloy that became known as 'stainless steel' and which was to become one of the primary materials of the modern industrial world.

Harry Brearley and Stainless Steel

The challenge of making a form of steel that could withstand rusting had occupied metallurgists around the world at the turn of the nineteenth and twentieth centuries, although many believed it was an elusive dream, with one authority remarking that 'the prospect of producing a cheap form of iron and steel which will be practically uncorruptible is extremely remote'. Robert Hadfield was one of those who had experimented with the inclusion of chromium in steel melts but without success.

Harry Brearley (1871–1948) was the son of a Sheffield steelworker who left school at the age of 12 to work in the same steelworks (Brown Firth) as his father. He got a job as general assistant in the company's research laboratory and at the same time worked at home and took evening classes in steel production and analysis. He became increasingly involved in work to solve the problem of erosion in gun barrels and the search for a material that would remain durable in use at high temperature. The research focused on adding chromium to steel, and in the course of his experiments Brearley discovered not only that the chromium alloys remained durable at increasing temperatures, but also that they were resistant to corrosion.

Brearley called his new alloy 'rustless steel' but was apparently persuaded by cutlers at Sheffield's Portland Works to change it to 'stainless steel' purely on aesthetic grounds. He was quick to realise the commercial application of his discovery and recommended to his employers that the material might be useful in cutlery. Although there was some initial reluctance among Sheffield cutlers to use the new material, commercial production was under way by 1915. This increased rapidly in the years after the First World War, when it was adopted widely not just by cutlers and manufacturers of household utensils but in large-scale industrial applications, most famously for the new chemical plant at ICI's Billingham Works on Teesside.

Portland Works.

Brearley left Brown Firth not long after his discovery and joined Brown Bayley's Steel Works, where he became a director in 1925. In his later years he acknowledged his own modest beginnings by founding a charitable trust to provide young working-class people with opportunities for travel, education and enjoyment of the arts.

The Growth of 'New Sheffield'

Until the Bessemer revolution, the skilled workers in the East End steelworks of Savile Street and Brightside Lane, and the crucible melters in particular, came from the industry's historic core in the town centre. Even in the 1860s, and despite the presence of the famous Huntsman works, Attercliffe could be still described as a village. Following the introduction of bulk steel production methods in the 1860s, the big movement of firms out to the East End onto lands of the former Fitzwilliam and Norfolk estates continued apace. The growth of the heavy steel industry in the second half of the nineteenth century was to a large extent fuelled by immigrant labour and inward-flowing capital. Roughly half of the population surge of the 1850s and '60s was accounted for by net immigration. By the end of the first decade of the twentieth century, the number of people employed in heavy industry had overtaken those in the traditional light trades.

The East End communities that developed rapidly in Attercliffe and Brightside were virtually a new settlement with few immediate connections to the long-established neighbourhoods of 'old Sheffield'. By the 1870s, endless rows of terraced houses had started to appear in the shadow of the great factories that were being built on former fields and meadows of the Duke of Norfolk's estates in the Lower Don Valley. These houses were slightly better constructed than those near the town centre, for most were built after the 1864 by-law that prohibited building of back-to-backs. Despite the fact that terraces were built close together, housing density was still lower than in most of the city.

From 16,900 people in 1851, the East End expanded six times to a population of 103,000 forty years later, so that by the end of the nineteenth century the former villages of Attercliffe and Darnall had changed beyond recognition. The majority of this population were immigrants from adjacent agricultural areas, particularly Nottinghamshire and Lincolnshire, drawn by steady employment and decent wages but unskilled in industrial work and unfamiliar with urban life. For a number of years, even when they brought their families with them, these new workers experienced lives somewhat detached from the city to which they had moved. Gradually, however, the new arrivals sought out former neighbours and formed clusters in particular streets and bonds with fellow workers. Gradually, too, some of the traditions of 'Old Sheffield' were adopted in the new setting so that it was 'St Monday' that became the day off for most steelworkers, when routine repairs to plant were carried out and, just like their predecessors in the cutlery trade, the workers found relief and comfort in the alehouse.

Generally speaking, the massive scale of immigration that occurred in the heavy steel areas in the decades leading up to the First World War worked against the trend towards 'respectability' that had been promoted by middle-class nonconformist citizens in the mid-nineteenth century. Instead, the society that developed in the industrial East End was vigorously working class and increasingly sceptical of the political liberalism of those above them in the social hierarchy. As progressive opinion looked to create a new urban society from the masses of people who made up Sheffield at the dawn of the twentieth century, the implications of this shift were to be profound.

Metropolis

Becoming a City

It is perhaps appropriate that the story of Sheffield's acquisition of metropolitan status began with a catastrophic failure of civic amenities. Indirectly, the Great Sheffield Flood had undermined the old Liberal establishment. Leading Liberal industrialists such as Frederick Thorpe Mappin and Robert Hadfield were directors of the Water Company and there was a general feeling that the Liberal-dominated town council had failed to act effectively against it in the aftermath of the disaster, in spite of demands that it should be taken into municipal control. At the same time, the transfer of social and political initiative from the local level towards regional and national networks that went hand-in-hand with the development of the heavy steel industry dominated by men such as Mappin had left the town council with few functions and little income.

Compared with the town council, the Cutlers' Company offered a more congenial social circle and an array of honorific offices; for example, John Brown was Master Cutler in 1865 and 1866 and was succeeded in the next three years by Mark Firth. The arrival of the new steel men in municipal politics had already been announced by the election of Brown as Sheffield's mayor in 1861 and 1862. In 1863, although the big steel manufacturers still only held ten out of a total of fifty-four seats on the council, that giant of the steel world, Thomas Jessop, held the position of mayor.

It was not until the council finally acquired the Water Company in 1888 that the balance of power began to shift. Four years later, in November 1892, Mayor Batty Langley (himself from a light trades background, and a Congregationalist rather than a Methodist like many of the prominent steelmen) proposed that the fiftieth anniversary of incorporation should be marked by elevation to city status. With this in mind he visited Birmingham, which had achieved the feat a few years earlier, for advice and guidance.

Against the background feeling that city status would increase their international esteem, and perhaps even make their inhabitants 'better citizens', in February 1893 both Sheffield and local rival Leeds petitioned for city status. Already by 1893, as a result of the phenomenal growth of the steel industry, Sheffield had overtaken Leeds as the most populous place in Yorkshire and had become the fifth largest town in England. The debate as to which of the two would take seniority in the region (figuratively represented in the local press as a contest between steel and wool) meant that this rivalry became embedded in Sheffield's collective consciousness for the next century and beyond. On 6 February, both towns had their petitions granted. Though it conferred no additional local powers, from this time on, Sheffield had the legal right to call itself a city.

In the event, the year of Sheffield's acquisition of city status was one of the least auspicious in its modern history, with a trade depression and high unemployment reflected by the more than 1,000 men on the newly formed register of those out of work. The solidarity of Sheffield working people during this time prompted Mayor Langley's comment that 'the poor people helped each other more than those in any other rank in life'. That this struggle

Sheffield's third Town Hall. Topped with a figure of Vulcan forging arrows, when it opened in 1897 it celebrated Sheffield's birth as a city and embodied its people's new-found civic pride.

against adversity was close to becoming outright class war was demonstrated by the rioting and destruction of property that broke out among Sheffield's mining communities as men faced mass lockouts when they refused to take cuts in their wages. As the nineteenth century gave way to the twentieth, the people from working communities across Sheffield would increasingly look to their city's officers to maintain the standards of relative prosperity and independence of living that had been enjoyed by their ancestors in the Hallamshire metal trades.

Despite the council's acquisition of a number of local services during the 1880s, the local Liberal establishment's focus on saving money meant that in the early years of municipal status it generally failed to promote Sheffield's interests or support civic projects such as the building of a new Town Hall. When this particular debate was settled, with the opening of the present building by Queen Victoria on 21 May 1897, a change in the manifestation of local loyalties among the population gradually became apparent, from a basis in the common bonds of Hallamshire craftsmen to a sense of civic pride in being citizens of Sheffield.

Civic Politics in the Liberal Age

Sheffield's civic functions began to develop after the turn of the century as pressure from working-class political organisations increased. The main trend was the capture of seats on the council by representatives of the Labour interest due to growing opposition to the power of the big industrialists, and the growth of clear working-class constituencies within large parts of the city. Working-class interest in Sheffield was increasingly something to be defended and fought over within the framework of the town's government.

In the two decades leading up to Sheffield's acquisition of city status in 1893, local politics had been characterised by Liberal/Conservative rivalry, with the rise of the Conservatives due in large measure to the big business interests of a heavy steel industry geared towards arms manufacture for central government. In terms of practical politics, however, and outside of election periods, there was little to divide Conservatives and Liberals, and council business was generally conducted away from party lines. Divisions within the Liberal group during this period meant that in the early days of the city council it was the Conservatives who took the initiative. The architect of Sheffield Conservatism was W.C. Leng, who was brought up a Wesleyan and a Liberal but became an Anglican and a Tory, in his own words due to his 'love of order and stability'. The basis of his success was the *Sheffield Telegraph*, of which he was proprietor and which he turned into an effective propaganda tool of the local Conservative party.

Conservative strength in the last two decades of the nineteenth century was based on five areas of policy clearly enunciated by Leng. The first of these was to cultivate the interests of Sheffield manufacturers through connections with the Chamber of Commerce and the Cutlers' Company and, in alliance with them, promote a fair trade ('Imperial preference') policy. The second was a strong advocacy of municipal ownership, which emboldened Leng to describe himself as 'a [true] socialist' at a time when the Liberals were being identified simply with making savings from the rates. Third, in alliance with interests associated with the brewery industry, was a strong opposition to the temperance movement promoted by the majority of Sheffield's nonconformists. Fourth was a specific targeting of the 'little mester' and skilled working-class vote, particularly through an appeal to patriotism and imperialism at a time when many jobs in the steel industry were dependent on arms contracts. Finally, Leng promoted the development of Conservative clubs in working-class areas, again supported by the 'drink interest'.

Despite initial gains, including victories in the strongly working-class Central and Brightside divisions, following Leng's death in 1902 and, in face of Labour gains in the years 1905 to 1908, Sheffield Conservatives lost direction and became increasingly aligned against working-class interests and any suggestion of collective ownership. For example, the incoming Conservative leader George Franklin expressed his opposition to the High Wincobank housing scheme on the grounds that it was 'socialistic' and driven by 'the suppression of individuals as holders of property'. In little more than ten years the coalition of working- and middle-class support that had been so carefully cultivated by Leng was destroyed.

In 1901 the Liberals gained the first majority on the council for almost twenty years. The main issues at the time were housing and education, and it was here that they had an opportunity to make lasting improvements. The Liberal leader was the autocratic Sir William Clegg, who was very much to the right of the party and closely aligned with the Liberal League that supported patriotism and imperialism, in contrast to the 'Little Englanders' who opposed the Boer War, and in Sheffield included a number of prominent nonconformists. This division played a more marked role in Sheffield politics than anywhere else in the country, the progressive group being sympathetic to socialism, while

Clegg and his allies adopted an overtly anti-socialist line following the success of Labour candidates in a few wards between 1905 and 1907.

Liberals were increasingly divided on the issue of the 'Lib-Lab ticket', a national arrangement whereby progressives in the party gave way to Labour candidates in areas they were more likely to win. Alarmed by this development, Clegg initiated a 'compact' with the Tories by which he intended to 'smash the socialists'. Following the 1909 election he stated his opinion that 'if the Liberal party wants to regain its position it must declare in no uncertain manner its determined opposition to revolutionary socialism'. The 'compact' of 1909 began an anti-socialist alliance that was in full swing by the time of the election of 1913, and which was formalised as the Citizens Association after 1918. Ultimately, it destroyed the Liberal group as an independent entity, since the polarisation of council politics provided Labour with a clear target.

The Rise of the Labour Movement

The Independent Labour Party (ILP) was founded in 1893 with socialist ideals that at the local level were practical rather than revolutionary: an eight-hour working day, an end to employment of children under 14, proper paid work for the unemployed and free education. The story of the Sheffield Labour movement in the years before the First World War is one of hard struggle between the well-established Lib-Labs who believed that working-class interests could be adequately represented by the Liberal party, and those who believed that the Liberals could never represent essentially working-class concerns and therefore argued that the focus should be put on developing the ILP.

The first few socialist councillors were elected after 1901, and three ILP members were elected between 1905 and 1906. Meanwhile, in 1900 the Labour Representation Committee (LRC) had been formed as an alliance of socialist organisations aimed at increasing representation of workers' interests in Parliament. In Sheffield, its members campaigned strongly on the issues of infant mortality, provision of school meals and universal old-age pensions. In 1906 the LRC was reconstituted as the Labour Party, and the next twenty years were notable for its meteoric rise in Sheffield and the rush towards anti-socialism by the other two parties. The election of Sheffield's first Labour MP in 1909 was a sign of things to come. Joseph Pointer had stood on a platform that included a maximum forty-eight-hour working week, free hospital treatment and free school meals.

Unlike the Tories and Liberals, Labour policy was driven by social need rather than providing dividends for ratepayers and aimed to use the entire profit from municipal utilities to finance improvement schemes. Generally speaking, Labour was in favour of high rather than low rates, since as the highest ratepayers were usually the most wealthy, high rates represented a clear and politically expedient system of redistributing wealth. The party put much effort into developing its base on a platform of interventionist local government, especially in the area of housing. Attention was directed particularly towards slum clearance, the construction of corporation housing, and direct employment of workers by the council.

The years in which the Labour movement came to prominence in Sheffield were ones of recession and significant hardship. The fact that men receiving financial assistance were classed as paupers and therefore lost the right to vote made unemployment a political issue. The employment committee that co-ordinated efforts to relieve the plight of the unemployed, mainly by providing work schemes, was of the opinion that such work should not just be charity but be of value to the community, and in the succeeding decades unemployed men were put to work on a number of municipal projects. In developing this policy, the council looked for co-operation from central government. Politicians in Westminster, however, refused to listen to councillors in Sheffield and gave little financial assistance in the new city's hour of need. Perhaps here we see the start of the antagonism between local and central government characteristic of Sheffield's political scene for much of the twentieth century.

In search of a more permanent solution to the problem of unemployment, Councillor Barton, one of the socialist members, carried a resolution in the distress committee demanding that central government put into effect measures recommended by the report of the Royal Commission on the Poor Law. As a result, in March 1910 the Labour Exchange Act of the previous year came into force and a Labour Exchange was established in Sheffield to help men look for work. In spite of the provision of work schemes both useful and otherwise, a significant section of the population faced great distress during these years, highlighted by the 389,985 breakfasts that were provided by the council to poor children at sixty-three schools in 1909.

In the winter of 1908–09 a significant programme of unemployment relief works was put into operation, including the replacement of inadequate sewerage, the improvement of public parks and recreation grounds and the construction of the Rivelin Valley bathing pool. New roads were built for

Labour Exchange, West Street; monument to the city's first period of mass unemployment.

the proposed housing estate at High Storrs and at the water company's site at Wyming Brook. A number of other road schemes were commenced using unemployed labour, including the construction of Whirlowdale Road and the widening of Abbeydale Road South, Abbey Lane and Middlewood Road. By the spring of 1909 work had been found for 3,948 men. No individual was allowed to work for more than sixteen weeks on these schemes so that the available work could be shared out. A significant reduction in infant mortality rates was achieved, largely through an improvement in milk supplies to the poor (opposed by the Liberals and Conservatives) and the establishment of a successful maternity and child-welfare scheme, both of which were among a number of successful policies pursued by Labour members of the council during this period.

War and Big Business

Metallurgical advances in themselves made possible the form and magnitude of warfare ... the modern battleship, destroyer, submarine, aeroplane and armoured tank, together with their armaments, were impossible but for the collaboration of the engineer and the metallurgist.

W.H. Hatfield, *The Application of Science to the Steel Industry*, 1928

The Crimean War (1853–56) established Sheffield's position as one of the main producers of armaments for the British government. From the late 1850s, John Brown pioneered the commercial production of armour plate in Britain to the extent that three-quarters of the Royal Navy's ironclad fleet used material made at Brown's Atlas works. By the early 1860s, Brown's and Cammell's had acquired a near monopoly in the British armour plate trade. Meanwhile, in the same period Firth's had become prominent in the manufacture of projectiles, guns and shells. Overall, from the 1860s onwards, the arms trade accounted for much of the expansion of the Sheffield steel industry, and it is during this period that the town's biggest firms became household names and counted among the largest companies in Britain.

As the science of explosives and the technology of guns developed, the demand for steel forgings, armour plate and projectiles increased. This was a level of demand that the Bessemer and Siemens methods of bulk steel production had been designed to meet. Brown's was one of the first Sheffield companies to stop producing rails and turn over production completely to armaments. The trade was of such high value that transport costs out of Sheffield were rendered virtually insignificant. In 1880, Hadfield's began the manufacture of shells, and before long Vickers had become pre-eminent in supplying all types of ordnance.

This phenomenon created a big shift in business perspectives, epitomised by the development of the Vickers company in close response to decisions made by the government in Whitehall. During a parliamentary debate in 1898, Sheffield was described as 'practically the inland naval arsenal of the country' and the British Association for the Advancement of Science declared in 1910 that Sheffield was 'at the present moment the greatest armoury the world has ever seen'. Commercially, the arms race filled the order books of Sheffield's leading steel firms. The five main steel producers in 1914 – Vickers, Brown's, Cammell's, Hadfield's and Firth's – grew massively as a result of the arms trade to the point where they were among the biggest business concerns in the world. Significantly, as a result of their increasing closeness to decision-making in London, these companies were no longer primarily steel makers nor Sheffield-based but national brokers of central government contracts.

The period between 1893 and 1918 was the high point of the Sheffield steel industry, and the marked recovery in the city's population at the end of the nineteenth century was closely connected with this massive growth in armaments work. War production meant that by 1918, Sheffield was the world's leading centre of electric steel production, with significant investments being made into

Former West Gun Works of Thomas Firth & Co., Savile Street and Carwood Road, built when Sheffield was 'the greatest armoury the world has ever seen'.

research and new technology. In terms of business development, the arms trade had two important impacts. First, it stimulated metallurgical innovation, for example into new heat treatments, alloys and production techniques. Second, it transformed the leading firms into integrated yet diverse arms conglomerates that took British industry to a new level of productivity and value. Perhaps even more significantly, through its contribution, for example, to the building up of Japanese armaments, it could be said that Sheffield was now playing a role in the emerging geopolitics of the twentieth century.

In a dark foreboding of events on the horizon, the technical competition between guns and armour plate became intense as experiments at the East End factories tested the forged steel shells of Hadfield's and Firth's against the all-steel armour plate of Vickers, Brown's and Cammell's. For the record, Hadfield's superior research and development facilities kept their shells ahead in this domestic battle in the years leading up to 1914. There is a tragic irony in the fact that Sheffield's period of greatest economic prosperity was directly related to the massive loss of its young male citizens in the trenches of Belgium and France. In the words of Sheffield historian David Hey, 'Sheffielders were to reap a bitter harvest from this arms race on the Western front in the First World War.'

The Inevitable Conflagration

One of the first indications in Sheffield of the impending global conflict of 1914–18 was a series of lectures given around the city by the new University's Vice Chancellor, the historian H.A.L. Fisher, who was a strong supporter of military action and a prime instigator in the formation of the Sheffield University and City Battalion (later to become the 12th Battalion, York and Lancaster Regiment). This volunteer unit, officially formed on 10 September 1914, soon reached a strength of 1,000 men and was based at a training camp at Redmires. A month earlier, the Lord Mayor had established a Sheffield Distress Committee to deal with the anticipated increase in unemployment and poverty that would come with an economy geared up for war. The trade unions and co-operative groups also established relief funds for their members.

Preparations for war were stepped up during the summer and autumn of 1914 to include police barriers being set up on all the main roads into the city, and power stations, reservoirs and other public utilities were placed under guard. In December, an anti-aircraft corps was formed in the city, originally with two guns on Wincobank – the ancient hill fort once again defending the Don Valley – and by 1916 two additional stations had been set up on the Manor and at High Storrs. One consequence of the outbreak of war was a sudden worsening in the housing situation, as a drop in private building coincided with an influx of munitions workers, for whom wooden huts had to be erected at various sites including Tinsley.

War memorial, Weston Park.

Starting in January 1916, thousands of Sheffielders between the ages of 18 and 41 were conscripted, the largest number destined for the mass slaughter at the Battle of the Somme six months later. A Sheffield military tribunal met a few times each week to organise public round-ups such as the one that took place with the closing of the gates of the Botanical Gardens on a Sunday afternoon in October 1916. In the course of this particular operation, soldiers working on behalf of the tribunal required all men of service age to prove their ineligibility for service, and around forty potential conscripts were taken for further investigation. By the end of the year, recruiting staff were going through factories looking to take men previously deemed 'indispensable' to industry in a process known as 'combing'.

War and Industry

From the time of the passing of the Munitions of War Act in July 1915, which gave munitions and related work priority over all other production, the conflict had a dramatic effect on Sheffield industry. The sectors most significantly affected were heavy steel and engineering, in which state-directed demand had already been growing rapidly before 1914. The war led to an immense increase in output, massive investment in new plant, a quickening of the pace of technological change and far greater government control. Whole firms, including Hadfield's and Firth's, were designated National Projectile Factories under direct control of the Ministry of Munitions.

An example of the increased scale of production can be seen at Firth's, where sales increased from £1.2 million to £4.9 million during the course of the war, which included the production of more than 4 million shells, more than 9,000 tonnes of gun forgings, 10,000 tons of marine shafts and turbine forgings, and 750 parts for torpedoes. A new Siemens melting plant was installed, and a 4,000-tonne press at the gun works. Firms such as Firth's, Cammell Laird, Hadfield's and Vickers were designated as official suppliers to the government, with workers' holidays cancelled and men ordered to work through the night.

Apart from the obvious need to increase capacity to meet the demands of war, there were two major effects on the development of Sheffield's larger firms: a shift away from competition and towards co-operation, and the formal merger of companies. As well as general business interaction, co-operation took the form of pooling technological knowledge, and a more united front on labour and wage rates. In many ways, wartime demands forced Sheffield businesses to make the structural adjustments that until then had been constrained by the small-scale nature of the city's industrial base. There was also increased co-operation between business and the new University, with Oliver Arnold, Professor of Metallurgy, in particular providing technical advice for a number of Sheffield firms.

Undoubtedly, such technical co-operation improved the ability of firms to meet war production demands more flexibly. For example, under the direction of the Ministry of Munitions, Spear & Jackson converted its agricultural and garden tool departments to the production of entrenching shovels and other equipment for use on the Western Front. Similarly, the hardening and heat treatment plant was diverted exclusively to the manufacture of armour plate for four months in 1915, with machinery operating at double capacity.

In terms of steel technology, the war forced rapid developments as firms took the opportunity to expand their research departments and invest in new techniques. One of the obvious areas was the development of stainless steel. By the summer of 1917, Firth's had produced more than 1,000 tonnes, much of it for use in armaments, and the scene was set for the full-scale exploitation of the alloy in the 1920s. The war also gave an enormous boost to the development of electric arc furnaces, which provided an ideal solution to the problem of recycling waste from machine shops: by 1918 Sheffield was the world's most concentrated centre of electric steel production. The major problem that Sheffield steel manufacturers faced by the end of the war was how to keep all this plant fully utilised once the demands of war production were over.

Anti-German Sentiment and the Jonas Affair

Between 1851 and 1910, more than 4 million people left Germany as part of a vast migration from Central and Eastern Europe in search of a higher standard of living. Although the great majority made their way to America, a significant minority went to Britain. Until 1891, Germans constituted the largest minority in Britain after the Irish. At the turn of the twentieth century, some 400 Germans had made their home in Sheffield, with several playing a significant part in the steel industry and the city's public affairs.

These included Carl Wilhelm Kayser (1841–1906), who was born in the cutlery centre of Solingen and first visited Britain in 1860 to study Sheffield's cutlery and steel trades. He decided to remain in England in 1864 and became a partner of the firm that in 1895 became Kayser, Ellison & Co. and went on to become one of the most successful in Sheffield. Two other Germans, Heinrich Seebohm and Georg Dieckstahl, founded a firm in 1865 that changed its name to Arthur Balfour & Co. at the height of anti-German sentiment during the First World War.

Probably the most famous German resident of Sheffield was Joseph Jonas (1845–1921), who came to Sheffield in 1869 and became a successful steel manufacturer, particularly after commencing a partnership with Joseph Colver. His civic career was equally spectacular, being elected a Liberal councillor in 1890 and Lord Mayor of Sheffield in 1905. In addition, he served as an alderman, a member of the University Council, was chairman of the Technical School and acted as Sheffield's consul to Germany. At the start of the First World War he was a naturalised British citizen, one of his sons was in the British Army and a daughter was married to a British officer. During his year as mayor, when he also donated £5,000 to fit out a foundry and laboratory in the University's Department of Metallurgy, he received a knighthood. No immigrant at this time could have been more completely integrated into British public life.

Hostility towards German immigrants first became noticeable at the beginning of the twentieth century as Britain began to feel threatened by growing German industrial, economic and naval power. With a good deal of government encouragement, members of the public began to think of Germans as potential spies. In October 1914, after the declaration of war with Germany, official rounding up of German and Austrian residents without British citizenship began in earnest. In Sheffield, 108 people were detained, ranging from managers of firms to waiters and mechanics, all of whom were sent for imprisonment in York. Some German-born Sheffield citizens attempted to defend themselves in the local press in the face of growing hostility from their neighbours. Firms with German names anglicised them; nevertheless, all firms with alleged German links were investigated and occasionally shut down.

Anti-German feeling reached its peak following the attack on the passenger liner *Lusitania* by German submarines in May 1915, leading to massive loss of civilian lives. Aggression was actively encouraged by the authorities, and in Sheffield two days of violence and looting broke out, mainly in Attercliffe, with around a dozen shops being ransacked, some with no obvious German connection apart from being purveyors of items such as sausage. Figures in the public eye were easy targets and soon came under attack, particularly politicians, businessmen and financiers such as the banker Sir Edgar Speyer and Liberal MP Sir Alfred Mond. In Sheffield, suspicion fell on Paul Kuenrich, manager of Marsh Bros cutlery and steel firm, but in particular on Sir Joseph Jonas.

Jonas was arrested without warning at his home, Endcliffe Hall, early in the morning of 13 June, 1918. During the summer he was prosecuted at the Central Criminal Court in London on charges of having contravened the provisions of the Official Secrets Act and, in collusion with his compatriots Carl August Hahn and Charles Alfred Vernon, communicating information of military value to the enemy in 1913. In fact, the type of communications Jonas was alleged to have had with German firms before 1914 were typical of Sheffield companies at the time, whatever their ownership. This was clearly a show trial. In the event, Hahn was found not guilty; Jonas and Vernon were cleared of felony but convicted of misdemeanour. Jonas was fined £2,000 and shortly afterwards stripped of his knighthood by the King.

Public opinion, and that of the press, was somewhat divided on the case but largely supportive of Jonas, considering him to have been badly treated. The workers in his company continued to refer to him as Sir Joseph. The man himself was broken by the experience, retired as a director of his company and suffered a stroke in December 1920 from which he never fully recovered. When he died in August 1921, large numbers turned out for his funeral procession, including many of his former workers, before his burial at Ecclesall church.

War and the Social Position of Women

The demands of wartime production placed a great strain on even the largest Sheffield firms. By 1915, up to 25,000 tonnes of steel a week was leaving Sheffield for use by the Allied forces, and there was a particular need to raise production of projectiles to meet the requirements of the massive bombardments taking place on the Western Front. Part of the response came through the Shells and Fuses Agreement of March 1915, which permitted women and young people to work on repetitive production tasks, leaving more skilled jobs to men. Similarly, the 'Dilutions Scheme' of October that year allowed the upgrading of semi-skilled workers. Finally, the 'General Substitution Scheme' of September 1916 allowed women to take up skilled roles in industry.

In March 1915, when the government announced its compilation of a register of women willing to do industrial work, more than 1,000 Sheffield women signed up. Membership of the Sheffield branch of the National Union of Women Workers increased from 350 in 1914 to about 5,000 by June 1918. Many women were involved in what was seen as 'traditional women's work', such as nursing in military hospitals both at home and overseas, in banks, local government and service industries. But due to the diversion of large numbers of men into the services and war production, women moved for the first time into previously male domains such as driving trams and heaving coal. On the railways, women were employed in signalling, station duties and locomotive and carriage cleaning. Female police patrols were formed from 1914 under the direction of the National Union of Women Workers to patrol parks, streets and public houses, partly to 'safeguard the moral welfare of women and young girls'.

In Sheffield, many women entered the cutlery industry, particularly to supply military equipment such as mess kits and razors. However, by far the largest number of women were employed in munitions, especially at large shell-filling factories such as Firth's Templeborough works (which temporarily became the National Projectile Factory) and Hadfield's East Hecla works, as well as the factories of the large armaments producers such as Vickers, Brown's and Cammell Laird, and at another 300 smaller firms that were turned over to war production. At Templeborough, no fewer than 5,000 women were employed under the direction of a skeleton staff of men.

The expansion of job opportunities for women during the war was in many cases short-lived. Though significant numbers of women remained in the clerical and administrative sectors, the majority were expected to return to their homes or pre-war occupations. The last female workers at Hadfield's were paid off in June 1919, although a small number of firms, such as Ibbotson Bros, did retain female workers. Indeed, as the country began to adjust to the realisation of the scale of loss of the male generation of working age as a result of the war, women were increasingly needed in industrial employment. Thus the 1921 Census shows that 4,000 women were employed in Sheffield's heavy industries, compared with only 255 ten years previously.

The other significant change to the position of women – the right to take an active part in the democratic process – also occurred during the First World War. In 1914, an amnesty was announced for campaigners for female suffrage who had been imprisoned, and in February 1918 their struggle met with partial success when the Representation of the People Act gave the vote to women over the age of 30. Votes for all women were finally secured in 1928.

War Comes to Sheffield: The Zeppelin Raid of September 1916
The technology developed by western nations in the lead-up to the First World War meant that the conflict was the first in history in which civilians could

be specifically targeted at a long distance from the main military action. By late 1915, the Germans had developed airships, known as 'Zeppelins' from the name of their inventor, with the range and capacity to bomb Britain. The first air raid took place on Hull on 6 June 1915, and during the rest of that year there were thirty-three raids on British targets, in which 127 people were killed and 352 injured. By the standards of later warfare, the bomb load of Zeppelins was small, but the raids caused widespread panic among the civilian population, particularly after a series of attacks on London in October 1915 that included the bombing of a primary school with large loss of life.

On the evening of 25 September 1916, a fleet of seven German airships set out to bomb inland English towns including Sheffield. Alarms were sounded in the city, and just before midnight a single airship was heard, and soon the massive Zeppelin L-22 appeared over the city from the south-east. After circling the city clockwise, the target was apparently determined as the dense residential areas just to the north and east of the centre. The first bombs were dropped on or near houses, a pub and a chapel across the Pitsmoor, Burngreave, Grimesthorpe, Darnall and Attercliffe areas. This was followed by repeated use of incendiary bombs and high explosives in which twenty-eight people were killed, nineteen seriously injured and many others suffered less serious injuries. More than eighty houses were seriously damaged and more than 100 others needed major repairs.

The raid presented a tragic lesson in the need for air raid preparations and defence in modern industrial warfare. Although a number of anti-aircraft guns and searchlights had been located around Sheffield, cloud prevented the crews from seeing the Zeppelin clearly in night-time conditions. A gun sited at Shiregreen was the only one to take action, firing two rounds in the general direction of the airship without result.

A report of the coroner's inquest into the raid appeared in the *Sheffield Independent* on 29 September and included an article questioning the lack of adequate warning. The victims had been ten women, eight men and ten children. The greatest number of casualties were in Corby Street, Burngreave, and included a family of seven. Some of the details reported, including graphic details of injuries and causes of death (the type of detail later forbidden due to government concerns about the effect on morale), bring out clearly the terror that the raid must have induced and which was undoubtedly its intention, as does this extract from the letter of a young girl who witnessed the bombing from her attic bedroom:

Suddenly we heard a droning sound overhead, which became stronger every minute, then there were two sounds that came from another direction and Elsie clutched hold of Harry's arm and screamed out 'they are here!' – she trembled like a leaf. The Sheffield people kept saying they [Zeppelins] will never get here. We got our big coats on and sat at my bedroom window and about two o'clock we saw a great red flash across the sky and a second later a terrific crash. Then another. They were high explosive shells and they shook the earth. They lit the entire sky up. They were incendiary bombs. There were 15 bombs dropped. I sat and watched it all through. I could not move. I felt numbed.

To a generation that was just getting used to the arrival of motor cars on the streets in place of horses, the appearance of a giant rocket-balloon in the sky from which men dropped carefully aimed explosives must have been terrifying. The horrific events of 25 September 1916 had given Sheffield its first taste of modern 'total war' and the people of Burngreave in particular were to go through much suffering again just twenty-four years later.

Labour Relations in Wartime

As a major centre of armaments production, Sheffield workers who avoided military service on the front generally fared well in employment and earnings during the war. Unemployment practically disappeared and long hours brought high earnings, though the hourly rates in engineering and related industries still failed to keep up with rising costs of living. In the long run, the transformation of industry during the First World War had an advantageous effect on the labour and workers' movements and led to a transformation of the city's industry and working life.

Initially, however, the signs were not encouraging. The 1915 Munitions of War Act made strikes illegal and restrictive practices exercised by the trade unions were suspended. At the same time, however, controlled employers were forbidden to lock out workers in dispute and companies could be subjected to large fines. In the first three years of the war, patriotic fervour tended to make all hardships bearable. Thereafter, war weariness was added to the dissatisfaction that came from profiteering and unfair distribution of food and other goods in short supply in which the co-operative societies and shops in working-class areas failed to obtain their rightful share. In addition, there was the exhausting effect of repeated 'comb-outs', in which officials scoured the factories for able-bodied men who could be spared for action on the Western Front.

At both national and local levels, the war had a significant effect on support for the Labour movement. The coalition government established in 1915 was seen as becoming increasingly dictatorial; ignoring union rights, diluting skilled labour markets and conscripting some exempt workers. Even moderate trades unionists were roused to militancy and inspired by the success of the Sheffield Workers Committee, an organisation of shop stewards that in November 1916 called a strike of the Amalgamated Society of Engineers in protest at the conscription of skilled workers, in which it is estimated some 12,000 Sheffield munitions operatives took part. Since Sheffield was a major centre of armaments production, coercive wartime powers were strongly exercised, but many workers felt empowered when the war effort depended on their skills.

However, as the war went on, a growing mood of rebelliousness spread among the working communities of the East End, and large numbers of workers and their families were ready to listen to arguments against the continuation of the war and turn against the jingoistic sentiments preached by the government. By the end of the war, Sheffield had become one of the centres of radical trade unionism, and the city's shop stewards, particularly the revolutionary socialist J.T. Murphy, together with those of Clydeside and Coventry, emerged as leaders of the movement

One of a number of Rolls of Honour commemorating Vickers' employees killed fighting in the First World War. The fact that the company had helped arm the world adds a bitter irony to their deaths.

for workers' committees and influenced the direction of industrial relations in the decades to come. Reflecting this trend, membership of the unions represented by the Sheffield Trades and Labour Council rose from around 12,000 in 1914 to 60,000 in 1920. While Sheffield did not become involved in the revolutionary events of the summer of 1919 to the same extent as cities like Liverpool, where the government moored a battleship outside the port and stationed tanks in the main square to 'maintain order', the scene was set for local challenges to government control in the decades to come.

Brave New World

Depression

The worldwide slump in the market for steel products that followed the end of the war meant that the effects of the economic depression of the 1920s and '30s hit Sheffield particularly hard. With the cessation of hostilities, many returning servicemen believed their suffering had given them the right to expect a job, a home and enough money to live on; instead they faced unemployment and poverty. The summer of 1919 witnessed widespread strikes in Sheffield, including walkouts by miners, railway workers and tramway operatives. There was a big surge in Labour Party membership in the city and the party gained seven new seats in the municipal election in November of that year.

In Sheffield, the mass unemployment of the 1920s was undoubtedly exacerbated by over-specialisation, and the steel industry was particularly badly hit. The total number of unemployed rose from 4,144 at the beginning of October 1920 to 30,000 in March 1921 and 69,300 during the coal strike of June and July, and never dropped below 25,000 before the late 1920s. The 1920 figure included more than 2,300 ex-servicemen, prompting the distress committee to move quickly in favour of devising road building schemes, such as that carried out in Rivelin Valley, to provide some relief. Construction of the new City Hall, which had been designed in 1920 but was held up due to lack of funds, eventually went ahead in 1929 as a way of giving work to the unemployed.

As in other towns and cities, Sheffield witnessed the inevitable social effects of large-scale poverty and unemployment, including an escalation of gang wars (in Sheffield based on 'pitch and toss' syndicates) and occasional running battles with police that were to foreshadow developments during the miners' strike of 1984. The feeling of 'them and us' became stronger after a

Sheffield City Hall, begun in 1929 as a public works project to tackle unemployment.

police baton charge on a mass demonstration outside the Town Hall in August 1921. Both nationally and locally, unemployed men took part in mass demonstrations on a weekly basis throughout the spring and summer months. Some demonstrations were in response to specific developments, such as that in June 1921 protesting at the reduced scale of poor relief imposed by the government on local authorities at the instigation of the Ministry of Health, and a notorious incident in 1923 when a number of unemployed residents of Walkley were evicted for failure to pay their rent.

Yet despite the fact that Sheffield ended the 1920s with one of the highest unemployment rates in the country, the city was notably free of extremist politics, with neither the extreme right or left able to gain a significant foothold in the context of a well-organised and popular local Labour movement. The General Strike of 1926 was well supported in Sheffield, where the Labour movement united in support of the miners and some 80,000 workers joined the action. Local women played a crucial role in the miners' cause, including the foundation of the Women's Committee for the Relief of Miners' Wives and Children, which was to be revived during the struggles of 1984. Encouraged by the success of this initiative, women in the city went on to set up self-help groups for the wives of unemployed men during the 1930s.

In addition to the economic recession, and in common with the rest of the country, Sheffield was hit by the effects of the worldwide influenza pandemic of 1918–20. At its height, more than 300 Sheffield people were dying each week and local hospitals were overwhelmed. Public health measures introduced at local level included school closures and regular disinfection of entertainment venues such as cinemas.

Labour Comes to Power

As the 'Great Depression' deepened, central government demanded stringent cuts in municipal spending and very few councils managed to survive this period with their reputation intact. In Sheffield, the Citizens Association that was formed in July 1920, with the Liberal Sir William Clegg as leader and Conservative leader Alderman Alfred Cattell as deputy, was effectively an anti-socialist alliance. The *Sheffield Independent* argued that they had 'no programme – just a few vague generalities'. This was perhaps a little harsh: the Citizens had the over-arching aim of reducing the financial obligations of ratepayers, their core constituency, and in this they were full supporters of the national government's austerity programme. Indeed, an editorial in the *Daily Mail* in December 1924 singled out Sheffield Council for praise for its policy of financial restraint, commenting that:

> the position of Sheffield as a municipality is perfectly sound. Its bank balances are in credit to the extent of nearly £400,000 … The municipal rates have been reduced by more than three shillings from what they were in 1921 to 1922.

Such 'sound economy' by the Citizens administration was maintained by building up huge debts, including £1 million on the Poor Law budget alone. Rates were kept artificially low, and the resulting worsening of conditions for thousands of working people, together with the group's opposition to Labour during the General Strike of 1926, contributed to their ultimate demise.

By 1926, the Labour group in Sheffield was in a strong position. The city was predominantly working class, with a much smaller middle class than other cities of comparable size. This might not necessarily have made it a Labour stronghold, but it helped, particularly when the Citizens, uniting Conservatives and Liberals, stood so firmly and exclusively on middle-class interests. Labour's achievement in gaining a majority on the city council that year was unique in the country. The party did well in municipal elections nationally because of the General Strike earlier that year, but in Sheffield, enthusiasm for the strike was overwhelming. It offered the chance for workers, especially engineers and miners, to hit back at a Conservative government that had continually cut pay and allowed massive job losses. In the words of Alf Barton, one of Sheffield's first Labour councillors, support for the strike in the city was 'a magnificent example of working-class solidarity'.

In the 1929 elections Labour won a massive victory and, with forty-seven councillors and sixteen aldermen, gained a majority of thirty. This apparent consolidation of Labour's hold seemed merely to confirm the impression of the general election of May 1929, when the party, as well as holding Attercliffe, Brightside and Hillsborough, won Central and Park for the first time in the victory that produced Ramsay MacDonald's second Labour government. Labour's municipal election victory of November 1926 had been the culmination of a long process, but the story did not end there. Between 1926 and 2020, Labour spent only a few brief periods in opposition on the council, and the years from 1926 to 1951 in particular saw the consolidation of Sheffield as a Labour stronghold. For much of its first half-century in power, the Labour administration oversaw a string of municipal successes in the areas of housing, education, health and social service provision.

Economic Recovery

With hindsight, it can be said that the First World War marked a watershed for the Sheffield steel industry, as indeed it did for the general development of Britain's economy. Before 1914, Sheffield had enjoyed a long period of growth, with full order books and equally full employment. This was a situation characteristic of a rising global demand for steel that had commenced in about 1870 and was linked to the large-scale replacement of iron by steel, the rapid development of new markets such as shipbuilding and railways, and the utilisation of new supplies of raw material. But it was a picture that changed abruptly in 1918.

Between the wars, the British steel industry experienced severe depression in the 1920s and steady recovery after 1933. In terms of business structure, the post-war economic downturn prompted the merger of a number of Sheffield firms and an increasing division of the industrial scene between large and small businesses. The first large conglomerate, United Steel Companies (USC), emerged in March 1918, and when the Birmingham Small Arms Company (BSA) acquired Jessop's in 1919 it was the first time an outsider had bought into the Sheffield steel industry. In 1928 the merger of the big two firms, Cammell Laird and Vickers, created the English Steel Corporation (ESC). Two years later, the historic giants Thomas Firth & Sons and John Brown merged to create Firth Brown, and in 1936 Sheffield industry became truly global with the purchase of J.A. Chapman by the American-owned Stanley Tools company.

In cutlery, the US market that had served Sheffield so well for the best part of 100 years finally collapsed. In response, manufacturers turned their attention to expanding colonial markets, but even these were badly affected by a universal decline in demand for luxury cutlery and plate that followed the war. The interwar period was characterised by competition between traditional methods in the cutlery industry and mass production in which the saving factor for Sheffield was its highly skilled workforce. Ultimately, however, this strength was to become a weakness in the face of cheaper foreign competition.

From 1933 the economic situation eased somewhat, and by late 1935 there were clear signs of a strong industrial recovery. Rearmament, which became embedded in government policy from 1937, obviously helped the heavy steel industry and enabled Sheffield to escape the worst of the renewed recession of 1937–38. In addition, the larger steel firms were able to weather the storms of depression, either by vigorously exploiting new export markets or introducing improved technology. For example, Arthur Balfour & Co. responded to the loss of the American trade by opening up new business in China, Japan, India, South America and Australia. Edgar Allen & Co. introduced high-frequency induction melting in 1927 and also led the way with super high-speed steels used in applications such as mining, cobalt steel magnets and tungsten carbide cutting tools, first introduced in 1939. Osborn's combined investment in the latest electric melting technology with more systematic exploitation of markets for its tool steels, castings and forgings, with the result that it was actually able to take on about 200 extra workers.

There was a recovery too of the light trades, including the traditional cutlery sector. The twentieth century saw slow improvements in working conditions in the cutlery industry, which included the replacement of natural grindstones, prone to breakage with occasionally fatal consequences, with carborundum in the late 1920s. A Cutlery Trade Board was set up by the government in 1934, which was able to raise wages for the poorest in the industry. Most workshop conditions remained poor, however, and regulations of 1937 aimed at improving the working environment were halted by the onset of war.

In terms of the technology of steel-making, the period witnessed the decline and final demise of the crucible process that had transformed Sheffield's fortunes from the time of its introduction by Benjamin Huntsman in the 1740s. While some smaller firms continued to produce high-quality steel using the old method, the introduction of high-frequency furnaces by Edgar Allen's, the first in the world with this new technology, meant that the days of the crucible were numbered. The new furnaces melted steel by induction and combined the economy and versatility of the electric arc method with the close quality control of the crucible.

Yet the positive economic trends had to be set against the residue of mass unemployment. Of 19,060 people applying for benefit at the Sheffield Labour Exchange during one week in late 1936, 5,254 had been out of work for two years or longer, and 2,125 for more than five years. The long-term effects of unemployment were to provide serious challenges for the new Labour council for years to come.

Homes Fit for Heroes

Following the end of the First World War, the desperate need for new housing was made more pressing by the large number of ex-servicemen wanting to get married and move into the 'homes fit for heroes' that they had been promised by a government keen to avoid social unrest. In Sheffield, the Citizens' Association failed them. Local councillors refused to finance the building of working-class houses from the rates and were content to let the private sector work at its own pace. At the 1921 election, the Citizens proudly announced a threepence in the pound cut in the rates at a time of severe unemployment and when extensive post-war development was needed, especially in housing and education.

The one exception to their austerity policy, a decision taken under political pressure from Labour, was the construction of the Manor estate, which started in 1924. However, although this was a council project, the work was contracted out to private firms and completed to a low standard. This, and other housing estates of the 1920s, ignored the potential of using Sheffield's hilly topography and instead settled for poorly built identical dwellings around geometric road patterns. Most of the houses required renovation, or even demolition, before the end of the twentieth century.

In contrast with the Citizens, Labour's performance in housing was increasingly impressive and brought Sheffield a reputation for innovation. The most imaginative of their early projects, High Wincobank, was influenced by the 'garden city' ideas of Ebenezer Howard, with an informal layout and a variety of cottage types. By the 1930s, the council was completing an average of 2,400 houses every year, the most significant projects being the estates at Southey

Parson Cross, one of the largest and more imaginative of the interwar council housing schemes.

Green, Parson Cross, Shirecliffe and Arbourthorne, characterised by well-spaced houses with gardens, built well away from the old slum areas.

By 1938, 24,000 houses classified as slums had been cleared, and almost half replaced by new houses. This was the highest number anywhere in England and Wales and involved the demolition of almost three-quarters of houses in the town centre, effectively consigning much of 'Old Sheffield', characterised by its crowded 'courts' and ramshackle workshops, to oblivion. The dramatic changes were the product of a radical attempt to improve working-class living conditions by the Labour council that was not without its critics. Some residents of the new estates protested against the lack of amenities such as libraries, community centres and parks. In response, the council provided additional funding for recreational facilities, though there was still some resentment at a perceived attitude of 'improving' the working classes through measures such as the prohibition of pigeon keeping on council estates, and protests continued for a number of years about the level of provision of public houses.

The bigger issue in the long run was that the demands of a second global conflict meant that virtually all new housing construction came to an end. The last pre-war council project to be completed, in 1943, was Edward Street flats in the recently cleared Crofts slum area. The scheme provided imaginative accommodation around a central green space for residents to meet and children to play and made use of the steeply sloping site to ensure lighting at a level barely imaginable by generations of slum dwellers. In their pronounced

Edward Street flats; with its multi-deck design and central play areas, a precursor to the modernist housing schemes of the 1960s.

use of horizontal lines, the flats were heavily influenced by the work of the Dutch modernist architect Willem Marinus Dudek and were a forerunner of the council's ambitious high-rise schemes of the 1950s and '60s.

Health and Education

The solid work undertaken by the Labour council in housing was matched by its public health policy. Between 1926 and 1938, rates of infant mortality were almost halved and maternal mortality was reduced by two-thirds. In both cases, the establishment of new maternity and child welfare facilities, including a new municipal domestic midwifery service and hospital rebuilding programme, clearly contributed to the successes.

Immediately after the end of the First World War, the city's education provision had been badly hit by the austerity programme introduced by the Citizens Association. Large numbers of working-class children were leaving the school system at an early age. To take just one area, fewer than half of the children on the Manor estate were attending school when Labour came to power in 1926, and one of the new administration's priorities was a progressive education programme. As well as significantly extending the school building stock, this included large-scale acquisition of playing fields, provision of swimming baths and gyms, music and other activities. Over the following decades the council was also to become a national leader in provision for children with disabilities and special needs, including the construction of open-air schools such as those at Whiteley Woods and Bents Green.

Work and Play

The Transformation of Working-Class Culture

Throughout the nineteenth century, the independence that Sheffield working people expressed through the regulation of their own working arrangements was a constant concern to the authorities. How was capitalist enterprise, which thrived on consistent and dependable work patterns, to incorporate a workforce that prided itself on working on its own terms and according to its preferred hours? Despite the remarkable resilience of the 'little mester' system, large cutlery firms were being formed, often under the management of men from the leading nonconformist families, in particular the Methodists. To men such as these, irregular work was anathema, and the long-established tradition of 'St Monday', by which workers in the cutlery and allied trades would take a whole day each week off work, drew particular criticism.

To the small but growing proportion of the population of Sheffield that counted itself among the 'respectable' middle class, the threat that came primarily from pub culture was not just that it involved drink, or even that it might lead to immorality, but that it constituted a rival social setting to the home. There was no surprise that the pub, with its warmth and relative comfort, was attractive to people whose home conditions could be tolerable at best and slums at worst. In opposition to Methodist ideals of home and family, the pubs apparently thrived on a rough culture of drinking, gambling and violent sports such as the dog fighting that shocked middle-class visitors to the town by the sheer scale of its popularity. If Sheffield's working class was to be controlled, it needed to be domesticated.

The drive towards 'respectability' as a facet of working-class culture was undoubtedly provided by the nonconformist chapels. Though only a tiny proportion of working people regularly attended services, their influence derived from the success of the Sunday School movement and the prominence of nonconformists in the city's administration. The main tenets of 'respectability' were regular work patterns, moderation (or preferably abstention) in consumption of alcohol, pride in possessions and personal appearance, and education. It was in an attempt to break the hold of the traditional 'rough' working-class culture, and to exercise greater control over the lives of working people, both within and outside the workplace, that the 'Saturday half-holiday' and 'rational recreation' movements were promoted so vigorously by Sheffield's middle class. If people were to be drawn away from 'the contagion of the pub and rough sports' then more 'healthy' pursuits at least as attractive would need to be found.

Up until the mid-nineteenth century, in addition to pitch-and-toss gambling and the ubiquitous dog fighting, the most popular leisure pursuits among working men included hunting with dogs, rabbit coursing, pigeon and sparrow shooting. Under middle-class pressure in favour of more 'respectable' leisure pastimes, fishing and pigeon racing were increasingly promoted, and by the early twentieth century a number of local firms had their own angling clubs. Some of the larger firms went further. In addition to its annual horticultural shows that it was hoped would instil a love of gardening, from the 1850s Sanderson's steel company, one of the principal proponents of 'rational recreation', was giving its employees tickets for art exhibitions and visits to museums, often in neighbouring towns such as Manchester and Leeds.

As a result of the campaigns of middle-class reformers, and business owners who wished to promote more regular work patterns, national legislation to provide Saturday half-holidays for manual workers was enacted from the late 1860s. In Sheffield, despite the continuing popularity of 'St Monday' among Sheffield's traditional workforce, the new arrangements caught on surprisingly quickly. This was in large part due to enthusiastic take up among the 'new' working class of the East End factories and the fact that organised sport in the form of football and cricket had already become established in the area. Over the next half-century, leisure pursuits in an almost infinite variety of forms, from mass participation to professional, were to reach levels of unrivalled popularity in 'steel city'.

Feeding the Mind

In 1856, Sheffield became the first Yorkshire town to establish a public library, and between 1870 and 1905 an additional six branches opened around the town. Interestingly, borrowing records show that the majority of library users at this time were members of the working class, including many servant girls. Following the lead taken by John Ruskin, who opened his Walkley Museum in 1875, in the same year the town council purchased the estate of Weston Hall and opened a museum in the converted house. In 1887, the Mappin Art Gallery opened in a newly built extension to the museum to house the collection bequeathed to the city by local businessman John Newton Mappin.

The opening of the new Central Library and Graves Art Gallery in 1934 signalled the beginning of a period of a general improvement of Sheffield's cultural facilities. The following year the Sheffield Philharmonic Society was founded, though the demolition in 1936 of St Paul's Church in the town centre, and its replacement by what was to become the Peace Gardens, was seen by many as an act of civic vandalism. On a more positive note, Sheffield took a national lead in the development of its greenbelt in the 1930s following Councillor J.G. Graves' purchase of Blacka Moor for the city in 1933. By 1938 the council had developed a trail along the Porter Valley into open countryside starting at Endcliffe Park, undertaken similar works in Rivelin Valley and at Wyming Brook, and had safeguarded the Duke of Norfolk's former shooting lodge at Longshaw for the enjoyment of the general public.

In the 1820s Joseph Hunter had made reference to a significant amount of land on the outskirts of Sheffield being given over to allotments for workers, which he said could 'afford the proprietors some profit, together with an amusement the most varied, innocent, and cheerful, and no doubt contribute much to the general health of the town'. Fifty years later, the town council was taking the first steps to acquire land for parks and recreation grounds to give some respite to the ordinary people of Sheffield from their crowded, smoke-polluted environment.

In 1875, Weston Park became the first open space in Sheffield to be purchased for public use and Robert Marnock, who had designed the landscaping of the

Meersbrook Park, with its view of Sheffield city centre, was painted by J.M.W. Turner in the 1790s.

Botanical Gardens, supervised the laying out of the grounds of the former Weston Hall. The Botanical Gardens themselves had opened to subscribers in 1836 but were only made available to the general public in 1898. The Duke of Norfolk had opened his Norfolk Park to the public in 1846 and finally relinquished ownership in favour of the council in 1909.

Between 1886 and 1890, the town council purchased Meersbrook Park, Endcliffe Woods and Hillsborough Park, and by 1900 the city had some 112 hectares of public parks and 19 hectares of recreation grounds. The variety and diversity of Sheffield's historic parks and gardens is impressive; not only do they represent some of the earliest recreational spaces in the country, no fewer than four are listed in the national register as being of special historic interest. In 1924 the Sheffield Association for the Protection of Local Scenery was formed, whose activities were ultimately instrumental in having the Peak District designated the country's first National Park in 1951.

Participatory and Professional Sport

The introduction of Saturday half-holidays took Sheffield's already well-established sports scene to another level. The game with the longest history in the town was cricket, and it was at Bramall Lane, the home of Sheffield United Cricket Club since 1855, that the Yorkshire Cricket Club was founded in 1863. As for football, Sheffield FC went into decline after the formation of the Football League in 1888. The Sheffield club was excluded from the new

Bramall Lane, early home of Yorkshire cricket and, later, Sheffield United FC.

competition due to disagreements about the rules, but by then it already had the distinction of being the first English club to play matches against opponents in continental Europe. And despite the relative eclipse of this venerable institution, by the 1890s there were no fewer than 880, mainly amateur, football clubs in Sheffield, demonstrating a remarkable level of participation.

Such was the popularity of the game that in 1867 the Wednesday Cricket Club formed a football team to keep members together with a purpose during the winter months. In 1878, Sheffield marked another landmark in the history of the sport when Bramall Lane staged the world's first floodlit football match, between teams made up of players from an assortment of local clubs. In 1889, Sheffield United Cricket Club also formed a football team that went on to have spectacular early success, becoming league champions in 1898 and runners-up twice in the following five years, as well as FA Cup winners in 1899, 1902 and 1915. The Wednesday Football Club (renamed Sheffield Wednesday from 1929) were FA Cup winners in 1896 and 1907 and league champions in consecutive seasons in 1903 and 1904. Indeed, the Edwardian period can be seen as a golden age for football in Sheffield.

At the outbreak of the First World War, Sheffield was a veritable 'city of sport', with participation at an almost fanatical level. By 1914 there were more than forty-eight bowling clubs affiliated to the Sheffield Amateur Bowling Association, fifty hockey clubs with both male and female teams, twenty tennis clubs, eleven privately owned golf clubs, a homing pigeon association and twenty cycling clubs, the latter part of a national craze that took hold in the 1880s. The first corporation swimming baths opened in 1869, and in the 1880s a number of running clubs were formed – including, most prominently, Sheffield United Harriers. The open-air swimming pool that opened at Millhouses in 1929 was seen as one of the best facilities of its kind in the country.

The 1930s were a second boom time for spectator and participatory sport in Sheffield. By this time, football had consolidated its position as the primary spectator sport, and Sheffield Wednesday followed its league championship of 1929 with an FA Cup victory in 1935. The following year their rivals Sheffield United were also to reach the FA Cup final but unfortunately lost. By the mid-decade Sheffield even boasted a baseball team (the Sheffield Dons) and a national boxing champion in Johnny Cuthbert. No fewer than 10,000 people turned out to witness the first greyhound meeting at the Owlerton Stadium, which also went on to host speedway motorcycle meetings.

Entertainment for the People

One of the first venues for public entertainment to be established in Sheffield for 100 years (after the Theatre Royal in 1773), the Albert Hall, opened in Barker's Pool in 1873. It was followed shortly afterwards by the Alexandra and the Adelphi Music Hall and, towards the end of the century, by the Empire Palace, the Alhambra (Attercliffe), City and Lyceum theatres, the last of which is the only one to survive. The most popular form of entertainment in these venues was 'music hall'. Following on from this success, the first cinemas opened in Sheffield early in the twentieth century. The new medium caught on particularly quickly in the city, partly on the back of its success in the form of 'bioscope shows' at travelling fairs. At first, the new medium was shown in converted theatres, such as the Empire that showed one of the first films, and the Albert Hall, which was holding regular Saturday evening screenings by the end of 1896.

Two local pioneers of early cinema, Jasper Redfern and Frank Mottershaw, were making such a quantity of films in the Edwardian period that Sheffield was seen by some as being a potential 'Hollywood of the North of England'. Many of Mottershaw's films were shot on location in the town, but by 1906 he had established studios in Upper Hanover Street. His firm's best-known film, *The Life of Charles Peace*, about the notorious murderer who shot and killed a man at Banner Cross in 1879, became something of a national sensation. Redfern was an optician and chemist who established the city's first permanent

Façade of the former Lansdowne Cinema of 1914, at the junction of London Road and Boston Street.

cinema within the Central Hall in Norfolk Street in 1905. Such was its success that by the 1920s it had been refurbished and, though officially called the Tivoli, was popularly known as the 'Ranch House' on account of the number of 'westerns' that were shown. By the 1930s, Redfern was the owner of a film theatre empire that extended to Liverpool, Manchester and even Windsor in the south of England.

The first purpose-built cinema was the Union Street Picture Palace, which opened in 1910, soon followed by the Electra in Fitzalan Square (1911), the Cinema House and the Colosseum (1913) and the Lansdowne Theatre, which opened on London Road in 1914 and whose elaborate 'pagoda' entrance still survives. By 1930 the city had forty-five cinemas, and when it opened shortly before the outbreak of war in 1939, the Carlton in Arbourthorne was the first all-concrete film venue to be built anywhere in the country.

Getting Away from it All

Another recreational activity with a long tradition among the working people of Sheffield was rambling, and a number of cross-country walking routes, such as those around the outlying village of Stannington, were in use by the mid-nineteenth century. Rambling, and the specialist pursuit of rock climbing that developed from it, became more organised in the early twentieth century. The lead had been taken by J.W. Puttrell, whose exploits at Wharncliffe Crags in the 1880s brought local and national fame, and one of the first clubs to be established for the enjoyment of the outdoors was the Sheffield Clarion Ramblers, with its ethos of socialism and fellowship that laid the seeds for the Kinder Mass Trespass of 1932.

From the 1890s, as the moors to the west of Sheffield became more intensively managed by aristocratic landowners for grouse shooting, a clash of interests with people seeking to enjoy Sheffield's dramatic landscape on their days off work seemed increasingly inevitable. The railways had made large areas of open country more generally accessible, but as people attempted to take advantage of the opportunities for recreation, they often came across gamekeepers who, acting on behalf of their aristocratic employers, aggressively turned them away. After a number of violent clashes, matters came to a head with the mass trespass of Kinder Scout organised by groups including the Sheffield Clarion Ramblers and the Young Communist League on 24 April 1932.

Around 500 people took part, and large-scale police action led to the arrest of six ramblers on grounds of unlawful assembly, upgraded later to the more

Memorial to the rambling and public access movements of the twentieth century, Sheffield Town Hall.

serious charge of riotous assembly, one that has had a history of use by the British establishment against working people from Peterloo to Orgreave, 165 years later. Those arrested were aged between 19 and 23, and half were Jewish, a fact that was pointed out specifically at trial by the judge to the jury consisting of army officers and country squires. Five of the accused were found guilty of riotous behaviour and sentenced to short periods in prison. Public reaction to the sentencing was almost universally hostile and undoubtedly provided impetus to the growing call for access to open land that ultimately led to Sheffield's reputation in the modern era as 'the outdoor city'.

Chapter Four

PHOENIX: 1935–2020

Blitz

Viewed from an increasing distance, the twentieth century emerges as a period in which the industrial capitalist world constructed by the imperial powers over the course of the previous half-century exploded into global conflict, not once but twice. As far as Sheffield was concerned, as one of the world's largest centres of concentrated arms production, the city had a uniquely tragic relationship with war and the machinery with which it was waged. Many Sheffielders must have read the news of a second impending conflagration with utter dismay, so fresh was the memory of the slaughter of the city's sons on the killing fields of Flanders, and the bombing of its working-class districts by a hostile power. Yet this was the city of steel, and put quite starkly, war meant work, full employment and busy factories. As the country braced itself for another clash of the global giants, the people of Sheffield looked towards the future in a chaos of mixed emotions. A few answered the call to the fight against fascism, and some fell, on the battlefields of Spain. Others, stirred to action by the Sheffield Jewish Refugee Council, founded in 1939, welcomed strangers fleeing fascist persecution into their homes. All of this was a fearful foretaste of what was to come in a world unsettled by the consequences of mass industrialisation.

A Second Call to Arms
In the two decades leading up to the outbreak of the Second World War in 1939, Sheffield once again played a major part in national armaments production, a development that further transformed the city's fortunes. With the East End factories working flat out to meet production targets, full employment was soon reached, and as the war progressed, a shortage of male workers meant that women were drafted in large numbers into less skilled jobs in engineering,

other industries and services. Sheffield's big firms all prospered, making large profits that helped pull the city out of the depths of global recession.

At the declaration of war, the government had once again taken over direction of the steel industry, and both the English Steel Corporation (ESC) and much of the cutlery trade geared themselves up for wartime production. But this time there was to be no great expansion of steel-making capacity as in the First World War; rather, the aim was to secure maximum output from existing plant. Thus, as far as the general history of Sheffield steel was concerned, the impact of the Second World War was much less dramatic than the first.

New developments in weapons technology meant increased demand for alloy steels in particular. The ESC soon became the country's largest producer of alloy steels, gun forgings and tank armour at its East End Vickers works, and the massive drop forge of the River Don works turned out crankshafts for the engines of Hurricane and Spitfire fighter aircraft, as well as the Lancaster bomber. Operated by a team of sixteen men, the 15-tonne drop hammer could be heard for miles around. Other military components produced in the big steelworks included parts for the British Army's fleets of Matilda and Churchill tanks, construction elements for floating harbours, the casings for 22,000lb

Steam hammer used by the Brown Bayley and Firth Brown companies, of a type used throughout the East End during the years of war production, now on display at the junction of Savile Street and Sutherland Street.

'Grand Slam' bombs and the bouncing bombs used in the 'Dambuster' raids. Output of special steels was greatly expanded, leading to a rapid development in electric arc steel capacity. The process had been growing in importance before the war, but now its output more than trebled.

Women of Steel

Just like in the previous generation, wartime production requirements and the conscription of men into the armed forces meant that large numbers of young women were drafted into the steelworks and related industries between 1939 and 1945. Women who had never been to work, or who had made a living from secretarial and administrative jobs, suddenly found themselves in the challenging surroundings of Bessemer converters and electric arc furnaces. In addition to steel production and munitions work, women were taken on in a number of roles, including crane drivers and machine operators. The work was extremely physically demanding and six-day shifts of up to twelve hours were common. Industrial injuries and, occasionally, fatalities were a reality to which women had to adjust quickly. Speaking of her entry as a 16-year-old into work at Tinsley Wire, Florence Temperton recalled:

> I'd never seen anything like it. It was a big and dirty place. The sharp wire could cut your hands to shreds, so before every shift I wrapped them in plaster-like material to protect them. [But] I didn't mind. I always achieved what the foreman asked of us, and in return we would be rewarded with cigarettes, so I didn't complain.

By the end of the war, women accounted for up to half the workforce in Sheffield, and the city played a leading role in the large-scale entry of women into employment in the twentieth century. But while women's wages rose faster than men's, and in some trades moves were made towards equal pay, in heavy steel and engineering average female pay was only half that of men.

After years of neglect, the testimony of women workers in Sheffield industries has now been systematically collected, and the true significance of the experience has become more fully appreciated. Women's lives were enriched by the friendships and camaraderie that got them through the most difficult times and transformed by the experience of seeing themselves as competent, equal comrades with men, self-aware, self-confident and independent.

'Women of Steel' memorial in Barker's Pool.

Following a campaign started by a small group of female steel veterans, general recognition for those who gave up so much of their young lives finally came in the form of a statue – 'Women of Steel' – unveiled outside City Hall in June 2016 in the presence of 100 of the women who had worked to help secure the nation's future.

Defending the City

At the national level, preparations for a potential outbreak of hostilities were well under way by 1935 with the establishment of the Home Office's Air Raid Precautions (ARP) department. By September 1936, plans were being made for selected buildings in Sheffield to be used as first aid and decontamination posts, though two years later the city had recruited fewer than half the number of air raid wardens required. In anticipation of conflict, prisoner-of-war camps were established at Potters Hill in Ecclesfield and at Lodge Moor, the latter being one of the largest in the country.

By March 1939, the Auxiliary Fire Service was almost up to full strength and Anderson shelters were being installed across the city more quickly than the Home Office could supply them. By the summer, air raid facilities were almost ready, though understaffing of the ARP service remained a concern for the authorities through the early months of the war, and it was fortunate for Sheffield that the anticipated large-scale air attack did not come as early as expected. Some fifty-eight public buildings were modified for use as communal air raid shelters, mainly by adapting existing cellars and vaults. A further 294 shelters were provided within shops, pubs, banks and other buildings requisitioned for war use. In September 1939, national plans for evacuating children from Britain's cities were put into effect locally, and 155 groups of children were taken in special trains to stay with families in rural Lincolnshire.

In December 1940, Sheffield had twenty-seven heavy anti-aircraft guns and a similar number of light guns that had been used in the previous conflict. The guns were located on three sites at Shirecliffe, Manor and Brinsworth. There were also searchlights and seventy-two barrage balloons designed both to obstruct enemy aircraft and to force them to fly higher, thus reducing the accuracy of bombing. The city's defences also included large oil tanks constructed on Strines and Burbage Moors, to be set alight as required to act as decoys and confuse enemy navigators. Though much had been achieved by the end of 1940, however, the city was soon to find that when tested, its defences were woefully inadequate.

Ring of Fire

Concentrated air attacks on Britain started on 10 July 1940 when the Luftwaffe began attacking airfields and coastal radar stations. On 7 September, daylight raids began on London that continued for seventy-six consecutive nights. On 14 November the Germans extended their targets to include industrial centres and ports, the first being Coventry, an important centre for aircraft production, which was bombed with devastating effect and provided a grim foretaste of what awaited other cities. In the days that followed, Southampton, Birmingham, Bristol, Plymouth, Liverpool and Portsmouth were all bombed. The people of Sheffield awaited what seemed an inevitable fate.

The first major raid on Sheffield came on 12 December, in clear conditions, two nights away from a full moon. The German high command code-named the operation 'Schmeltztiegel' (crucible) and allocated 406 aircraft to the raid. The first alert, known as the yellow warning, was issued at 6.15 p.m, followed by purple at 6.45 and the red warning to take cover at 7 p.m. No sooner had the red alert been issued than the first wave of aircraft, a squadron of Heinkel 111s from a base at Chartres in northern France, arrived over the city. This unit had a reputation for navigational accuracy and was armed with incendiaries and small high-explosive bombs used to illuminate targets. By the time their work was complete at around 8.45 p.m., fires had encircled a large area of the south-western residential district, and a second group of aircraft approaching from the south along the Sheaf Valley followed this up by dropping incendiaries on a large area from Millhouses in the south to Owlerton and Burngreave north of the city centre.

This terrifying ring of fire provided a target area in which 350 tonnes of high explosives were dropped over the course of the next four hours, with bombs dropping on Sharrow, Glossop Road, Meersbrook, Wybourn and Neepsend, where the gasworks was hit. A direct hit on Nether Edge hospital destroyed an entire ward, killing five people. Jessop Hospital for Women was also hit and had to be evacuated, and the Royal Hospital on West Street was badly damaged. From 10.38 p.m. to 2.15 a.m. the bombing was intense, particularly over the city centre. In the worst single incident of the night, seventy people lost their lives while taking shelter in the cellars of the Marples Hotel in Fitzalan Square.

By midnight, the fires in the city centre were out of control. Every single building on Angel Street had been bombed or was on fire, King Street was completely ablaze and the Moor was bombed to virtual oblivion. The emergency services were completely overwhelmed by the situation and could do little but try to contain the fires and wait for the bombing to cease. From around 2.15 a.m. the intensity of the attack diminished and at 3.50 the last bomber departed. After eleven hours of bombing, the all-clear was finally sounded at 4.17 a.m.

Daylight

Morning brought the revelation of the devastation visited on Sheffield in the course of this terrible night. Much of the city centre was destroyed, and an area bounded by Millhouses, Norfolk Park, Pitsmoor and Nether Edge had suffered extensive damage. Much of the city was without gas, and about half of all homes had no electricity. The water supply was contaminated, and many people had to rely on water carts for weeks to come. Communications were severely disrupted, especially the tram system that radiated from the city centre, and craters obstructed many roads. The Midland Railway line was blocked at Heeley, Millhouses and at Midland Station, and the LNER line at Wicker Arches and Darnall was badly damaged. Some 106 out of the city's 154 schools were damaged, and eight completely destroyed.

Rescue work and clearing up was severely hampered by unexploded bombs, many of which were equipped with time-delay fuses to cause maximum terror. Relief for the homeless came from the emergency services, which

Devonshire Green – an open space left when three whole streets were obliterated by a single high-explosive bomb in December 1940.

opened evacuation centres at High Storrs and Carterknowle schools and organised billeting of affected residents to areas that had escaped the bombing. Rationing was suspended so that people could obtain food wherever it was available and meals were served at the City Hall. Learning from the experience of the earlier bombing of London, and the importance of maintaining morale, great emphasis was placed on getting things back to some kind of normality as quickly as possible.

The Enemy Returns

The process of clearing up had hardly begun, however, when the Luftwaffe returned. On 13 December, 130 aircraft took off from France, but in deteriorating conditions some were diverted to less distant targets, such as Bristol, and it was a smaller raiding party of ninety-four bombers that reached Sheffield at around 6.50 p.m. Between 7.30 and 9 p.m. a heavy concentration of aircraft focused its bombing on an area to the immediate north and east of the city centre and along the Lower Don Valley. The success with which the previous raid had been able to create a circular fire storm around principal targets had obviously been noted, as this time the Germans dropped even more incendiaries. The first bombs fell along Prince of Wales Road, with a group of sixteen Heinkel 111s dropping 11,520 incendiary canisters, starting fires in Attercliffe, Grimesthorpe and Burngreave over a period of fifty minutes.

The second raid paid more attention to the industrial East End of the city, and the large quantities of high explosives dropped had a considerable impact on the densely packed terraced housing. On this occasion there was also significant damage to industry. Brown Bayley's steelworks, where a parachute mine caused the complete destruction of one rolling mill and damage to others, was worst affected. Elsewhere, there was damage to Hadfield's Hecla and East Hecla works, Arthur Lee's on Bessemer Road, and the English Steel works on Brightside Lane. Other factories were partially damaged, and loss of gas and electricity continued to affect production. Once again, unexploded bombs, including one at the English Steel works at Grimethorpe, held up recovery operations.

Aftermath

Overall, in the course of two nights of bombing, more than 600 Sheffielders were killed and 488 seriously injured. On 20 December, 134 of the casualties were buried in a mass grave in City Road cemetery. Some 78,000 homes across the city were destroyed or significantly damaged, leading to more than

40,000 people being made homeless. Many areas were without gas and water for a number of weeks. Cold and draughty houses, coupled with the bitter winter of 1941, made living conditions very hard and undoubtedly led to a large number of premature deaths, particularly among the elderly population.

On the whole, Sheffield suffered much but coped well with the terror of the Blitz. The official government report into the raids mentioned that there had been no panic, nor the mass exodus that had occurred in some cities after bombing. However, fire-watching was found to have been inadequate, and as a result of Sheffield's experience, more systematic fire watching procedures were instituted across the country in early 1941. The only industrial facility to suffer major damage, Brown Bayley's steelworks, had to be closed completely for a week while debris was cleared, and normal production levels were not attained until November 1941.

It was long assumed that the Germans' main target must have been the heavy industry of the East End, and the fact that most of the damage and loss of life was sustained by residential areas was due to navigational errors. This seemed surprising, however, given that one of the most experienced Luftwaffe squadrons was involved in the first night of bombing. More recently uncovered German bombing maps of Sheffield reveal that the areas where the majority of bombs and incendiaries fell, including hospitals, were actually the main targets. It is clear that the primary intention of the first raid, in particular, was not to take out industrial capacity but to cause terror in both densely packed working-class areas and middle-class suburbs alike.

In this context, despite the loss of life and huge destruction, the bombing operation cannot be counted as a great success, since the swift efforts at both national and local level to uphold morale were largely effective. Locally, the information bureau housed at the Central Library, the first of its kind outside London, provided a valuable service in co-ordinating information between the local authority and the people of Sheffield that did much to sustain morale.

Sheffield had to withstand major bombing for a third time on 14 March 1941, as a secondary target of a mission headed for Glasgow. On this occasion, 117 aircraft were involved, with the majority of bombs falling in the Southey Hill area where eighteen people were killed. A final raid on 12 October 1941 killed nine people in Burngreave, the part of the city that in all enemy bombing operations since the Zeppelin raid of 1916 had suffered the most. Again, both of these raids were concentrated mainly on working-class housing areas and no serious attempt appears to have been made to consolidate damage to industrial installations. While it might be difficult to make sense of German objectives in these missions, one thing emerges very clearly from the city's experience of the Blitz: the strength of spirit and collective solidarity of the people of Sheffield.

Reconstruction

Post-War Industry

The new Labour government of 1945 was elected on the premise that a nation that had planned so effectively for war should be able to organise society successfully in peacetime. Accordingly, plans for the post-war reconstruction of the steel industry were set out just as they were for other parts of the economy. Those who supported this vision saw it as strengthening the case for nationalisation, particularly in the steel sector where ever-larger plant was required, though there was much opposition to state control among the owners of Sheffield's steel firms. Whereas the larger companies like United Steel and Firth Vickers were able to invest in bulk production facilities such as their joint venture at the Shepcote Lane rolling mills, smaller firms struggled to raise the necessary capital. There was little surprise, therefore, when the Labour government nationalised the iron and steel industry in 1949. However, management structures were left virtually untouched and plans to rationalise the industry made little progress.

The way was therefore left open for the incoming Conservative government to restore the status quo, and in 1953 the industry was duly returned to the private sector, though under much-increased levels of government scrutiny. Supervision of the industry at national level was facilitated by the establishment of the Iron and Steel Corporation of Great Britain, which in order to exercise some control over those companies with the largest capacity brought firms such as the ESC, United Steel, Firth Brown, Brown Bayley's and Hadfield's under its wing.

Whether industry was in private or public hands, Sheffield's traditional advantages of technical prowess, a large, skilled workforce and a unique grouping of metalworking and engineering concerns continued to uphold the city's competitive edge. Sheffield was also able to maintain its position as a major centre for research into steel production methods, and the best of its firms adapted quickly to emerging technologies. The research laboratories operated by United Steel and Firth Brown were as impressive as any in the world, and Jessop-Saville, though not one of the larger firms in the city, still employed 200 physicists, metallurgists and engineers in its research department.

In terms of jobs, unlike the city's experience after the First World War, the Second was not followed by an economic slump. Instead, the full employment that was to continue through the 1950s and '60s laid the foundation for what would later be seen as a high watershed in the peacetime fortunes of Sheffield. In Sheffield itself the ESC was the major employer, with a workforce of 16,500 in the mid-1950s. Firth Brown was the next largest with some 6,000 workers, followed closely by Hadfield's, Jessop's, Osborn's and Brown Bayley's, with between 3,000 to 5,000 workers. Nearby Rotherham was dominated by the giant United Steel, with some 35,000 employees in 1953, making it one of the largest companies in the country.

By the beginning of the 1950s, the steel industry was enjoying peak production and full employment, and by the end of the decade the ESC regularly made annual profits in excess of £4 million. These were years of strong economic growth, and major producers such as Britain and France were starting to exploit the new continental trading areas such as the European Economic Community founded in 1957 and the European Free Trade Area in 1960, which made up for much of the loss of their former colonial markets.

The mid-1950s saw big government investment in the UK steel industry. By 1958, some £500 million had been provided over a ten-year period,

English Steel Corporation's Brightside Lane machine shop (1956).

enabling a significant rise in output. The largest single investments were at United Steel's new Templeborough works based on the latest electric arc furnaces, which opened in 1963 and enabled production of more than a million tonnes of steel a year; the ESC's new Tinsley Park works, which opened in the same year; and Tube Investments' Park Gate works, where new electric-arc and oxygen-production equipment was installed at a cost of more than £30 million. In the post-war years, markets for steel grew significantly, led by the major consumers in car and aircraft production, and the range of products manufactured in Sheffield expanded to include turbine rotors for power stations, specialist components for power plants and castings for the offshore oil industry.

Away from the heavy steel and engineering sector, Sheffield's business structure continued much as it had been in previous decades, with just under 2,000 firms, only 450 of which employed more than ten people. Almost half of sales in cutlery and tools were for the export market. In addition to the cutlery and tool manufacturers themselves, there was a flourishing sector supplying Sheffield firms with machinery and materials for processes such as grinding and polishing. This myriad of small firms was linked by long-standing bonds of mutual support, and took pride in the knowledge that 'Made in Sheffield' continued to be a brand associated around the world with the highest standards of quality and workmanship.

At this time about 90 per cent of the metal tableware and 40 per cent of cutting and hand tools made in the UK was produced in Sheffield. In addition, there was what Sheffield artisans themselves referred to as cutlery: fixed-handled knives, spring knives (pen knives), scissors and traditional cut-throat razors. In the 1950s some 50 million of these items were being produced each year for both the home and export markets. As for agricultural and other specialist tools, at least 80 per cent of the national output of scythes, sickles and hooks was made in Sheffield in the mid-1950s. That such high levels of production continued in the face of the increasing mechanisation of the agriculture sector was largely due to a buoyant global export market. Similarly, more than 90 per cent of the country's garden shears, hacksaws and light edge tools, and 75 per cent of all files and rasps, were made in Sheffield.

Between 1939 and 1960, with steel production almost doubling, and a massive expansion in the manufacture of cutlery, tools and other steel products, Sheffield was among the most prosperous industrial areas of the country. The future of the city, and the prosperity of its citizens, seemed assured.

Immigration from Overseas

A visible sign of Sheffield's post-war economic success and increasingly outward-looking ethos was the growth in non-indigenous immigration in the decades after 1945. The first wave of immigration, in the form of some 1,200 Polish ex-servicemen and a sizeable Somali community drawn to high wages in the steel industry, had taken place in the immediate post-war years. They were soon to be followed by others from what were then East and West Pakistan (the former to become Bangladesh in 1971), Yemen and the West Indies.

By the mid-1950s the austerity of the immediate post-war years was giving way to a growing mood of optimism, and an acute shortage of labour in key industries attracted increasing numbers of immigrants from the Caribbean, Southeast Asia and elsewhere, significantly transforming the city's traditionally insular character. By the early 1970s an estimated 12,000 overseas immigrants had made Sheffield their home, the greatest numbers coming from the West Indies, Pakistan and Bangladesh, but there were also significant communities from Somalia, the Port of Aden and Hong Kong. The majority settled in the old industrial areas of the city.

Mindful of the fact that there were elements, even within mainstream politics, that wished to inflame racial tensions in Britain's cities, in 1966 the council established a Sheffield Committee for Community Relations and appointed Syed Rasul, himself an immigrant from Bangladesh, as Sheffield's first Community Relations Officer. The initial aims of the committee were to help immigrants integrate into the community and to foster harmonious relations between the various ethnic and cultural groups within the city. At the same time, the council established the Sheffield Unified Multicultural Education Service (SUMES) in an attempt to adapt its education provision to the needs of growing ethnic diversity within the city. The scheme included a community languages and bilingual resources unit, special provision for the under-5s and children with special educational needs, and a network of community liaison teachers.

Rebuilding and Extending the City

In the immediate post-war period, as the rubble was gradually cleared from the bomb sites, Sheffield's elected representatives were determined to leave behind its reputation as a second-rate, smoky industrial city. Plans were drawn up for the reconstruction of the city centre, and at the same time, the enlargement of the local authority boundaries. The most ambitious plans included the construction of a local airport. At the national level, the prime focus of the post-war Labour government was the creation of a Welfare State with its flagship National Health Service. Locally, though this meant that certain responsibilities, such as maintenance of hospitals, were lost to central government, the Sheffield Labour Council grasped the opportunities presented by the commensurate expansion of local authority responsibilities in planning, housing, education and social welfare.

Plans for rebuilding and reconfiguring the city centre included a central core of municipal and cultural facilities that would provide the basis for a new regional shopping centre to compete with rival cities such as Leeds. A key part of the strategy was the refusal of planning permission for out-of-town shopping centres. Another component was the aim of retaining housing within walking distance of the city centre, and within the central area priority was to be given to pedestrians within safe and pleasant precincts.

These plans included deliberate symbols of the forward-looking image the city was seeking to project to the outside world, such as the Crucible Theatre with its contemporary design and thrust stage reaching out into the audience, itself a metaphor for a futuristic city in touch with its people. Similarly, the redevelopment of Castle Square in the form of an underground precinct open to the sky – soon to become known locally as 'hole in't road' – signalled the

The Moor – bombed almost to oblivion in December 1940 and extensively rebuilt in the post-war period.

planners' ambitious, futuristic ethos. Critics of the council's radical plans, however, lamented the transformation of a much-loved – if somewhat incoherent – old town into a city that seemed to have been remade for concrete and cars.

Councillors were keen to raise the status of the city in keeping with both its size and industrial importance, and a key component of this policy was to be the creation of a national benchmark for high standards of municipal services. Over the next two decades, Sheffield's approach to tackling problems in housing, education and personal social services was to become recognised as innovative both nationally, and in the case of housing, internationally. In regard to housing, all new construction had come to an abrupt end at the outbreak of the Second World War. Following the cessation of hostilities, in September 1945 the decision was taken to build 20,000 new houses over the next three years. The post-war estates were generally more successful than the often-substandard buildings that had been put up under interwar austerity. An example was the Norfolk Park estate, which provided homes for more than 1,000 people while keeping pedestrians safely away from traffic.

In the short term, however, demands from central government to increase house building forced local authorities to lower standards. The resulting 'peoples' houses' were first built in Sheffield at Greenhill and Bradway and included a combination of 'maisonettes' and thirteen-storey blocks of flats. After 1955, government housing grants were reduced in favour of assistance for slum clearance and housing for the elderly. However, unlike many other parts of the country, construction of council houses continued in high numbers in Sheffield throughout the 1960s. A shortage of land had been anticipated by the council's development plan of 1952, when it was calculated that land for accommodation of 74,000 people would be needed outside the city boundaries in Derbyshire if the city's housing challenges were to be met.

Sheffield had already constructed a number of small estates in Derbyshire, but this had caused administrative problems, and the loss of population within the city's boundaries led to a drop in government grants. In response, the council sought permission for a southern boundary extension in the vicinity of the Derbyshire village of Beighton. In 1951, Parliament refused the request, mainly on the grounds that there was still much vacant land within the city boundary. However, the council's long-standing commitment to the greenbelt principle meant that much of that land was unavailable for housing, while so-called 'brownfield' sites were required for industrial and commercial development.

In the search for additional land for housing, the city was faced with two options. The first was to maintain the existing policy of raising housing densities by constructing flats up to six storeys high and to negotiate an overspill agreement with Derbyshire, whose council was keen to develop a new town to consolidate the mining villages in the vicinity of Mosborough. The second was to increase the densities on estates within the city by building higher and bringing into use sites that had previously been ruled out because of their steep slopes or because they were used as recreational spaces. In choosing the second option, the way was cleared for the iconic developments of Park Hill and Hyde Park in the 1960s. At the same time, many of the government's objections to expansion were eventually overcome, and from April 1967 the city's boundaries were extended to include most of the parish of Beighton, the Mosborough and Gleadless areas of the parish of Eckington, and parts of the parishes of Holmesfield, Killamarsh and Ecclesfield, together with some small additions from the county borough of Rotherham.

However, it was not reconstruction projects or territorial expansion that were to have the greatest impact on the national perception of Sheffield, but the Clean Air Act of 1956. The first smoke control order came into effect on 1 December 1959, and by the mid-1960s the clean air zone had been extended across the city. The burning of coal, which had taken place on a massive scale both industrially and domestically for more than 100 years, had not only made visibility difficult, and been injurious to public health, but had left the city's sandstone buildings covered with a layer of black soot. The gradual cleaning of public buildings, starting with the Town Hall in 1959, seemed to symbolise Sheffield's emergence from a polluted industrial past into the bright light of modernity. Certainly, the effects of the Clean Air Act were more dramatic in Sheffield than in any other urban centre in the country, and within ten years of the legislation coming into force Sheffield boldly claimed to be 'the cleanest industrial city in western Europe'.

The Peace Movement

Sheffield's significance as one of the country's most important centres of armaments production was central to the emergence of a well-organised local peace movement in the immediate post-war years. No doubt this was driven partly by the fear that the city would be a major target for enemy bombing, and not all workers were persuaded that temporary armaments contracts provided the most secure foundation for the modern development of the steel industry.

Another important impetus for the peace movement came from the strength of the political left in Sheffield, expressed both in the working-class character of the city and the highly organised local unions, particularly in the heavy steel and engineering sectors. The contribution of the unions to the peace movement was exercised primarily through the Sheffield Trades and Labour Council, and to a lesser extent through the internationalist perspective of the Communist Party. Local churches also played an important role and, true to its historical foundation in nonconformity, the Methodists were one of the drivers of pacifism in the city.

Following on from the strengthening of the position of women in the workplace during the First World War, in the 1930s local women had become increasingly influential in shaping the city's response both to worsening unemployment and the renewed threat of global conflict. This can be seen in the impressive network of self-help groups for the wives of unemployed men, and in the active role played by many women in the peace movement at both local and national level. Youth groups, too, became increasingly active, and in Sheffield this can be seen in the popularity of the Woodcraft Folk, an organisation open to both boys and girls that had been established in south London in 1925. The organisation's foundation largely in opposition to the masculine, militaristic ethos of Baden-Powell's scouting movement was particularly attractive in Sheffield, where it enjoyed close links with the co-operative movement in a shared objective 'to educate and empower young people to be able to participate actively in society, improving their lives and others' through active citizenship'.

After the end of the Second World War, Sheffield citizens were prominent in the international peace movement that developed in response both to the horror of that conflict and the threat of devastation to civilian populations on an unimagined scale in the wake of the atomic bombs dropped on the Japanese cities of Hiroshima and Nagasaki. Prominent among local promoters of the movement was Alan Ecclestone, vicar of Darnall and member of the Communist Party, whose election as chair of the Sheffield Peace Committee coincided with the local collection of a remarkable 50,000 signatures towards a post-war global peace petition.

The success of the Sheffield petition led to the choice of the city as the venue for the second World Peace Conference in November 1950. The conference was initially supported by the local Labour Party, but Britain's involvement in the Korean War and the American-sponsored 'crusade against communism'

Peace Gardens, Hiroshima Memorial.

divided opinion, with the Bishop of Sheffield prominent in denouncing the peace movement as an instrument of communist propaganda. On 10 November, the Home Office refused visas for two-thirds of the 2,000 delegates, including the black American singer Paul Robeson, the Russian composer Dmitri Shostakovich and Frederic Joliot-Curie, president of the Peace Movement. Undaunted, 4,500 delegates still arrived in Sheffield on the scheduled opening day on 16 November, despite the fact that in the face of determined opposition by the British establishment, the conference had formally been moved to the Polish capital of Warsaw. Notwithstanding these initial setbacks, Sheffield was to remain a major centre of the peace movement during the Cold War period, symbolised by the formal adoption of the 'Peace Gardens' as the name for the city's main public square.

City on the Move

On the back of a buoyant industrial sector, Sheffield entered the 1960s looking confidently towards the future. By 1964, about £150 million had been spent on the modernisation of the steel industry, with investment schemes such as the complete refitting of the Templeborough works, then the largest concentration

Former Templeborough works, Rotherham, now Magna Centre.

of electric steel-making facilities in the world. The size of this capacity was based on a confident forecast of annual demand for steel of more than 1.2 million tonnes. At the same time, the ESC opened its new Tinsley Park works at a cost of £26 million and based around two giant 100-tonne electric arc furnaces able to produce up to 300,000 tonnes of special steel a year. What these new developments had in common was their foundation on the almost universal assumption of ever-expanding demand for steel.

By the early 1960s Sheffield was revelling in its increasingly clean air and almost futuristic stainless steel image, with this spirit of optimism and modernity well captured in the council-sponsored promotional film *City on the Move*. Released in 1972, the film captured the mood of the times with its portrayal of a thriving modern city, developing both socially and economically on the back of a booming steel industry. Workers in the engineering, steel and related sectors enjoyed some of the highest wages in British industry and all areas of the local economy prospered as a result. These were days when working-class youngsters, starting work at 15, had money to spend on an increasing range of leisure options at weekends, and were encouraged to relax in the assurance of a job for life and a comfortable future.

During the course of the 1950s and '60s, Sheffield's central shopping area, much of which had been destroyed during the war, was almost entirely rebuilt, and local officials boasted that no city north of London had a greater range of department stores. *City on the Move* revealed to cinemagoers a thriving metropolis, with good motorway and rail access and a range of shops that made Sheffield a natural retail destination for a large area of south Yorkshire and the North Midlands. As for residential improvements, the film highlighted the case of Mosborough, where 'a whole new town within a town is being created' and where land was set aside to develop small local businesses.

Yet amid this headlong rush to the future, Sheffield still managed to retain a thriving working-class culture based around the local pubs and working men's clubs. These were at the heart of working-class communities whose bonds were still as strong as in the days of the nineteenth-century alehouse poets. Some of the more successful institutions, such as the Dial House Social Club in the Wisewood area of the city, put subscriptions towards support for members during periods of enforced unemployment, trips to the seaside for children during the summer holidays and fielded football and cricket teams. Dial House also boasted a concert room, bowling green and a billiard room. Founded in 1932, by the mid-1960s the club had 2,400 members, including 800 women, and remained an important social hub for the community up until the 1980s.

Dial House – nucleus of its community in the boom years of the twentieth century.

A major symbol of Sheffield's self-confidence in the 1960s was the annual Lord Mayor's Parade and Sheffield Show. By the mid-decade this had transformed into a major public celebration, including a fly-past of military aircraft, marching bands and floats highlighting the best of Sheffield's industry and entrepreneurship. This period also saw the highpoint of Sheffield's civic provision, with the city able to boast over 100 municipal sports pitches, nine swimming pools, 130 tennis courts, seven golf courses, eight riding schools and numerous bowling greens spread around the city.

A sure sign of Sheffield's booming economy was the rapid development of the entertainment and leisure sector. The high point was the opening of the Epic complex on Arundel Gate in 1968 with a nightclub, ballroom, shops, cinema and a car park all on a single site. It was joined two years later by Club Fiesta, promoted as the 'largest nightclub in Europe'. The club scene expanded in the 1970s to follow the money wherever it was, from the sophisticated Josephine's in the city centre with its strict dress code and *à la carte* menus to popular dance venues such as Samantha's and Tiffany's on Queens and London Roads respectively. In the 1960s and '70s, whatever the perception of Sheffield from the outside, to its largely working-class inhabitants who were enjoying unprecedented standards of living, the city was – in the words of *City on the Move* – 'swinging'.

Streets in the Sky

Despite this unassailable optimism, however, Sheffield still faced a significant housing shortage. By October 1947, only 824 permanent and 1,357 temporary homes had been constructed of the 20,000 that were estimated to be needed in the city's post-war reconstruction plan. After considerable debate, therefore, the council's housing committee took the decision in April 1949 to consider the construction of high-rise flats for the first time. During the summer, members of the committee made visits to London and cities in Scandinavia to look at suitable models. Although relatively few, mainly isolated, 'tower blocks' were built in Sheffield at this time compared to other cities, the precedent had been set for a 'high-rise' revolution in the city that was to find its full expression in the radical schemes of the early 1960s.

The first major programme of slum clearance since the 1930s got under way in 1953 with the question of where residents should be rehoused still unsolved. Here, Sheffield's post-war struggle to extend its boundaries was to have dramatic consequences both for the people who needed to be rehoused and on the physical appearance of the city. Faced with government restraints on the city's expansion beyond its traditional boundaries, the demand for housing would need to be met within considerably more restricted boundary constraints than had been envisaged by planners in the immediate post-war period.

Part of the solution was to emerge from the council's appointment in 1953 of J. Lewis Womersley as the city's new forward-looking chief architect. His approach to Sheffield housing requirements in the context of constrictive boundaries had three main aims. First, to develop medium-density neighbourhoods in suburban areas, including those such as Gleadless Valley, which had been previously considered too hilly for successful development; second, to concentrate urban development on a limited number of sites in the central area; and third, and most revolutionary, to design high-density blocks with deck access on three main sites close to the city centre. It was this aspect of Womersley's scheme that was to lead to the construction of complexes of approximately 1,000 homes at Park Hill, Hyde Park and Kelvin that, with their wide deck access, popularly known as 'streets in the sky', were to attract international attention to a city that, in architectural terms at least, had hitherto been largely ignored. Together, these three developments constituted the largest public housing scheme in Western Europe.

The architects responsible for the scheme's conception, Ivor Smith and Jack Lynn, had already made their mark with innovative designs on behalf of London County Council. In meeting the challenges of rehousing the inhabitants of former slums in Sheffield, Smith and Lynn looked to Le Corbusier's 1952 Unité apartment block in Marseille, with its 'street decks' being the most obvious common feature, as well as to the most ambitious of Sheffield's own pre-war schemes, the Edward Street flats. They were also influenced by the 'brutalist' designs of British architects Alison and Peter Smithson, which utilised exposed structures and undecorated concrete to evoke a rough, industrial quality. Drawing on this dual inspiration, the resulting buildings made a dramatic, if controversial, contribution to the urban landscape and arguably provided Sheffield with its most imposing gateway from the Don Valley since the destruction of the castle in the seventeenth century.

As an experiment in community living, the Park Hill scheme was carried out with bold vision, and some 3,500 people were housed in standards clearly superior to those they had left behind in the slums. Each flat had a door opening onto a wide, covered street deck by which the architects hoped to provide the benefits of the street culture working-class communities had previously

Park Hill flats – simultaneously helped solve the housing crisis and brought Sheffield international recognition in the 1960s.

enjoyed with the added bonus of protection from the elements. Integral to the scheme was the inclusion of shops, schools, pubs, play areas and other social facilities that formed a central feature of the estate.

In terms of meeting Sheffield's housing needs, these high-density developments enabled people to be rehoused in close proximity to the areas that were cleared, while at the same time gaining maximum advantage from the government grants that favoured such clearance schemes from the mid-1950s. The flats' proximity to the city centre also had the benefit of replicating traditional residence patterns and allowed ready access to commercial and civic buildings. Finally, and of no little significance, the national and international attention attracted by the Park Hill scheme, in particular, helped contribute to the changing, modern image of the city that the council was striving to project.

Overall, between 1963 and 1971 Sheffield saw the construction of 2,000 new council homes, and an additional 1,000 privately built houses every year. The international recognition that was given to Park Hill came soon after the widespread acclaim accorded to the Gleadless Valley development of 1955–62 with its award-winning mix of low, medium, and high-rise housing and community buildings in close harmony with the natural topography. By 1973 the number

Gleadless Valley – making the most of Sheffield's topography.

of houses under the local authority's management had grown to about 75,000, and at 45 per cent, a greater proportion of the inhabitants of Sheffield were in council housing than in any other city in the country.

Education for the Future

Following the end of the Second World War, Sheffield was the first city in the country to have its school building programme approved by central government. During the 1950s, 19,000 additional school places were provided in thirty-six new or modified schools, of which 11,000 were in eighteen new secondary schools. The 1944 Education Act also required Local Education Authorities (LEAs) to provide special education for children with disabilities. Sheffield responded to these obligations with vigour and by 1961, 937 children were receiving special education in the city. Sheffield also took the lead in provision for children with specific disabilities such as cerebral palsy, and the visually and hearing impaired.

A noticeable trend in Sheffield education in the 1960s was a more assertive approach by parents towards the education of their children. The Confederation for the Advancement of State Education (CASE) and other parents' organisations became very active in the debate surrounding the introduction of comprehensive education. They also argued effectively for parental involvement in the management of local schools, an area in which Sheffield set the pace nationally. In response to parental initiative, in 1969 the council introduced a plan 'to promote the widest participation in the running of schools by parents, teachers, trades unionists [and] people from all walks of life within the locality'. From 1970, every school in the city had a governing body that included a wider representation of local people than those appointed by the LEA. Some 2,000 places were available, and in many schools, elections were required as parents showed their enthusiasm for the new system. At the time of its introduction, the Sheffield scheme for civic representation in school governance was the most radical of any in the country.

The twenty years from around 1965 to 1985 can be said to have been a golden age of education in Sheffield. In 1968 the Labour government's scheme of comprehensive education was enthusiastically adopted in the city with cross-party support, and there was to be no return to a selective schools system in Sheffield. Many aspects of education thrived in this period, from special needs resources to outdoor activities, music provision and foreign exchanges. Community education was driven by the establishment of the South Yorkshire Open College and the Northern College, and youth clubs were created to help avoid 'inner-city problems' and provide what the council hoped would be a 'systematically ordered structure' for young people's lives. There is no doubt that Sheffield's vision of how to achieve the provisions of the 1944 Education Act was clearer than in most cities, and a coherent comprehensive system of education provision can be seen as one of the main drivers of the post-war 'city on the move'.

Learning for All

At this time Sheffield also established its further education provision, beginning in 1953 with work on the new Pond Street site for the Sheffield College of Commerce and Technology, which had been established immediately after the war. The College of Art's Psalter Lane site was expanded, and in 1967 the two institutions combined to form the Sheffield Polytechnic under control of the LEA. From 1976 it came under direct council control as Sheffield City Polytechnic, and in 1992 became Sheffield Hallam University. From its inception, it was envisaged that the institution would work closely with local industry and business, and it soon gained a high reputation for the quality of its work-integrated 'sandwich' courses and qualifications. Also at this time, the central Sheffield College of Further Education was established with five satellites spread across the city.

Owen Building, opened in 1969 for Sheffield City Polytechnic (now Sheffield Hallam University).

As for higher education, the University of Sheffield expanded rapidly from the mid-1950s. By this time its links with local industry included joint research laboratories for the glass, steel and iron industries. In 1956 the University combined with the United Steel Company to complete the purchase of a cutting-edge 'electronic digital computer' that allowed significant advances in research to be made right up to the 1980s and kept Sheffield at the forefront of academic endeavour. Away from the fields of science and engineering, the University's School of Social Studies, founded in 1948, was engaged in the training of social workers and carried out detailed research into solutions for local social problems.

In the post-war period, following the introduction of direct government grants, students from outside the region started to outnumber those from Sheffield itself, and by the mid-1960s there were more than 4,000 students at the University. The continuing significance of engineering and metallurgy was reflected in this period by the opening of a new thirteen-storey metallurgy building at the St George's campus in 1965. Other new buildings opened at this time to accommodate the rapid growth in student numbers included the iconic Arts Tower (which for many years remained the city's tallest building) and Western Bank Library. New facilities for the Medical School, one of the founding components of the University, coincided with the opening of the Royal Hallamshire Hospital in 1978.

Arts Tower and Library of the University of Sheffield (1959–66), among the most impressive of Britain's post-war university buildings.

Hitting the Wall

Between 1845 and 1979, Sheffield was among the most prosperous industrial areas of the country. In the boom years of the 1960s, the city's industrial base of special steel-making, heavy engineering and toolmaking looked set to provide a comfortable living for the majority of its population well into the future. In the event, Sheffield's equivalent of the Gold Rush was to be tragically short-lived. The strong growth of the UK economy in the first two decades after the end of the war began to slow before the end of the 1960s, and by the mid-1970s the steady expansion of world steel production began to level off in the face of declining demand. To reduce costs, manufacturers around the world looked to reduce the amount of steel used in products and at the same time there was competition from other materials such as plastics and ceramics.

The unforeseen oil crisis of the early 1970s only served to exacerbate problems and expose Sheffield's over-reliance on the special steels on which it had built its reputation from the 1890s onwards. Changes in weapons technologies and developments in modern warfare meant that Sheffield lost much of its preeminence as a global armaments centre. Even special steels were becoming 'just another product' that was most efficiently produced in large quantities wherever energy and labour costs were cheapest. In these changing conditions, a local industry that had consolidated its position on the discovery of new types of steel was to learn to its cost that the development of modern production technology was of paramount importance. Locally too, the owners of many steel businesses argued that environmental regulations that came into force with the Clean Air Act of 1956 added an intolerable burden to production costs.

British Steel

The Labour government elected in the mid-1960s made the revitalisation of the UK steel industry a priority. Its aim was to pursue an expansionist strategy based on the Japanese model of giant integrated steelworks that could compete in the world market in terms of volume. To put this into effect, the industry was renationalised around the British Steel Corporation (BSC), created in July 1967. A merger of fourteen major companies, the BSC was a giant on a par with the largest steel concerns in the world.

The government's policy allowed the smaller companies to continue in private hands. Only firms producing 475,000 tonnes a year were to be included in the BSC, which took over about 90 per cent of raw steel production, but the majority

Massive engineering sheds in Carlisle Street, of a type that colonised the old East End in the decades before the industrial collapse of the 1980s.

of the forging, rolling and processing was kept in the private sector, much of it in Sheffield. The result of this arrangement was that of the companies that operated in Sheffield or its immediate region, only three – the ESC, United Steel and Parkgate – were nationalised, the remaining fifty or so firms being left in private ownership. The impact of steel nationalisation on Sheffield is therefore difficult to assess. Supporters have argued that through its special steels division in particular, the BSC was able to provide the investment necessary to compete in world markets for mass-produced materials such as stainless steel. Critics allege that the years of uncertainty that preceded renationalisation prevented firms from investing and then triggered an overhasty rush to modernise. Moreover, they claimed that the creation of competing private and public sectors in a single city was a recipe for business chaos.

In the event, no sooner was the renationalised industry up and running than the business world was turned upside down. The global economic chaos that followed the world oil crisis of the 1970s came as a shock to the almost carefree optimism of previous decades, as mergers and rationalisation were forced on a rapidly fragmenting Sheffield steel industry. The government responded in 1976 with the creation of BSC Stainless as six separate profit centres, and work began on the transformation of the Shepcote Lane site into the biggest purpose-built stainless steel plant in Europe. The project was a significant achievement, but the cost was considerable, rising from a projected £130 million to nearly £200 million in what was to be the last great development in the history of the Sheffield steel industry.

Collapse

For a while, special steels continued to fare better than bulk product, but as world steel production stagnated and overcapacity became an increasing problem, individual companies attempted to restructure rapidly and move towards manufacture of higher-quality steels. By the mid-1970s a frantic pattern of mergers, plant closures, strikes and redundancies unfolded as firms desperately attempted expensive and long-overdue modernisations during a period of acute recession and overcapacity. The immediate casualty was the collapse of the traditional industrial centres such as Neepsend and Brightside. But it was the big East End firms such as Hadfield's that were the focus of union action in the national steel strike, in which 100,000 workers walked out in early January 1980 in a dispute centred on pay. The biggest industrial action since the 1920s, the strike was seen at the time as a test of resolve for

Margaret Thatcher's new Conservative administration and its hard-line 'monetarist' policies. Despite fourteen weeks of bitter struggle on the part of the workers, it was a battle the government won.

As the confident expectations of the 1960s were rapidly revised, the BSC's expansionist strategy was the most significant casualty. Attempts were made to restructure the giant Firth Brown company and stem its losses, but by the early 1980s the dramatic decline of the forging industry, in which the BSC's River Don Works shared, was unabated. In 1973 some 13,000 people had been employed at the River Don and Shepcote Lane sites, but by 1983 the number had fallen to 5,000. The break-up of Sheffield's once proud industrial base soon attracted business 'predators' who, in the words of one local historian, 'saw the industry through the eyes of cost accountants rather than metallurgists'.

Like heavy steel, the cutlery sector was also badly affected, in particular by the entry of foreign competition into the market, including Hong Kong, Taiwan and South Korea, and by the imposition of import duties in Australia, traditionally one of the strongest markets for Sheffield goods. From the mid-1960s, East Asian imports flooded the market and few Sheffield firms were set up to respond effectively. By the late 1980s, closures, mergers and mass unemployment had drastically reduced Sheffield's historic staple trade. Only

Preserved entrance to Thomas Firth & Sons' Siemens Melting Shop, Savile Street, memorial to Sheffield's devastated steel industry.

the tool industry was able to ride out the worst of the storm, saved partly by the contemporary DIY (home improvement) trend, in addition to improved technology and more effective marketing. But by the mid-1980s, even this sector of local industry was under relentless assault.

Following so closely from an immediate post-war period characterised by high demand, full employment and sky-high business optimism, the collapse of Sheffield's steel and associated industries at the end of the 1970s came as a great shock. On one level, there was something inevitable about the sharp decline of the steel industry, since a high-investment, high-technology business had ended up in the hands of a very small number of producers and a small but highly productive group of workers. Yet, almost half a century later, questions remain as to the causes.

Should more have been spent on research and development? Was it a combination of poor management and an inflexible workforce? Among the causes pointed to by those who worked in the industry themselves are an arrogance towards emerging East Asian competitors, stifling parochialism, outdated sales techniques, slow investment and a reluctance to merge unsustainable smaller units. However, there has also been significant criticism of the role of central government. First, it is argued that the government should have stood firm against foreign 'dumping' of cheap steel on the UK market. Second, the continuation of the chaotic mix of private and public structures in a single, critical industry has been criticised. Above all, the devastating effects of the Thatcher government's rapid deflationary economics on a sensitive industrial sector, sharply reducing demand for manufactured products based on steel, seem beyond dispute. The fallout, when it came, was not just economic. The cost over the decades to come was all too human.

The Human Cost

From 1979, Sheffield was shattered by redundancies on an unprecedented scale, two-thirds of which were in a steel industry reeling from the wholesale closure of production and engineering works. For the first time in its history, unemployment in Sheffield rose above the national average, peaking at just over 16 per cent of the workforce in 1987, amounting to some 50,000 people. In the tool sector, the number of workers fell from 20,000 in 1970 to 1,200 in 1991. In the South Yorkshire steel industry as a whole, the number of people employed fell from around 60,000 in 1971 to 16,000 in 1987, and below 10,000 by the early 1990s. From the mid-1980s, the social effects of

Meadowhall Road, approaching the retail centre built on the ruins of the former Hadfield's steelworks, the major employer in this area until its collapse in the mid-1980s. At that time, no fewer than sixteen residential streets branched off the former Brightside Lane at this point, all subsequently obliterated from the landscape.

mass unemployment in the traditional steel, engineering and cutlery sectors were to be devastating.

By any standards, the effects of the wholesale closure of steel and engineering works of the early 1980s were brutal. Coming on top of the slum clearances of the previous generation, many parts of the city's East End were utterly devoid of either industry or housing. By 1988, fewer than 300 people lived in what had been Sheffield's beating industrial heart and almost half of all land was either vacant or derelict. The great leviathans of Sheffield's once-proud steel industry – Firth Brown's, Hadfield's and Brown Bayley's – had all been completely flattened.

About two-thirds of the registered unemployed were former steelworkers. Given the nature of the job, these were men who had worked, as their fathers and grandfathers had done, in close-knit teams, each depending on the other. The sudden cutting of close ties like these, with their origins far back in Sheffield's traditional cutlery industry, was to be catastrophic for generations to come. In addition to this human tragedy, in the space of just a few dramatic years, the whole Sheffield and Rotherham region was to lose its distinctive character as a centre for heavy industry that it had built up since the establishment of the East

End works more than 100 years before. In the words of labour historian Sidney Pollard, 'a significant chapter in the history of the city and the country, a distinguished chapter of success and achievement, had come to a close'.

In 1981 the council established an employment department to promote retraining for new skills and jobs, and began to devise policies to stimulate new investment in the city and investigate the creation of new employment opportunities. Already, by 1981, the male steelworker was no longer typical of Sheffield's workforce, and in his place female workers in the service industries dominated the employment market, and the city's main employers had become the council, the health authority and the institutions of higher and further education. Unemployment in Sheffield, which for decades had been lower than the national average, was now consistently higher. In parts of Sheffield, entire communities were out of work. Everywhere across the city there were families whose lives and futures were irredeemably changed, almost overnight. The choice facing those who governed the city in these dark times was stark. It was a choice of whether to accept the human cost of this tragedy or to fight back.

People's Republic of South Yorkshire

On 1 April 1974, as part of a massive reorganisation of local government across the UK, Sheffield became part of the newly created metropolitan county of South Yorkshire. From this time onwards, the relationship between centre and locality in English politics and administration shifted from one of general co-operation to increasing tension and conflict, a situation that was at its most marked in the years following the election of Margaret Thatcher's Conservative government in 1979. Thatcher herself was ideologically opposed to public spending on social welfare and, at a time when councils in the distressed industrial areas of the north of England were desperately trying to maintain provision of services, was determined to reduce both state benefits and central subsidies for local councils. The main instrument of government policy in this period was the 1984 Rates Act, which enabled the government in Westminster to set limits (known as 'rate capping') on local authority spending and to take legal sanctions against individual councillors who refused to comply. Outside of London, all the councils that declared their intention to maintain social service spending despite the new legislation were in areas devastated by the damaging effects of government policy.

It was against this background that in the 1980s Sheffield City Council, and by extension the city and region as a whole, gained the popular epithet 'People's (or socialist) Republic of South Yorkshire'. The exact origin of the tag is uncertain, though it was possibly first voiced by Irvine Patnick, leader of the South Yorkshire Conservatives and subsequently MP for Sheffield Hallam. Those who used it as a slur saw its most obvious expressions in actions such as the council's declaration of Sheffield as a nuclear-free zone in November 1980 and, most notoriously, in the flying of the red flag over the Town Hall on May Day 1981 in honour of International Workers Day. For those who proudly accepted the description, it was the reflection of a legitimate struggle for local justice and democracy that had its roots deep in Sheffield's past.

Sheffield's response to the economic and social crisis of the 1980s coincided with the emergence of a new, more outward-looking element within the Sheffield Labour movement based around a group of councillors in the Brightside ward known as the New Urban Left. The group had come to promi-nence following the opportunities presented by the creation of the South Yorkshire authority in 1974 and, under the leadership of the charismatic David Blunkett, attained dominance in the local Labour Party. Blunkett, who grew up on one of the city's working-class estates, was an advocate of decentralisation and community politics very much in the mould of nineteenth-century reform-ers such as Isaac Ironside. However, although Blunkett's individual reputation was forged not only by his role in local politics, but as a minister in the later Blair government, he was just one member of a very able group of Labour councillors at local level. This group, in contrast to the contemporary Militant activists in Liverpool, were particularly skilled in reconciling rival factions in left-wing politics and thus formed a credible opposition to the increasingly hard-line Conservative government.

Putting People First

In 1978, a joint District Labour Party and city council working party headed by David Blunkett and Clive Betts produced a comprehensive report on the local service needs of vulnerable groups across the city, including the elderly, those with physical and mental disabilities and young people. The report concluded that to provide the support that was desperately needed, the people of Sheffield would need to pay higher rates. In return, the report's authors pledged that the city's social provision would be the best in the country. As the decimation of local industry continued, and the number of unemployed continued to rise,

Sheffield council was determined to maintain the city's strong tradition in the provision of local services that had been established in the 1930s. Significant expenditure was directed towards the poorest areas and, as just one of the outward expressions of the community-centred ethos of Blunkett's group, council tenants were included in the development of housing policy.

Determined to maintain Sheffield's reputation for far-sighted local social policies, the council pressed ahead with initiatives such as cheap bus travel (a flat 2p fare for any journey within the South Yorkshire boundaries) and led a national campaign against rate capping. In the area of industrial strategy they provided direct assistance, mainly in the form of research, to the steel unions fighting to maintain production levels in Sheffield, encouraged the formation of workers' co-operatives and set up training schemes for redundant workers. From 1981, a rapid reduction in central government contributions to council finances meant that, in order to maintain current levels of service provision, Sheffield's business rates would need to be raised by almost 60 per cent. In response, the government declared its intention to enforce the new legislation and the stage was set for confrontation between Sheffield council and the Thatcher administration.

Protest

Against this background, the 1980 steel strike and 1984 miners' strike became emblematic of the confrontation, and the New Urban Left group increasingly positioned Sheffield as 'an example of what we could do as a socialist government at national level'. Directing much of their effort into making the local authority a model employer, Blunkett and his allies increasingly envisaged Sheffield as a beacon of resistance to the Thatcherite ideology that was transforming Britain from the post-war political consensus that favoured social welfare into a country based on free-market principles and American-style individualism.

In 1981 the council refused to allow Sheffield to be made into one of the government's new Enterprise Zones intended to introduce free-market principles to local economies and, in a decision that did not go unopposed, cut the local business community out of discussions of the future economic development of the city. The conflict between two distinct and opposite views of what type of Britain would emerge from the economic upheavals of the late 1970s and '80s came to a symbolic head with popular demonstrations against Margaret Thatcher's visit to Sheffield in April 1983. Local business leaders were becoming increasingly unhappy both at the council's anti-business stance and the destructive effects of the government's anti-industrial policies. It was arguably in this context, rather than as a statement of outright support, that the Cutlers' Company invited the Prime Minister to their annual feast. On arrival at Cutlers' Hall, Thatcher was met by a noisy demonstration of some 6,000 people. In the face of such protest, the Prime Minister was smuggled quickly into the Hall before most in the crowd realised she was there.

Inside the Hall, almost all the after-dinner speakers referred to the disastrous effect of Tory policies on the local steel industry, though the hardening opinions both for and against her regime were reflected in the fact that a significant number of those present gave Mrs Thatcher a standing ovation. Nevertheless, in its reporting of the event the *Sheffield Star* noted that at the very least, there must be a public image problem if the Prime Minister needed 1,000 police officers to provide protection during a visit to a provincial English city. Certainly, from this point on, Sheffield's once-significant Conservative group started to lose support rapidly, so that by the 1990s they were no longer the main opposition to Labour in Sheffield.

Conflict

A national rally against rate capping was held in Sheffield on 6 March 1984, and the next day the council set a budget over the government limit, declining to set a rate. Later in the month it passed a resolution explaining that it would not set a rate until it knew the outcome of a judicial review that was to be held on 12 April at the behest of Greenwich borough council in London. A further meeting on 24 April again postponed setting a rate. By the beginning of May cracks began to appear in the campaign at leadership level, as both Blunkett and his deputy Alan Billings acknowledged the full risks of their stance.

At a crucial council meeting on 7 May, the leadership put forward a motion that refused to set a rate until the government was prepared to negotiate, a position that it was understood would provoke immediate legal action. In the event, during the course of a five-hour meeting, twenty Labour councillors voted with the Liberal and Conservative groups on the council to set a rate within the capped limit. Ultimately, Blunkett's campaign had failed, though his national reputation was enhanced by the principled stand he had taken. However, the main significance of the crisis is that for local authorities such as Sheffield, which had to deal with the financial implications of mass unemployment, the socially destructive effects of government interference in local authority spending were to be felt for decades to come.

The years during which the 'rate-capping crisis' was coming to a head were ones when Sheffield was at the forefront of confrontations between local and national government, with the city's councillors giving tacit support. The most prominent examples were the steel strike of 1980 and miners' strike of 1984–85, when mass pickets confronted management at the Hadfield works in Sheffield's East End and British Steel's Orgreave coking plant on the border between Sheffield and Rotherham. On the latter occasion events escalated following the government's decision to draft large numbers of police from forces outside the region, with the intention of staging a set-piece confrontation aimed at bringing the tactic of mass-picketing to an end.

The inevitable conflict came to a head with the events of the so-called 'Battle of Orgreave' of 18 June 1984. In the course of one of the most violent clashes in British industrial history, 6,000 police officers from eighteen different forces, equipped with riot gear and supported by police dogs and forty-two mounted officers, corralled the pickets, estimated to number around 8,000, into a field overlooking the coke works. Officers with riot shields were positioned at the bottom of the field and mounted police and dogs on either side. At the moment the pickets surged forward to meet the first convoy of vehicles bringing coal to the plant, the officer in charge of operations, South Yorkshire Police Assistant Chief Constable Anthony Clement, ordered a mounted charge. According to official figures, which are disputed, fifty-one pickets were injured in the subsequent struggle and seventy-two police officers.

In a direct echo of government tactics going right back to the Peterloo Massacre of 1819, official reports blamed the violence on the pickets for throwing bricks and stones, to which act of aggression the police had no choice but to respond. In support of the establishment line, BBC news bulletins were edited to suggest that the charge by mounted police came after the throwing of missiles, but even supporters of Margaret Thatcher's industrial policies were shocked at the sight of mounted officers charging into lines of demonstrators, recalling images of the infamous events in Manchester more than 150 years earlier. Two more mounted advances were ordered by Clement, followed by a third supported by 'short-shield snatch squads' whose tactic was to deliver quick-fire rounds of baton beatings to the unprotected pickets. By the time a final charge was ordered, the majority of pickets had fled the scene and were pursued into Orgreave village, where Clement ordered a 'mounted police canter' described by historian Tristram Hunt as an 'out-of-control police force [attacking] pickets and onlookers alike on terraced British streets'.

In the following weeks, ninety-five pickets were charged with riot, unlawful assembly, violent disorder and related offences. However, all the subsequent trials collapsed due to lack of evidence, all charges were dropped, and a number of lawsuits were brought against the police for assault, unlawful arrest and malicious prosecution. South Yorkshire Police (SYP) later agreed to pay £425,000 in compensation and £100,000 legal costs to thirty-nine pickets in an out-of-court settlement. No police officers ever faced disciplinary charges. Following the end of the miners' strike, chief constables of police forces that had been involved were invited to drinks at the Home Office and congratulated by senior government figures on their part in 'defeating' the miners and unions.

Despite government refusal to hold a formal inquiry into police tactics at Orgreave, there was widespread criticism of the system whereby officers who made arrests were not held responsible for their 'prisoners' or required to write out statements detailing the arrest, but instead handed them over to a holding station and then returned to action. At the end of the operation they were simply required to sign pre-prepared statements written by other officers not involved in the arrest. Officers had also been instructed not to write anything in their pocketbooks. All of these actions were contrary to established police procedure, and these and other significant changes in the culture of British policing were to come back to haunt SYP, not to mention relatives of the victims, in the aftermath of the events of the Hillsborough Disaster in 1989.

The site of Orgreave coking plant, focus of the infamous Battle of Orgreave and now the location of the Advanced Manufacturing Research Centre and Waverley housing development.

A notable aspect of the miners' strike of 1984–85 was the prominent role played by women. Taking leadership from miners' wives, large numbers of local women found their voice politically through their defence of jobs and the fight for the survival of their communities. Although a core of the membership of Sheffield Women Against Pit Closures (SWAPC) had connections with the Communist Party of Great Britain and other established affiliations, many women were becoming involved in political struggle for the first time in 1984. As well as joining the picket lines themselves, members of SWAPC addressed public meetings, organised demonstrations and raised funds in support of the cause. During the course of the strike the Sheffield committee raised more than £100,000, used mainly to supply food parcels and clothing to the families of striking miners. This work was formally recognised by the leadership of the Trades Union Congress, which was of the belief that the strike could not have lasted so long without the involvement of highly organised groups of women. An important legacy of the strike was the empowerment of women in working-class communities like Sheffield and the confidence it gave them to take part in, and lead, direct political action at both the local and national level.

The Hillsborough Disaster

The death of ninety-six football supporters, and injury to a further 766, at the Hillsborough football stadium on 15 April 1989 was the worst disaster in the history of British spectator sport. Shortly before the kick-off of the FA Cup semi-final match between Liverpool and Nottingham Forest, in an apparent attempt to ease overcrowding at the entrance turnstiles at the Leppings Lane end of the ground, the senior policeman in charge of crowd safety, Chief Superintendent David Duckenfield, ordered an exit gate to be opened, leading to a surge of even more supporters into the already crowded holding pens.

Over the following days and weeks, senior police officers fed fabricated versions of events to the media, in particular suggesting that the main cause of the tragedy was drunken and thuggish behaviour by Liverpool support-ers. Despite the fact that the Taylor Report into the disaster that reported in the following year found that the main cause of the events was a failure by the police to control the situation, the blaming of Liverpool supporters per-sisted. In his summing up, Lord Justice Taylor described senior SYP officers as 'defensive and evasive witnesses' who refused to accept any responsibility for their actions. However, in response to the report, the Director of Public Prosecutions ruled that there was insufficient evidence to justify prosecu-

Leppings Lane stand, Hillsborough stadium.

tion of any individuals or institutions. In terms of general safety at football grounds, the Taylor Report led to a number of improvements, most notably the elimination of standing terraces where groups of supporters were fenced in pens, in favour of all-seater stadiums at the top levels of English football.

The first coroner's inquests into the deaths that were released in 1991 ruled that all the casualties were accidental. This led to concerted action by the families of the victims, who rejected the findings and commenced a campaign to have the case reopened. However, a second report in 1997, by Lord Justice Stuart-Smith, came to the conclusion that there was no justification for a new enquiry. In response to this setback, private prosecutions were brought by the Hillsborough Families Support Group against Chief Superintendent Duckenfield and his deputy Bernard Murray in 2000, though these again failed.

As a result of continued campaigning by the group, a Hillsborough Independent Panel was formed in 2009 to undertake a fresh review of the evidence. This resulted in the previous findings of accidental death being overturned, and the commencement of new coroner's inquests. In 2012 the panel concluded that 164 witness statements produced by the police had been altered after the event. Of these, 116 were amended to remove or modify negative comments about South Yorkshire Police. The report also concluded that the then Conservative MP for Sheffield Hallam, Irvine Patnick, had passed inaccurate and false information from senior police officers to the press.

The second coroner's inquest, held from April 2014 to April 2016, ruled that the victims were unlawfully killed due to gross negligence on behalf of police and emergency services in fulfilling their duty of care. The inquest also found that design flaws and irregularities in safety certificates at the Hillsborough stadium had contributed to the initial crush. Public anger at the actions of the SYP in the aftermath of the verdict led to the suspension of Chief Constable David Crompton. In June 2017, six people were charged with various offences including manslaughter by gross negligence, misconduct in public office and perverting the course of justice for their actions during and after the disaster, though the Crown Prosecution Service subsequently dropped all charges against one of the defendants. On 25 June 2019, it was announced that David Duckenfield would be subject to a retrial, scheduled to start on 7 October at Preston Crown Court. On 28 November he was found not guilty of a charge of gross negligence manslaughter.

Cutting the Social Fabric

Inevitably, the city's much-praised system of social provision was to suffer from the cuts imposed by central government restrictions on local spending. The council house building programme came to an abrupt halt, and repairs and renovations to existing stock were no longer carried out. As a result of the government's council house purchase scheme, those council tenants either unemployed or on the lowest incomes who could not afford to buy found themselves dependent for survival on state benefits. Old people's and children's homes were closed, the home-help scheme was much reduced, and retiring social workers were not replaced.

In the area of education, in which Sheffield had been a leader of post-war developments, the school building programme was brought to an end and maintenance of existing buildings was curtailed significantly. Teachers and equipment were not replaced and class sizes were increased. Specialist provision, such as music teaching, which had been a flagship of the Sheffield system, was reduced and significant cuts were made to further education provision. Leisure and recreation facilities were restricted, charges increased, local libraries closed and for those that remained, book-purchasing budgets were slashed and opening hours reduced.

In 1989, after almost a decade of cuts to social spending, the council produced an update of its study of poverty in the city, first conducted in 1983.

This concluded that deprivation had increased markedly, the number of home-less people was five times higher, and economic disparities across the city had widened. By the end of a decade of rising unemployment, one in five households in Sheffield were dependent on income support, with the greatest proportion (41 per cent) being in the traditional working-class district of Burngreave.

For Sheffield, a city in which the quality of life of its citizens had improved considerably since the end of the Second World War, the 1980s had been a dis-aster. In the early 1970s it was a city with an impressive social fabric and notable strengths in schools, community health provision, transport, libraries and parks. Twenty years later, the quality of life – whether measured by the availability of public transport, traffic congestion, school buildings and educational provision, or the number and quality of old peoples' homes – had deteriorated significantly. As Sheffield marked its centenary as a city in 1993, the challenge faced by its leaders was how to rebuild its shattered economy and to restore the bonds of community that had been one of its greatest strengths since its foundation among the hills and streams of Hallamshire a millennium earlier.

Coming Up for Air

Economic Regeneration

Faced with the reality of a drastically reduced budget, Sheffield councillors had little choice but to move, albeit reluctantly, in the direction of business-led reconstruction favoured by the government. The first concrete result of this change of policy was the Sheffield Economic Regeneration Committee (SERC), established in December 1986 with the aim of regenerating the Lower Don Valley in a collaboration between the public and private sectors. The council's original intention had been to restore manufacturing to the area, stimulated by the creation of an 'employment zone'. Unlike the government's preferred 'enterprise zone', this would have been led by public sector initiatives such as the workers' co-operatives the council had set up in the early 1980s. In addition, it had recommended the building of new housing as a central element of the physical and environmental regeneration of the historic former heavy steel and engineering sector of the city.

However, by 1986, in the face of diminishing central funding, the council effectively gave in to the government's preferred public–private initiative (PPI) model, as evidenced by the abandonment of its previous policy of prohibiting

A sculpture by Robin Bell commemorating Sheffield's traditional crucible steel teams, Meadowhall Shopping Centre.

the development of out-of-town shopping centres. In a landmark change of direction, approval was given to the redevelopment of the former Hadfield's East Hecla steelworks as the Meadowhall shopping centre. When it opened on 4 September 1990, Meadowhall was the second largest shopping centre in the UK with more than 280 retail units. It was undoubtedly aided in its ascendancy by the construction of the adjacent transport interchange, making it the only large-scale retail outlet in the country to include a bus, rail and tram hub, so that it was accessible to a large region beyond the immediate Sheffield area. As such, it was not long before it was widely blamed for the large-scale closure of shops in both Sheffield and Rotherham town centres.

In 1986 the short-lived South Yorkshire Council was abolished by the government, which, expressing alarm at the amount of public funds that had been spent on the much-vaunted cheap fares policy, put a cap on the new transport authority's spending as part of its drive to privatise local authority-run bus services across the country. By 1988, the city council had given up further ground to central government by allowing the establishment of the Sheffield Development Corporation with powers to provide services and acquire, manage and dispose of land over much of the former industrial area of the Lower Don Valley. The underlying principle behind these new bodies was the government's conviction that economic regeneration would be more effectively stimulated by business than by local government. An equally significant development was the report by a council working party that recommended a diversification of the city's economic base to be led by developments in the leisure, tourism and technology sectors.

In these areas, the city council took the lead with a number of ambitious initiatives, including a bid to host the World Student Games in 1991, a new light rail tram system ('Supertram') that started operation in 1994, a city airport in the Tinsley Park area close to the M1 aimed at the business sector, and a science park on former industrial land near the railway station. A key element in the Student Games initiative was the construction of the Don Valley Stadium, which was earmarked as the flagship development of the regenerated former industrial East End of the city. Although the games proved successful as a sporting event, and the city attracted praise for its decision to refurbish some of the vacant Hyde Park flats as the athletes' village, in terms of finance and project management there was a good deal of criticism. Despite the significant boost to the city's self-image in terms of visitor numbers, the event ended up with an operating loss of some £10 million and much recrimination between all the parties involved that lasted beyond the end of the twentieth century. At the local level, much of the criticism centred on the question of whether the acquisition of a small number of top-class sporting venues was worth the loss of numerous community facilities, such as sports pitches, that followed from the council's inevitable sale of assets. Sheffield City Airport, too, failed to thrive. Opening just at the beginning of the low-cost air travel revolution, its short-hop business flight model was soon obsolete. The last scheduled airline pulled out in 2002 and the facility closed completely six years later. The city did manage to regain some civic pride in this period, however, when in 1991 Sheffielder Helen Sharman became Britain's first astronaut and the first western European woman to go into space.

As for Sheffield's once-famous steel industry, this presented two faces to the world at the end of the twentieth century. The immediate impression was one of catastrophic decline, with steel-making long since absent from its roots in the city centre and Neepsend, and the later industrial heartlands of Attercliffe and Brightside a scene of apocalyptic devastation. However, less obvious was the fact that the Sheffield region was at this time home to some of the most technologically advanced and productive steel melting facilities in the world, based in three main centres of Stocksbridge, Rotherham and Tinsley (Shepcote Lane).

Indeed, the region was now producing more steel than it had during the Second World War and the early 1950s, with the two massive electric fur-

Ponds Forge aquatic centre, constructed for the World Student Games on the site of the former steelworks of George Senior & Sons Ltd.

naces at Stocksbridge alone having a combined capacity of some 250 tonnes. Special steels were starting to find new applications in the aerospace and nuclear power industries, and at the same time stainless steel had found new mass markets, from the massive scale of offshore oil platforms to the micro level of beer kegs and cans. But while in one sense business was booming, the outer face of Sheffield was heavily scarred. In large part this was because the great bulk of this modern steel production was automated. To protect jobs, generations of Sheffielders had resisted mechanisation; now the future was there for them to see – a productive steel industry that no longer needed them.

The Devastation of the 1980s on Screen

At the height of the Cold War, and as Sheffield plunged into the mass unemployment of the 1980s, the city found itself on the map as the location for the TV drama *Threads* (1984), Barry Hines' dramatic exploration of the social, environmental and economic consequences of a potential nuclear conflict. Based around an imagined 1-megaton strike on the South Yorkshire capital, the programme was broadcast on BBC TV on 23 September 1984 and attracted almost 7 million viewers. With its brutal realism, the film sent shockwaves throughout the country, and brought the anti-nuclear proliferation movement into sharp focus, not only in the UK but, arguably, around the world.

In the mid-1990s, two British films highlighted aspects of the economic and social disintegration of the South Yorkshire region that had begun ten years previously. The comedy drama *Brassed Off* (1996) focused on the challenges faced by a colliery brass band following the closure of their pit. The final winding up of the coal industry in the wake of the 1984–85 miners' strike made little impression on the country as a whole, but devastated regions such as South Yorkshire. The drama was based on the real-life struggle of the Grimethorpe colliery band, which provided the soundtrack for the film. Within a darkly comic setting, the film dealt with the hopelessness faced by once-proud working-class communities (in a particularly shocking scene, one of the characters tries to hang himself while wearing the clown costume in which he attempts to scrape a living as a children's entertainer) and the resulting fight-back, led largely by miners' wives.

In the guise of a light-hearted comedy romp, *The Full Monty* (1997) can be seen as a subtle exploration of themes of masculine identity as a metaphor for a failing heavy industrial city experiencing mass unemployment, and with it the first generation of working-class men to question their role within society. Unemployment, fathers' rights, depression, impotence, homosexuality, body image, working-class culture and suicide are among the themes explored in this bittersweet tale of six unemployed men, four of them former steelworkers, who decide to form a striptease act both to relieve their boredom and make some money. The film was a major critical and commercial success on its release and at the time was the highest-grossing film ever in the UK.

Reshaping the City Centre

Away from the East End, redevelopment projects of the 1990s and new millennium that focused on the city centre generally had the twin aims of providing up-to-date facilities while preserving the city's industrial heritage. One of the first areas to receive attention was the former Sheffield Canal Basin, which had been completed in 1819 as the terminus of the Sheffield canal and included the Grade II listed Terminal Warehouse from that date, as well as other storage facilities and a crescent terrace of coal merchants' offices from the later nineteenth century. The basin had ceased operation as a cargo port in 1970, and the area was largely neglected until restoration and redevelopment commenced in 1992 to provide new office and business space, small retail outlets and berths

Section of the Five Weirs Walk at Spider Bridge.

for leisure boats, rebranding as 'Victoria Quays'. A parallel project, aimed at reclaiming former industrial land on the banks of the River Don and the canal, led to the creation of long-distance urban pedestrian routes such as the Five Weirs Walk, linking Sheffield city centre to Meadowhall and Rotherham.

From 1998, regeneration of the city centre became a key council policy, and in February 2000 the government set up an Urban Regeneration Company known as 'Sheffield One' to help put plans into action. Its initial report highlighted the fact that the city centre was falling behind developments in its main regional rivals, Leeds and Manchester, as well as increasingly losing ground to Meadowhall. However, progress was slow and the city centre retail scheme known as 'Sevenstone' was put on ice as a result of the global financial crash of 2008, and eventually killed off altogether by the withdrawal of the main investor in 2013.

In terms of civic identity, the council's flagship project, known as 'Heart of the City', was launched in 2004 and its first phase completed in 2016. First to receive attention was the Peace Gardens that had originally been laid out in 1938, following the controversial demolition of the historic St Paul's Church. Originally named St Paul's Gardens, the public space was given its present name in 1985 as part of the council's stance against the nuclear arms race. In 1997 work commenced on remodelling the gardens with water channels representing the rivers of Sheffield. The second phase followed the demolition of the Town Hall Extension in 2002 and included monumental water features representing both Sheffield's industrial rivers and the city's economic foundation based on the working of molten metal. Opened in 2004, the city council took the decision to name these the 'Holberry Cascades' in commemoration of Sheffield's revolutionary hero of the Chartist period. A combined project on the site of the former Town Hall Extension saw the creation of the Millennium Gallery which opened in 2001 and, as well as displaying the Ruskin collection (originally housed in his own St George's Museum in Walkley), holds what is probably the most extensive collection of Sheffield metalwork ever to have been assembled. The other part of the project saw the construction of the imaginative Winter Garden, opened by the Queen in May 2003 and home to more than 2,000 plants from around the world.

For much of the two decades between 1990 and 2010, redevelopment of the inner-city landscape and preservation of its industrial heritage went hand-in-hand, with commercial archaeological teams working with architects and planners. A good deal of valuable information about Sheffield's industrial past emerged during the construction of new stretches of the inner ring road from 1999 and residential developments such as Riverside and Millsands that took place at the same time. The involvement of skilled archaeological teams ensured sympathetic restorations of important industrial sites such as Cornish Place and Butchers Wheel. The Cornish Place site, formerly the premises of James Dixon & Sons, is generally regarded as the most impressive cutlery works still

The Winter Garden, opened in 2003 on the site of the Town Hall Extension known popularly as 'the egg boxes'.

Former cutlery works at Cornish Place, one of a number of industrial buildings renovated for residential use from the late 1990s.

surviving in Sheffield, rivalling the Lancashire textile mills in terms of architectural quality and heritage value. From 1998 the building was cleared, cleaned and converted into apartments. The restoration and remodelling of Butchers Wheel, a significant former cutlery and tool works near the city centre, was completed in 2007, and as well as apartments included workshops, a gallery and café. Both of these developments allowed generations who had grown up in a post-industrial Sheffield to gain some impression of the layout of integrated cutlery works at the height of the city's prosperity.

A City of Sport

Some relief from the gloom of the 1980s came in the field of sport. This had already begun with the staging of the World Snooker Championships at the Crucible Theatre from 1977, which from that time onwards firmly associated Sheffield with the sport. The relative success enjoyed by Sheffield Wednesday FC under their manager Ron Atkinson in winning the League Cup in 1991, the club's first trophy in fifty years, brought a sense of cheer to much, if not all, of the city. As at 2020, this was the last time a team from outside the top flight of English football was to win one of its major trophies. To add to the triumph, Wednesday achieved promotion to the First Division in the same year. Under the management of Trevor Francis, in the 1992–93 season the club visited Wembley four times for a League Cup final, an FA Cup semi-final, final and replay. In the FA Cup semi-final they recorded a historic 2–1 win over their rivals Sheffield United, an encounter that generated real excitement across the city. However, Wednesday failed to win either competition, losing to Arsenal in both League and FA Cup finals.

A professional sport that seemed to epitomise Sheffield as a working-class city fighting back against adversity was boxing. Of particular significance was the gym presided over by Irish-born trainer Brendan Ingle in the deprived Wincobank area of the city. First to emerge to national prominence was the middleweight Herol 'Bomber' Graham, a popular figure in the 1980s, followed by 'Prince' Naseem Hamed, a Sheffielder of Yemeni heritage, who fought at bantam and featherweight levels, winning the WBO featherweight title in 1997. Hamed was later to prove the inspiration for Kell Brook, who emerged from the same gym and held the IBF welterweight title from 2014 to 2017.

In 1982, the city obtained its first new professional sports team for many years in the form of the Sheffield Eagles rugby league club. Following stints at the Owlerton Stadium and Bramall Lane, the Eagles became established at the Don Valley Stadium following its opening in 1991. After changes of ownership, the club was refounded in 2000 and played again at Don Valley Stadium from 2012 until the facility's demolition in 2013 (see below). In recent years they have been playing at the Olympic Legacy Park on the site of the demolished stadium. Another new sports franchise that benefited from the facilities constructed for the World Student Games was the Sheffield Steelers ice hockey club, formed in 1991 at the time of the opening of the Sheffield Arena.

Following the landmark action of the Kinder Mass Trespass of 1932, in the 1950s and '60s Sheffield started on its path to becoming an acknowledged 'outdoor city'. In addition to walking and rambling, it was rock climbing that led the way, following the earlier lead of J.W. Puttrell who, after starting out at Wharncliffe, began to develop climbing routes on the millstone grit (or 'gritstone') edges to the south-west of the city. The big leap forward in the sport came with two working-class young men from the Lancashire side of the Pennines, Joe Brown and Don Whillans, but in the 1970s further technical advances were made by Sheffielders such as John Allen and Steve Bancroft, as well as their fellow Yorkshireman Ron Fawcett.

To date, perhaps the most ambitious attempt to harness local enthusiasm for outdoor pursuits was in the construction of an artificial ski slope in the Parkwood Springs area of the city in 1988. The facility proved immediately popular; by the end of 1990 it had eight slopes and over the next five years underwent a significant redesign including the addition of a ski lodge, bar and shops, as well as specialist features for use in freestyle skiing and snowboarding. By then it was believed to have been the largest artificial ski slope In Europe. A number of winter sports professionals first developed their skills at the so-called 'Sheffield Ski Village' and there was much sadness in the city and wider region when a number of major fires, both deliberate and accidental, destroyed the facilities in 2012. In January 2019, Sheffield City Council agreed a loan of just under £5 million towards a scheme for redeveloping the site as an extreme sports centre.

A Post-Industrial City

The Early Twenty-First-Century Economy

After a slow start, the regeneration schemes put in place from the late 1980s started to bear fruit. Indeed, in 2008, by which time they had been under way for some twenty years, Sheffield was ranked among the top ten UK cities as a business location, with initiatives aimed mainly at the modern technology and sports sectors. The global financial crash of the same year therefore came just as the city's regeneration was becoming embedded, and flagship schemes such as the Victoria Quays canal-side redevelopment and the projected city centre retail quarter came to a halt. From 2010, the austerity programme implemented by the Conservative and Liberal Democrat coalition government in response to the crash meant that many of the plans that had been made for the city in the 1990s had to be re-evaluated. For a number of years, Sheffield struggled to attract significant inward investment and many redevelopment schemes were shelved, or abandoned altogether. Since 2010, the context within which Sheffield has attempted to rebuild itself has once again been economic recession, and a government polity of financial austerity led by cuts in public services that disproportionately affected the former industrial cities of the north of England.

In 2012, in an attempt to keep the worst effects of recession at bay, the Sheffield City Region Enterprise Zone was established to promote regeneration in a number of areas of the city and its wider region. By 2018 these efforts were beginning to pay off, with the Advanced Manufacturing Research Centre (AMRC) – a joint enterprise between the University of Sheffield and companies including Boeing and McLaren on the site of the former Orgreave coking plant – leading the way. In early 2021 it was announced that the

University had collaborated in a management buyout of Castings Technology International, a world-leading provider of technology to the cast metals sector. The reconstituted company was scheduled to operate from purpose-built premises at the AMRC.

At the same time, the council launched its 'Heart of the City II' project, channelling some £500 million of investment into a revised version of the abandoned Sheffield Retail Quarter scheme. Partly in response to the general downturn in high street retail profits in the face of increased online shopping, the new plans placed greater emphasis on office space and residential accommodation and included new offices for HSBC, one of the city's largest private sector employers. Redevelopment of the adjacent site of the Moor included a new flagship cinema, shops and restaurants to add to the indoor market that had replaced the old Castle Markets in 2013. One project that just managed to survive the 2008 crash was St Paul's Tower, a thirty-two-storey residential block that, when it was completed in April 2011, took over from the University's Arts Tower to become the tallest building in Sheffield.

As for the steel industry, after the original revival of the 1990s this struggled to keep afloat amid increasingly volatile global markets and, in particular, the rise of China as a major steel producer. The guarded optimism of the 1990s was severely dented by the fallout from the financial crisis of 2008 and in its worst year, 2015, the UK steel industry lost 4,000 jobs in just three months – though fortunately for Sheffield, the majority of these were in the other steel heartlands of the North-east and Scotland. In view of the undoubted importance of steel manufacture to the continuing viability of Britain's industrial base, there was widespread criticism of the government for not intervening in what it viewed as the commercial decisions of private companies in the face of the massive dumping of cut-price Chinese steel on the UK market.

By this time, large-scale steel interests in Sheffield and its region were in the hands of foreign owners. BSC Stainless, the former flagship of the nationalised industry, became part of the Swedish Avesta group in 1991, and ten years later merged with the Finnish conglomerate Outokumpu to form the largest stainless steel company in the world. In 2005 much of the Shepcote Lane plant in the historic Tinsley steel-making area, home of the world-famous 'Staybrite' brand, was closed with the loss of more than 500 jobs. Three years later the former Stocksbridge plant of Samuel Fox & Co. was also shut down, with operations moving to Outokumpu's Meadowhall site. In February 2020 the company announced that it was considering the cessation of its Sheffield operations, leaving not just a further 500 jobs but the very survival of the city's most famous product in doubt.

In the special steels sector, major capacity in Stocksbridge and Rotherham that had been acquired by the Indian Tata group was taken over by the British–Indian Liberty House company in 2017 as part of the creation of Liberty Steel UK. Initially, the future for steel-making in both these areas looked bright, as Liberty recommissioned mothballed plant for the production of high-value steels to be used in the automotive, aerospace and energy sectors. At the same time, Liberty's owner, Sanjeev Gupta, announced that by massive conversion of plant for the use of recycled material, Liberty Steel would aim to be the world's first carbon-neutral company by 2030. However, in January 2020 the company announced the axing of 250 jobs at the Stocksbridge plant while attempting to soften the news with the confirmation that some 1,500 jobs would remain in the South Yorkshire region as a whole. By the end of the year, Gupta's entire business dealings had come under the spotlight and the Stocksbridge steel operations faced an uncertain future.

Perhaps surprisingly, the sole survivor in Sheffield's once-famous heavy castings and forgings sector, Sheffield Forgemasters, continued in business, like its predecessor Vickers, due to a close association with the country's defence industry. Under threat of significant redundancies in 2016, the company managed to secure a £30 million loan from US bank Wells Fargo, underwritten by the companies responsible for supplying the UK's Trident nuclear submarine programme in view of Forgemasters' vital role in supplying nuclear reactor casings. At the same time, the company secured £6.5 million of investment from Sheffield City Region Local Enterprise Partnership. Together, this investment enabled the company to construct plant capable of pouring the largest single steel casting in Europe, an achievement that recalled memories of the golden age of Sheffield's heavy industrial past.

Sheffield Forgemasters: An Industrial Survivor

By the early twenty-first century, the city's single remaining big independent steel producer was Sheffield Forgemasters. The company could trace its origins back to the Sheffield miller Edward Vickers, who moved into the metal-working trade in 1805, making it possibly the oldest surviving steel business in the world. By the 1850s, the Vickers company was producing the largest steel castings in the world and the company expanded further with the adoption of the Bessemer process and the establishment of the enormous River

Don Works in the 1860s, which within ten years had become one of the largest steel engineering works in the world.

Sheffield Forgemasters came into being in 1983 through the amalgamation of Firth Brown with the BSC's River Don Works. The following year, in the face of huge losses, the shareholders fired the board and brought in new management with a survival plan. With the BSC due for privatisation in 1987, Forgemasters agreed to a management buyout. In the next ten years the company bucked the trend of the local steel industry and saw a significant return to profit, largely on the back of expanding export markets. However, the company's reputation was dented due to its role in the 'Iraqi Supergun' affair, when customs officials in Middlesbrough seized parts of what were believed to be a massive weapon on a ship bound for the regime of Saddam Hussein in Iraq. In their defence, Forgemasters claimed they had been told the castings were to be used in a petrochemical project.

In 1998 the company was sold in two parts to American buyers, who failed to develop the business and it went into liquidation in 2003. Soon afterwards, the River Don plant experienced another significant turnaround in business, which prompted a second management buyout in 2005. In March 2010, the company secured an £80 million loan from the Labour government, enabling it to install a 15,000-tonne press for making massive civil nuclear forgings. Despite the fact that a few months later the incoming coalition government withdrew the loan, the company was able to survive through increased diversification.

Continuing the tradition that Vickers had established in the construction of battleships at its shipyard in Barrow, the company developed expertise in critical components for Britain's nuclear submarine fleet in addition to specialist products for the civil nuclear, energy exploration, power generation and marine sectors. Through its apprentice system and lifelong training programmes for employees, Sheffield Forgemasters can be said to have rekindled old-established Sheffield traditions based on a highly skilled workforce.

At the smaller end of Sheffield's original industry, remnants of the skilled cutlery trade managed to survive the ravages of the 1970s to '90s to supply the market for quality handmade products. One of the most famous names from Sheffield's past, the Taylors Eyewitness trademark established in 1838 by John Taylor, was bought in 1975 by Harrison Fisher & Co., which continued to use the brand and in 2007 changed its name to Taylors Eyewitness Ltd. Until 2018, the business was still based in the Eyewitness Works on Milton Street, one of the biggest industrial complexes to have been constructed when the steel and cutlery industries made the transition from water to steam power in the 1850s. As the company continued to thrive, particularly in the export market, it moved to new, more suitable premises on the outskirts of the city.

Another success story has been Arthur Wright & Son Ltd, formed in 1947 to make traditional Sheffield penknives and pocket knives, as well as scissors. The company continued to make all its pocket knives by hand, using traditional methods passed on through apprenticeship, with every part of the process – from blanking out of blades to the final polish – carried out in-house. Similarly, scissors manufacturer Ernest Wright, founded in 1902 but taken into receivership in 1988, was able to re-establish itself from 2014, largely on the back of a documentary film that enjoyed significant online popularity. Another Sheffield firm that has seen recent success through the combination of historical methods and modern technology is HD Sports. The company claims a 330-year history, based on descent from the skate blades made by the toolmaker John Wilson from 1696, which included a royal appointment to King William III. It is now the world's leading manufacturer of figure skating blades under the John Wilson brand.

A traditional Sheffield industry that has witnessed a revival on the smaller scale is brewing. In the nineteenth century, Sheffield had been home to about thirty breweries, the last of which closed in the 1990s. From this time, the fashion for real ale stimulated the development of a thriving microbrewery sector. One of

A rare survivor of a Georgian house in the city centre, in Charles Street, currently home to A. Wright & Son, traditional cutlers.

the pioneers was the Kelham Island Brewery, which commenced operations in 1990 in the beer garden of the newly opened Fat Cat pub. It was the first new independent brewery in Sheffield for over a century. Into the twenty-first century, the continuing interest in craft beers stimulated further entries into the sector, which by 2018 included around fifteen independent businesses.

Despite the continuing survival of both large- and small-scale manufacturing, by the second decade of the twenty-first century, Sheffield had transformed into an essentially post-industrial city. By this time the largest employers were all public sector services, with the two universities, hospitals and local government heading the list. A major boost to the local economy came from large numbers of international students, particularly from China, who were estimated to be responsible for some £120 million per year in net economic benefit to the city.

A Diverse Community

Arguably the most land-locked city in the country, by the early twenty-first century, in population terms, Sheffield was no longer the isolated backwater it had once been. Immigration from overseas, which had accelerated in the 1970s, diversified over the following decades. By 2011, 32,400 Sheffielders were of South Asian origin, with the largest sub-groups being from Pakistan and Bangladesh, and with a community centred on the old steel areas of Darnall,

Madina Masjid, confident symbol of the vitality of Sheffield's South Asian community.

Burngreave and Attercliffe, as well as Sharrow and Nether Edge. A visible sign of the growth of Sheffield's South Asian community was the establishment of the Madina Masjid, otherwise known as the Wolseley Road Mosque, in between the Nether Edge and Heeley areas of the city. Since its construction in 2006, the building has been a prominent landmark to the immediate south of the city centre.

The second-largest immigrant community, from Somalia, was also one of the longest-established from that region in the country. The first migrants had arrived in the period between the First and Second World Wars, followed by a second wave attracted by the booming steel industry of the post-war period and 1960s. However, the greatest numbers settled in Sheffield as a result of the civil war and droughts of the 1980s. The Black Caribbean community of just over 9,000 is also one of the largest in the country and since 1986 has been represented by the Sheffield and District African Caribbean Community Association (SADACCA) centre on the Wicker. One of the most recent and fastest-growing ethnic groups in the city is Black African, originating mainly in Zimbabwe, Kenya, Nigeria, Liberia, Burundi, Ethiopia, Eritrea and the Democratic Republic of Congo.

An eastern European population that started with Polish immigrants in the immediate post-war period grew significantly with the post-2004 expansion of the European Community and the arrival of immigrants from Latvia and Slovakia, as well as more from Poland. In addition to having one of the largest populations of Spanish descent in the country, Sheffield's established left-leaning politics is a contributory factor for the presence in the city of former residents of countries such as Chile that have been subject to fascist dictatorship. This tradition was formalised in 2007 when Sheffield declared itself the first UK 'City of Sanctuary' to welcome political asylum seekers and refugees.

Sheffield's ethnic diversity came into sharp focus after 2010, with perceived tensions among the residents of Page Hall, one of the city's poorest areas. Originally a white working-class area of terraced housing built on the estate of the former mansion of the same name, it was settled by families from the Pakistan-controlled part of Kashmir from the 1970s. From 2004, a small number of asylum seekers from the Slovakian and Czech Roma communities, fleeing discrimination and persecution in those regions, were housed in the area. Following the expansion of the European Union in the same year, and the relaxation of some controls on movement, some 6,000 Slovakian Roma arrived in Sheffield within a few years.

Other areas of Sheffield that accommodated Slovakian Roma immigrants included Burngreave, Fir Vale, Tinsley, Darnall, and Firth Park – all among the most economically deprived parts of the city. From 2008, reports began to emerge of tensions in these areas, particularly Page Hall, with much of the blame – including implicitly from the former head of Sheffield City Council, Lord Blunkett – attached to the Roma community for failing to integrate following their moves from impoverished villages in Eastern Europe. Problems were highlighted in a number of lurid stories in both the local and national press and in the Channel 4 series *Keeping up with the Khans* (2016), which focused on the experience of the Roma, asylum seekers from both the Middle East and African countries, and white residents, in the context of the relative increase in prosperity of the earlier Pakistani immigrants.

In the face of growing hostility, a Sheffield Roma Network was set up by members of the community themselves with the aim 'to accelerate the process of bringing the Roma community to a level of maturity and engagement where they can stand equal with other communities in their participation, representation and responsibility in, and to the city of Sheffield'. While acknowledging that there were responsibilities for assimilation on the community itself, the founders of the network, as well as a growing number of social commentators, highlighted the fact that the main problems in these areas stemmed from growing inequality, social and economic deprivation, and poverty, rather than simply inter-community tension. Like many of the challenges faced by Sheffield from the second decade of the twenty-first century, the roots lay in the large-scale withdrawal of public funding to former industrial cities that was initiated under the Thatcher government in the 1980s and continued thereafter. By the same token, solutions to community tensions are likely to be found through the proper funding of social provision in the city's most deprived areas.

Arts, Culture & Entertainment

A positive long-term initiative to arise from the SERC partnership was the establishment of the Cultural Industries Quarter aimed at encouraging the development of music, design and media enterprises on underused sites near the city centre. This also benefited from the fact that Sheffield's Labour council had become involved in support of the local music scene at a much earlier stage than most local authorities. As early as 1972, at the height of the city's post-war manu-facturing boom, the council was funding school holiday music facilities for the city's young people. Such initiatives led in time to a thriving local music scene, with experimental electronic groups including Cabaret Voltaire and The Human League (later to transform into an internationally successful pop act) at the fore-front. By the early 1980s, in an attempt to ameliorate many of the economic and social problems caused by high unemployment, the council's support for music creation developed into the Red Tape Studios, in which it provided recording facilities, rehearsal space and technical instruction for out of work young people.

Red Tape Studios, a cornerstone of Sheffield's civic socialism and late-twentieth-century music scene.

Recent decades have seen significant developments in the artistic and cultural spheres. A number of nationally recognised festivals have been held in the city, starting with the 'Off the Shelf Festival of Words' in 1991, a collaboration between Sheffield City Council and Arts Council England. This went on to become one of the country's largest festivals dedicated to writing and reading, and as well as being a popular addition to Sheffield's cultural calendar, has attracted some of the biggest names in literature and media to the city. The festival also plays an important role in community and outreach provision, especially through its programme of events for children and young people. Established a few years later, Sheffield Doc/Fest is now one of the biggest celebrations of film and television documentaries in the world. The Tramlines festival, first held in 2009, was originally a free event that celebrated mainly local music-making at more than seventy venues around the city over a single weekend. In January 2018 it was announced that the festival would be moving to a permanent home at Hillsborough Park.

Following the prominence of musical groups such as The Human League (in the field of electronica) and Def Leppard (heavy metal), a number of Sheffield acts in various genres have flourished since the 1990s. These include the avant-garde pop group Pulp, formed in 1978 by Jarvis Cocker and fellow pupils of City School that found belated success on the back of the mid-nineties 'Britpop' phenomenon. In the lyrics and vocal style of singer Alex Turner, the Arctic Monkeys, formed in 2002, gave a worldwide voice to the city's dialect, as did the singer-songwriter Richard Hawley, who took much of his inspiration, song and album titles from his native city. As well as becoming an increasingly well-known artist in his own right, Hawley's collaboration with playwright and fellow Sheffielder Chris Bush on her musical *Standing at the Sky's Edge*, which celebrated the life and times of the iconic Park Hill flats, became a major Sheffield event on its premiere at the Crucible Theatre in the spring of 2019. Refurbishment of the flats themselves, which were granted listed building status in 1998, had begun in 2007 under developer Urban Splash, and to some commentators became the most potent symbol of the gentrification of Sheffield's working-class past.

An artist whose work has become particularly associated with Sheffield's attempts to regenerate since the 1990s is Pete McKee, the son of a Sheffield steelworker who grew up on the Jordanthorpe council estate. Thwarted in his ambition to attend art college, and getting a job in a factory instead, McKee nevertheless established himself in later life as a painter and commercial artist

Jarvis Cocker mural, Kelham Island, by Bubba2000.

Site of former Arches nightclub, Wicker.

whose move into the realm of public art includes a number of popular murals around his native city.

Mirroring the popularity of the disco and nightclub scene in Sheffield from the mid-1960s to the late '70s, the city once again became associated with a ground-breaking club scene from the late 1990s. Most fondly remembered by those involved at the time is probably the Arches club, built into the historic railway bridge at the Wicker and which provided a home for many of the

The former National Centre for Popular Music, now home to Sheffield Hallam University Students' Union.

city's 'techno' music fans from the mid-1990s. Better known nationally was the Gatecrasher brand that moved from Birmingham to be hosted at a number of Sheffield venues at around the same time.

However, an attempt to celebrate the new millennium by showcasing Sheffield's historic contributions to the field of popular music failed spectacularly. The Lottery-funded National Centre for Popular Music, which opened its doors in March 1999, had closed them by June of the following year following a failure to attract visitors in any significant numbers. By 2001 the eye-catching building with its four colossal steel drums surrounding a glass-roofed atrium was operating as a live music venue, before being taken over by Sheffield Hallam University in 2003 and going on to serve as that institution's Students' Union.

Urban Revival

Once council regeneration policy had shifted from the services model of the early 1980s to the commercial initiatives of the '90s and beyond, an inevitable consequence was the 'gentrification' of former industrial areas. At the end of the second decade of the twenty-first century, areas subject to significant investment and redevelopment included the riverside locations of Kelham Island and Castlegate. Reconstruction of former industrial sites at Kelham Island included the building of zero-emission homes powered entirely from renewable sources, as well as consolidation of some of the area's key heritage such as the historic Green Lane Works dating from 1795. Much of

Eco-friendly housing development, Cotton Mill Walk, Kelham Island.

the success of areas like Kelham Island and Meersbrook has been down to the conversion of former industrial and commercial premises to new uses including coffee shops, cafes, independent restaurants and craft beer shops. Notable successes have included Peddler Market and the Cutlery Works, two former industrial venues in the Neepsend area converted to use as a night market and food hall respectively.

The redevelopment of Castlegate, in particular the site of the former markets, had the aim of reconnecting the city centre with its prime waterways of the canal basin and the rivers Don and Sheaf. Plans included the uncovering of part of the canalised River Sheaf, which at this point ran through a concrete culvert under the market site, the creation of a small urban park, and significant excavation and display of remains of the medieval castle by archaeologists under the supervision of the University of Sheffield.

A significant feature of the city's regeneration since 2012 has been the contribution of investment from China. The most visible early sign of this development was the release of plans for New Era Square on a prime site at the corner of St Mary's Gate and Bramall Lane. Financed by several multi-million-pound Chinese investors, the project included some 4,000 units of student accommodation as well as retail and cultural facilities. With financial involvement also coming from members of Sheffield's Cantonese community, the site was partly chosen in recognition of its proximity to the city's traditional Chinese quarter. In 2015, the city council concluded a deal with a prominent

New Era Square, the fruit of Chinese investment on the site of former working-class terraced streets leading up to St Mary's church, Bramall Lane.

Sichuan construction company to invest in a number of projects in Sheffield and the wider region, including the New Era Development. The following year the council stepped up its efforts to attract Chinese investment, focused particularly on its twin city of Chengdu (capital of the Sichuan region), and given greater urgency following the referendum vote to leave the European Union. Plans at around the same time to sell the iconic Central Library building to a Chinese hospitality company were eventually abandoned following significant protest from Sheffield residents.

A sharp reminder of the realities of the years of austerity after 2010, however, was the fate of the Don Valley Stadium, flagship of the regeneration of Sheffield's former industrial East End in the late 1980s. The stadium had been completed in September 1990 in time to be the main venue for the 1991 World Student Games. The award-winning design featured an innovative sunken track that gave the stadium the aspect of a 'bowl' and, in addition to the positioning of the track for optimum conditions with regard to wind direction and sun, offered athletes every opportunity of producing optimum performances. It therefore came as a shock to the people of Sheffield when it was revealed in January 2013 that the city council planned to close the stadium due to the urgent requirement to save £50 million as a result of government-enforced austerity measures. At the time of its closure, Don Valley was the second-largest athletics stadium in the UK, with a seating capacity of 25,000. Only the London Olympic Stadium offered more impressive facilities. Less than ten years earlier, the stadium had been praised by the *Pevsner Architectural Guide to Sheffield* as 'a distinctive landmark in the city'.

In some mitigation of the loss, it was announced in October 2014 that an Olympic Legacy Park would be constructed on the site, which would include an advanced Wellbeing Research Centre, an indoor sports arena, a sports pitch that would provide a new home for Sheffield Eagles rugby league club and a University Technical College backed by Sheffield College and Sheffield Hallam University. The plans built on the earlier creation of the English Institute of Sport, established with Lottery funding in 2003. The Olympic Legacy Park as a whole was a joint venture between Sheffield City Council and Sheffield Teaching Hospitals NHS Foundation Trust, and at the end of 2020, a ten-year investment plan was announced that would include a National Centre for Child Health Technology.

New Era?

Environmental Challenges

In addition to redeveloping the city centre, during the early 2000s local efforts were targeted at improving the water quality of the formerly heavily polluted River Don. From 1884, the city's main sewage treatment works had been established at Blackburn Meadows, and despite this facility still being at the forefront of treatment methods in the first half of the twentieth century, high ammonia levels were allowed to build up in the river below the works, which had a devastating effect on fish populations. This came on top of the industrial pollution of the river, which by the end of the twentieth century had all but eradicated wildlife. From 2012, significant modernisation and improvements were begun at Blackburn Meadows that, since completion in 2016, led to great improvements in the water quality of the Don, and it is now viewed as being cleaner than at any time since the Industrial Revolution. In July 2016 sightings of otters were confirmed, and within a few years it was evident that populations were becoming established at a number of sites, to join the salmon that had first been seen back in the river about ten years earlier. In addition, local projects were promoted to reclaim increasing lengths of the River Sheaf and

Sport fishing has returned to the River Don in the twenty-first century.

Porter Brook that had been canalised beneath the city in the industrial period, and one of the early successes was the creation of a 'pocket park' behind a new school on Shoreham Street.

A less frequent problem with the River Don has been flooding. The most serious event in recent years came in June 2007, when prolonged heavy rain led to the river breaking its bank and causing widespread flooding through much of the lower valley and the Wicker. To a lesser extent, the tributaries were also affected, and in one tragic incident a 14-year-old boy was swept to his death by the swollen River Sheaf in Millhouses Park as he walked home from school. In the city centre, a 68-year-old man died after attempting to cross a flooded road. The seriousness of the flooding of 2007 prompted the city council and local environmental agencies to look into improving the city's flood defences.

The environmental concern that attracted the widest attention in the second decade of the twenty-first century was the city's highways policy insofar as it concerned the maintenance of street trees. In 2012, the council signed a twenty-five-year contract with the public works company Amey as part of its 'Streets Ahead' programme. Over the following three years there was increasing public concern that trees that were neither obstructing highways nor pavements and were in good health were being felled. In response, protest actions became increasingly direct, and in the most notorious incidents local residents were arrested while attempting to obstruct tree-felling operations that had been scheduled by the council for the early hours of the morning.

At the prompting of protesters, a fifteen-month investigation by the Forestry Commission into the felling of more than 5,400 trees in the city found that about 600 may have been felled illegally, and by 2018 information had come to light that the council was planning to fell 200 trees per year regardless of street issues. In the face of mounting criticism, including controversial use of the police and private security personnel by the city council, the tree-felling programme was halted in March 2018 and a number of protesters who had been prosecuted for breaching council injunctions took action to have their convictions overturned. At the same time, an independent investigation into the council's actions found that they fell far short of good practice. While there is no doubt that heavy-handed council action was disproportionate and caused deep resentment, more than anything the street tree affair revealed the murky world of Private Finance Initiative (PFI) agreements signed at a time when the local authority was burdened by debt and starved of central funding and desperately trying to maintain a basic level of social services.

One of the main objections raised by protesters against the tree-felling programme was the importance of street trees in absorbing airborne pollutants. By 2010, Sheffield was consistently in breach of European clean-air regulations and air pollution was considered to be contributing to around 500 premature deaths in the city each year. In 2019, the city council introduced a consultation on its plans to reduce air pollution, which included charging what it had identified as the most polluting vehicles – including taxis, buses, vans and HGVs – to enter a clean-air zone within the inner ring road. Private cars were, however, exempt, and environmental protesters argued that the scheme did nothing to tackle Sheffield's long-standing traffic congestion and public transport problems that had increased markedly since the privatisation of bus services in the 1980s. To many people, as long as large numbers of Sheffield residents drove to their places of work such as the universities and hospitals, and such a large proportion of parents drove their children to school, no meaningful reduction of the city's appalling air pollution was likely to occur. In the context of debates around public transport, in January 2018 the Chinese company Ofo introduced a few thousand dockless shareable bicycles to Sheffield, along with a number of other UK cities. However, within eighteen months the scheme had been abandoned nationally, and an experiment in green transport in a city facing mounting air pollution problems came to an abrupt end.

In the face of growing worldwide concern about human-created climate change, Sheffield council began introducing a number of schemes to combat emissions. In August 2019, residents were asked to give their views on plans to vary street lighting levels across the city, aimed at achieving a 380-tonne annual reduction in CO_2 emissions, as well as reducing light pollution. In September of the same year, a trial started, using refuse collection lorries powered by the waste they collected. Under this scheme, old diesel vehicles that were going to be scrapped were fitted with batteries charged by electricity produced by incineration of household waste. The scheme was believed to be the first of its kind in the world.

A New Kind of Politics?

Under the Cities and Local Government Devolution Act of 2016, a new elected office of the Mayor of the Sheffield City Region was created to chair a combined authority for South Yorkshire with powers over transport, economic development and regeneration. The post was tenable for four-year periods, and the first election in May 2018 led to the selection of Dan Jarvis, Labour MP for Barnsley Central, as the first mayor. Meanwhile, the selection of Magid Magid, a Somali refugee who came to Britain with his mother and five siblings at the age of 5 in 1994, to the ceremonial office of Lord Mayor of Sheffield in May 2018, brought a good deal of attention to the city. As well as being the first ethnic Somali, the youngest ever and the first Green party councillor to hold the role, Magid created a stir with his political activism and disregard for convention. Though he attracted criticism in some quarters, there was a general feeling, particularly among younger residents of the city, that his tenure of the role helped to break down a number of social barriers and encouraged political engagement. In May 2019, Magid was elected to the European Parliament as a Green Party MEP for Yorkshire and the Humber, in the event one of the last people to be elected to the role.

In the referendum of June 2016, Sheffield voted to leave the European Union by a slim majority of 51 per cent to 49 per cent on a turnout of 67 per cent. If this came as a surprise to many Sheffielders, so did the defeat of former Deputy Prime Minister Nick Clegg as MP for the Hallam constituency in 2017. A committed pro-European, Clegg had also notoriously supported a party pledge to scrap university tuition fees in 2010, only to abandon the policy following his decision to join a coalition government with the Conservatives. Some commentators attributed Clegg's defeat largely to the success of left-wing activists in working to ensure that large numbers of students were registered to vote in their university city. To many young people, Clegg could never be forgiven for his abandonment of their cause. Clegg's removal meant that for the first time in the city's history, every one of Sheffield's parliamentary constituencies returned a Labour MP.

In 2019, divisions emerged among the ruling Labour group on the city council as a result of the development of a cabinet style of government by which only the council leader and nine cabinet members were involved in key decision-making. The system led to significant disquiet across the political spectrum and the raising of a petition that gained more than the 26,000 signatures required to trigger a referendum of voters. Through the course of 2019 a number of Labour councillors resigned from the cabinet in protest at the system and to enable them to campaign for democratic reform. One of those who resigned, deputy leader Olivia Blake, called for 'a wider debate on how to rejuvenate our democracy' and said that it was 'important that Labour voices contribute to this debate'. Blake subsequently stood as Labour candidate for the Sheffield Hallam constituency, which she won in December 2019 in the face of a determined and well-organised campaign by the Liberal Democrats.

Sporting Achievements

Recent years have seen some significant local success in sport. Leading the way was Jessica Ennis-Hill, a track-and-field athlete specialising in multi-eventing disciplines. The peak of her career came at the 2012 London Olympics, where she won the gold medal in the heptathlon, and a giant portrait hung over her home city throughout the duration of the games. It is a tragic irony that Ennis-Hill's introduction to athletics came as a 10-year-old when her parents took her to a participatory event during the summer holidays at the new Don Valley Stadium; the stadium was demolished in 2013, less than twenty-five years after its construction had seemed to herald a new age of optimism for the city.

Golfer Danny Willett came to world attention in April 2016 when he won the prestigious Masters tournament in the United States, his first major championship. In so doing, Willett became only the second Englishman to win the Masters, following Nick Faldo's success twenty years earlier. Since 2003, English cricket has had two captains, Michael Vaughan and Joe Root, with Sheffield connections.

In 2014, Sheffield found itself firmly on the world sporting map when Stage 2 of the 'Grand Depart' of cycling's famous Tour de France was staged in the city. The challenging final hill climb to the finish line, known as the 'Cote de Jenkin Road', was historically significant in being close to both the centre of the East End steel industry and in rising steeply up to the Wincobank Iron Age hill fort. The winner of the stage, the Italian Vincenzo Nibali, went on to win the Tour as a whole.

In 2019 the prestige of the city was undoubtedly enhanced by the promotion of Sheffield United FC to the Premier League for the first time since 2006. Against all expectations for a team that had been in the third tier of English football only two years previously, United finished ninth and attracted much positive comment for their brand of fast-flowing attacking football. Unfortunately, the team's exploits were not maintained during the following season, in which they were once again relegated.

A University City

By the late twentieth century, the two universities were, along with the NHS and the council, the two biggest employers in the city. Both the University of Sheffield and Sheffield Hallam University (until 1992 Sheffield City Polytechnic) expanded student numbers rapidly from around 2010, so that by

London Road, home to an increasing ethnic diversity of restaurants and cafes.

2020 the city had a combined population of some 60,000 university students. It is largely due to the presence of two major universities that in 2020 the largest age group within Sheffield's population of 570,000 was between the ages of 20 to 24. An increasing proportion of students were from outside the UK; one third of the University of Sheffield's students were from overseas at this time, with one in five of the student population as a whole coming from China.

As well as making a significant contribution to the local economy, the presence of large numbers of international students has had a marked effect on the built environment of the city through the construction of large-scale accommodation schemes aimed at this sector. By 2020, some 27,000 private accommodation units had been provided, and at least one local developer was of the opinion that this represented saturation point. An example of the marked impact of this phenomenon can be seen in the St Vincent's quarter, the former poor immigrant area of the Crofts, earmarked in the city council's new millennium plans for the city for low-rise development focused on the church and utilising views across the city centre. Instead, within less than twenty years of the new millennium it had been completely covered by high-rise student accommodation blocks, within which St Vincent's church and its hilltop location were completely obscured.

Large-scale student residential developments have rapidly transformed the face of the city since 2010. Here, a sole-surviving Georgian house stands on Broad Lane.

Social Challenges

Not for the first time in its history, the years following 2010 saw Sheffield struggling locally to combat the effects of a nationally imposed austerity programme. Among a number of significant challenges facing both the city council and the newly elected mayor of the city region were homelessness and rough sleeping, economic deprivation in general and child poverty in particular, and increasing levels of crime.

For most of its history, statistics had consistently shown crime rates in Sheffield to be relatively low compared with other towns and cities in the country. However, a marked rise in incidents of antisocial behaviour was evident from the commencement of the government's austerity policy in 2010, and for the first time in 2017 there was clear statistical evidence that crime in Sheffield was rising. The figures highlighted the growing levels of inequality in the city from the late twentieth century, with the least safe areas being Burngreave, Darnall, Firth Park and Manor, all among the most economically deprived parts of the city. More specifically, knife crime almost doubled in the ten years up to 2019, one of the biggest increases outside London. In a single year up to September 2019 the police recorded nearly 1,000 offences in which a knife had been involved.

A significant factor in the rise of crime was undoubtedly the sharp decline in police numbers that resulted from cuts in government spending. Between 2010 and 2020 there was a 16 per cent decrease in the workforce of South Yorkshire Police, slightly higher than the national average. In 2020 there were 3.5 police officers per 1,000 people, again slightly below the national average. In addition, long-term questions had hung over the effectiveness of SYP, particularly in the light of events such as those at Orgreave and Hillsborough. More recently, the force had come under significant criticism for its handling of allegations of child sexual exploitation in Rotherham. In 2019, HM Inspectorate of Constabulary concluded that these issues had contributed to problems of policing in the Sheffield region. However, the Inspectorate also believed that SYP's approach to tackling serious and organised crime was generally effective, as were its procedures for gathering intelligence and preventing people from becoming involved in crime. In 2019 a new SYP Head of Investigations in Sheffield was appointed with a remit of keeping communities safe, and to step up preventative work at community level. An injection of government funding also established a violent crime task force in Sheffield, largely in response to concerns about knife crime.

Growing social and economic inequality in Sheffield, exacerbated by the government austerity programme from 2010, was highlighted by the growing dependence on charitable interventions such as so-called 'food banks'. The deprivation in which an increasing number of children were growing up was particularly concerning. In 2018 the first 'hunger event' was held, partly funded by the city council, aimed at improving the health and well-being of people in the poorest areas of the city, and more particularly to ensure that children got adequate meals during the school summer holidays. In the summer of 2019, twenty-one such hunger events were held in some of the most deprived areas of the city. The long-term social problems caused by the industrial collapse and mass unemployment of the 1980s were coming home to roost. They could be seen also in the growing problem of homelessness, with the number of people living on the streets and sleeping rough in the city increasing threefold between 2010 and 2018.

A potential radical solution to the challenges of poverty and inequality came in the form of growing calls for the introduction of a Universal Basic Income (UBI) that, it was argued, would do away with the need for welfare payments as every citizen would be given a fixed sum to cover the basics, whatever their level of income or whether or not they were in employment. In 2019, Sheffield moved closer to becoming one of the first UK cities to trial the system after the council formally lent its support to the idea. In the view of Jason Leman, chair of the Sheffield project, the city was uniquely predisposed for a pilot scheme:

> It's like a collection of towns, it isn't a monolithic city. Every city has its neighbour-hoods, but Sheffield is particularly divided. There is a real disparity between the north-east and the south-west in terms of wealth, life expectancy and life experience. Within Sheffield districts you have communities that are almost self-supporting.

These were divisions and disparities that Sheffield people had struggled collectively to resist since the time of the French Revolution, and which had brought the city into frequent conflict with central government at moments of economic crisis in the twentieth century. They were shown up all too vividly with the arrival of the coronavirus pandemic in the spring of 2020, during which Sheffield was one of the cities worst affected and in which the citizens in its poorest areas suffered the most. The radical reformers of Sheffield's past, from the eighteenth to the twentieth centuries, would have looked aghast at the fundamentally unequal society that had been created by the twenty-first.

In hindsight, the abrupt change forced on Sheffield in the late 1980s, from a successful model of social inclusion to a capitalist programme that put the welfare of the city's people at the mercy of market forces, might be seen as a turning point. Certainly, the systematic removal of central government support from cities such as Sheffield, coupled with inevitable debt and the effects of successive austerity policies, have presented a massive challenge over the past forty years. The economic depression that came in the wake of the COVID-19 pandemic threatened the very survival of a city still struggling to recover from the seismic shocks of the 1980s and 2008. The pandemic brought many of Sheffield's structural weaknesses into sharp focus – not least the economic decline of the city centre, which had begun with the construction of the Meadowhall shopping centre a generation earlier.

Yet throughout the course of their story, the people of Sheffield have repeatedly demonstrated the ability to summon collective strength in the face of adversity, whether the struggle has been against forces of oppression from within the country or enemy assault from outside. For half a century from 1926 to 1976, Sheffield led the way in showing how a city can be run for the good of its people, and how an inclusive, caring society brings benefits to all. In the light of this experience, and if the clear lessons of the early 2020s can be learned, there is the possibility of a positive future, both for Sheffield and its people, and for the country as a whole.

SELECT BIBLIOGRAPHY

Anderson, N., *Sheffield's Date with Hitler: The Story of the Blitz* (2010).

Belchem, J., *Popular Radicalism in Nineteenth-Century Britain* (1996).

Bevan, B., *Ancient Peakland* (2007).

Binfield. C. et al (eds), *The History of the City of Sheffield 1843–1993* (3 vols, 1993).

Downing, A., The 'Sheffield Outrages': violence, class and trade unionism, 1850–70, *Social History*, 38:2, 162–182 (2013).

Edmonds, M., Seaborne, T., *Prehistory in the Peak* (2001).

Engels, F., *The Condition of the Working Class in England* (1993 edn).

Harman, R., Minnis, J., *Pevsner Architectural Guide to Sheffield* (2004).

Hey, D., *The Fiery Blades of Hallamshire: Sheffield and its Neighbourhood, 1660–1740* (1991).

Hey, D., *Historic Hallamshire* (2002).

Hey, D., *A History of Sheffield* (2010).

Hey, D., *A History of the Peak District Moors* (2014).

Holt, J.C., *Robin Hood* (1982).

Hunter, J., *Hallamshire: The History and Topography of the Parish of Sheffield in the County of York* (revised edn by A. Gatty, 1869).

Jones, M. (ed.), *Aspects of Sheffield: Discovering Local History* (vol. 1, 1997; vol. 2, 1999).

Jones, M., *The Making of Sheffield* (2004)

Keeble Hawson, H., *Sheffield: The Growth of a City 1893–1926* (1968).

Leader, J.D., *The Records of the Burgery of Sheffield* (1897).

Lewis, C., *Samuel Holberry: Chartist Conspirator or Victim of a State Conspiracy* (2009).

Linton, D.L. (ed.), *Sheffield and its Region: A Scientific and Historical Survey* (1956).

Machan, P., *The Dramatic Story of The Sheffield Flood* (1999).

Mathers, H., *Steel City Scholars: The Centenary History of the University of Sheffield* (2005).

McGlynn, S., *Robin Hood: A True Legend* (2018).

McWilliam, R., *Popular Politics in Nineteenth-Century England* (1998).

Pawson & Brailsford's *Illustrated Guide to Sheffield and Neighbourhood* (1862, reprinted 1971).

Price D., *Sheffield Troublemakers: Rebels and Radicals in Sheffield History* (2008).

Rawlins, M., *Women of Steel* (2020).

Reynolds, S., *Rip it Up and Start Again: Postpunk, 1978–1984* (2005).

Royle, E., *Revolutionary Britannia? Reflections on the threat of revolution in Britain, 1789–1848* (2000).

Smith, D., *Conflict and Compromise: Class Formation in English Society 1830–1914, A Comparative Study of Birmingham and Sheffield* (1982).

Stevenson, J., *Artisans & Democrats: Sheffield and the French Revolution, 1789–97* (1989).

Taylor, J. (ed.), *The Illustrated Guide to Sheffield and Surrounding District* (1879, reprinted 2012).

Warr, P., *Sheffield in the Great War* (2015).

Walton, M., *Sheffield: Its Story and Its Achievements* (3rd edn, 1952).

Walton, M., Lamb, P.J., *Raiders over Sheffield: The Story of the Air Raids of 12th & 15th December 1940* (1980).

Online Articles

The Archaeological Discoveries at Whirlow Hall Farm, www.thetimetravellers.org.uk/whirlow-project-report.html

The Dragon of Wantley: A Major Reappraisal Revealing Ancient, Medieval and Hitherto Unrecognised Early-Modern Roots of the Famed English Legend, https://stevemoxon.co.uk/dragon-of-wantley-reappraisal-legend-myth

Reports

Jamroz, E., Tyler, P., *Roma in Sheffield: Mapping Services and Local Priorities*, South Yorkshire Roma Project 2017.

Video

City on the Move (Sheffield City Council, 1971).

Menschen in Sheffield (People in Sheffield), Peter Nestler for Südfunks Stuttgart (1965).

INDEX